Translation in the D

Translation is living through a period of revolutionary upheaval. The effects of digital technology and the internet on translation are continuous, widespread and profound. From automatic online translation services to the rise of crowd-sourced translation and the proliferation of translation apps for smartphones, the translation revolution is everywhere. The implications of this revolution for human languages, cultures and society are radical and far-reaching. In the information age that is the translation age, new ways of talking and thinking about translation which take full account of the dramatic changes in the digital sphere are urgently required.

Michael Cronin examines the role of translation with regard to the debates around emerging digital technologies and analyses their social, cultural and political consequences, guiding readers through the beginnings of translation's engagement with technology, and through to the key issues that exist today.

With links to many areas of study, *Translation in the Digital Age* is a vital read for all students of translation studies.

Michael Cronin is Professor of Translation Studies at Dublin City University. He is author of *Translation Goes to the Movies* (2008), *Translation and Identity* (2006) and *Translation and Globalization* (2003), all published by Routledge.

New Perspectives in Translation Studies

Series editor: Michael Cronin holds a Personal Chair in the Faculty of Humanities and Social Sciences at Dublin City University.

The *New Perspectives in Translation Studies* series aims to address the changing needs in translation studies. The series features works by leading scholars in the field on emerging and up-to-date topics in the discipline. Key features of the titles in the series are accessibility, relevance and innovation.

These lively and highly readable texts provide an exploration into various areas of the field for undergraduate and postgraduate students of translation studies and cultural studies.

Cities in Translation
Sherry Simon

Translation in the Digital Age
Michael Cronin

Translation in the Digital Age

Michael Cronin

Routledge
Taylor & Francis Group

LONDON AND NEW YORK

First published 2013
by Routledge
2 Park Square, Milton Park, Abingdon, Oxon OX14 4RN

Simultaneously published in the USA and Canada
by Routledge
711 Third Avenue, New York, NY 10017

Routledge is an imprint of the Taylor & Francis Group, an informa business

British Library Cataloguing in Publication Data
A catalogue record for this book is available from the British Library

Library of Congress Cataloging in Publication Data
Cronin, Michael, 1960-
Translation in the digital age / Michael Cronin.
p. cm. -- (New perspectives in translation studies)
Includes bibliographical references and index.
1. Translating and interpreting--Technological innovations.
2. Machine translating. 3. Internet. I. Title.
P306.97.T73C76 2013
418'.020285--dc23
2012027030

ISBN: 978-0-415-60859-6 (hbk)
ISBN: 978-0-415-60860-2 (pbk)
ISBN: 978-0-203-07359-9 (ebk)

Typeset in Sabon
by Taylor & Francis Books

Printed and bound in Great Britain by the MPG Books Group

For Fionnuala and Lasairfhíona, brightness of brightness

Contents

Acknowledgements

In an era dominated by images of the virtual, it is easy to neglect our indebtedness to the physical. The writing of any book gains immeasurably from the support and comradeship of colleagues and friends and this work is no exception. The constant stimulus provided by colleagues and research students in the Centre for Translation and Textual Studies has greatly enriched my reflections on the themes addressed in this book. The wider community of the School of Applied Language and Intercultural Studies has proved over the years to be the ideal multilingual and multicultural milieu for thinking through what it means to dwell in globalized settings. I would like to acknowledge my gratitude to the Head of School Dr Aileen Pearson-Evans and the Governing Authority of Dublin City University for allowing me to avail of sabbatical leave in 2011–12 so that I could work on the present volume. Special thanks go to those friends whose conversations and insights have always challenged my own unreflective prejudices, in particular Gavan Titley, Caoimhghín Ó Croidheáin, Peter Sirr, Barra Ó Séaghdha, Evelyn Conlon, Claude Aschenbrenner, and Michael Cunningham who first alerted to me to what was shocking about the digitally new more than fifteen years ago. My son, Máirtín, as a native inhabitant of the digital world, deserves my thanks for his genial tolerance of his father's endless enquiries.

Translation is, of course, both a local and a global enterprise. The advice and opinions of scholars too numerous to mention have been of much assistance, but I would like to take the opportunity to express my gratitude to the colleagues in the following institutions that allowed me the space and freedom to test drive a number of the ideas in their earlier states of formulation: Barnard College, New York, USA; Centre for Irish Studies, Leuven, Belgium; Yale University, New Haven, USA; Centre for Translation Studies, American University in Cairo, Egypt; Société des Gens de Lettres, Paris, France; Pusan National University, Korea; University of Warwick, England; Humboldt University, Berlin, Germany; University of Helsinki, Finland; Rikkyo University, Tokyo, Japan; University of Kent, England; University of Gdansk, Poland.

A special word of thanks also goes to the editorial staff at Routledge, in particular Louisa Semlyen and Sophie Jaques, for their kindness and patience in bringing this book to publication.

There are few words adequate to describe my debt to Fionnuala Mac Aodha who has been unwavering in her support throughout the preparation and writing of this book. She has been the best companion imaginable, and her emotional and intellectual honesty inform every line in this volume. If this book is about, among other things, the birth of new ways of doing and thinking about translation, it is partly because genesis was never too far from my thoughts in a period that saw the joyful event of the birth of my daughter, Lasairfhíona. This book is dedicated with affection and gratitude to Fionnuala and Lasairfhíona.

Introduction
The translation age

> I open my eyes and I don't know where I am or who I am. Not all that unusual – I've
> spent half my life not knowing. Still, this feels different. The confusion is more
> frightening. More total.
>
> (Agassi 2010: 3)

Andre Agassi has just woken in his hotel suite in New York City. He is playing
in the US Open that will turn out to be his last US Open, in fact, his last
tournament ever. A cocktail of health problems and personal issues will cause
him to retire from the world of professional tennis at the age of thirty-six. His
sense of confusion will be familiar to anyone engaged at whatever level with
translation in the present moment. The omnipresence of online translation
options, the proliferation of smartphone translation apps, the relentless drive
towards automation in large-scale translation projects, the fundamental changes
in literacy practices as reading migrates from page to screen, the unforgiving
instantaneity of electronic communication as responses are demanded 24/7, the
ever-changing wardrobe of digital translation props such as endlessly mutating
translation memory software – all of these factors contribute to the sense that
'this feels different'. There may have been changes before but this time, the
'confusion is more frightening. More total.'

This book addresses that sense of confusion. Over the last decade, speaking
to audiences in different parts of the world, the same questions keeps returning:
Is there a future for translators? In the age of Google Translate, is the human
translator condemned to large-scale extinction, or to the quaint peripherality of
the Sunday hobbyist? The demand for translation keeps growing apace in the
contemporary world, but will humans continue to be asked to service this need,
or will it be our machines that will do the bidding?

What the questions express is a feeling, which I believe to be well founded,
that translation is living through a period of revolutionary upheaval. The
effects of digital technology and the internet on translation are continuous,
widespread, and profound. They can no longer be quarantined into geekish
conclaves, evaluating the most recent software or ritually ridiculed in the

humourless recitation of the latest machine-translation howlers. Students, scholars, and, indeed, anyone interested in the future of human cultures and languages, would be well advised to watch carefully what is happening to translation in a digital age.

This book is a work of interpretation not prophecy. In an area where there is an endless stream of technical innovations, it would be foolish in the extreme to try to predict what might or might not be the ultimate success of automated systems in dealing with problems or questions of translatability. Its aim is rather to understand in a broader sense the implications for language, culture, and society of translation's engagement with technology. In order to do this, it takes in disciplinary perspectives from anthropology to zoology and deals with historical examples ranging from the river settlements of the Tigris and the Euphrates, to the changing fortunes of the Australian military in the contemporary world. Throughout the book, there is a deliberate avoidance of the idle partitioning of evidence, and literary translation is discussed alongside technical, commercial, and scientific translation. There is repeatedly the contention that technology is not simply an accessory, an adjunct to translation, but that it has been central to the definition of translation activity in many different societies and in many different historical periods up to and including, of course, our own.

Frances Yates, the eminent historian of the European Renaissance, has commented on the seeming paradox of the march forward being subject to the look backwards:

> The great forward movements of the Renaissance all derive their vigour, their emotional impulse from looking backwards. The cyclic view of time as a perpetual movement from pristine golden ages of purity and truth through successive bronze and iron ages still held sway and the search for truth was thus of necessity a search for the early, the ancient, the original gold from which the baser metals of the present and the immediate past were corrupt degenerations.
>
> (Yates 2002: 1)

In any examination of translation in the digital age, there are the twin perils of what might be termed the 'backwards look' and the 'forwards look'. The backwards look is the temptation to see the digital present as evidence of an irredeemably fallen state of translation affairs. In the pristine golden age of the translator's youth people knew how to spell, they read books, they could concentrate on a page for more than five seconds, and they knew the names of all fifty states of the United States of America without having to unholster their smartphone. The forwards look is the equally strong temptation to see the digital present as a world of miracles and wonders, narrated in the breathless corporate prose of 'Isn't it amazing that …'. In the excitable hyperbole of the cyber apostles, automated translation will mean the end to all human strife, grief, and misery as humans unite in the higher communion of mutual intelligibility.

Translation in the Digital Age seeks to avoid the dual dangers of terminal pessimism and besotted optimism by examining closely what is happening in today's translation world. It does, however, make a larger claim which indicates the wider importance of translation for any student of contemporary culture and society. This claim is that our present age, which is often referred to as the information age with its corollary, the knowledge society, should more properly be termed the translation age. The extreme flexibility of digital tools means that they can generate a wide variety of outputs. The most basic laptop with the correct software and internet connections can function as archivist, accountant, game console, library, photo album, estate agent. The variability of outputs of these machines is made possible, in part, by the universal convertibility of binary code, the ability of words, images, sounds to be converted to the universal language of code. In this sense, the radical changes that have been wrought in all areas of life as a result of the advent of information technology are to be placed under the sign of convertibility or translation. It is precisely the metamorphic or transformative effects of the convertible which are at the heart of the digital revolution that makes translation the most appropriate standpoint from which to view critically what happens to languages, societies, and cultures under a regime of advanced convertibility, and to understand what happens when that convertibility breaks down or reaches its limits.

Chapter 1 begins by situating a digital engagement with translation in the long material history of humanity's interaction with tools. It is argued that humanity is not distinct from, but is rather defined by, the possibilities offered by its tools. This centrality of tool use is not, however, used to justify a debilitating form of technological determinism. The chapter goes on to explore both the importance of kinship arrangements for the opening of human communities to the possibility of translation, and how, through the notion of entailment, social and organizational infrastructures are central to the flourishing of material cultures. As societies develop, these cultures are faced repeatedly with the challenge of managing translation relationships over distance, and examples are taken from antiquity and the late Middle Ages to show the emergence of an ethics of proximity in translation, an attempt to deal with the spatial and cultural consequences of expansion. Central to this chapter is the elaboration of what is referred to as the '3T paradigm': trade, technology, translation. In tracing the evolution of early urban cultures, the claim is made that trade, technology, and translation are inseparable in their development, and that any balanced history of these cultures must take into account the close interaction between all three. The interaction is all the more important in that the tendency to exclude any of the three components tends to lead to isolationist or exclusivist readings of particular cultures. As cultures and societies interact, the question of power is inevitably present, and ancient Rome is investigated as a site of acute cultural anxiety around the linguistic consequences of technical and commercial growth. More generally, these anxieties are related to the unforeseen consequences of a new medium, and Marshall McLuhan's notion of the medium as message is revisited for what it might tell us about a material history of translation.

Sixteenth-century England is explored in the context of the relationship between translation and the emerging intellectual ethic of the printing press, a medium that profoundly shapes the message of translation. How the technology of print continues to shape the fortunes of translation is examined in the case history of a nineteenth-century Irish translator, Lady Jane Wilde. Wilde's translations in the late 1840s were a crucial contribution to the emerging imagined community of Irish nationalism, a movement that, like so many similar movements elsewhere, was sustained by the virtual constituency of print. The chapter concludes with a consideration of how, at different moments in human enquiry, space or time has been privileged as a way of understanding human experience, and how both categories are open to the constant interrogation of translation and material culture.

Chapter 2 focuses on questions of language, power, and translation in the digital age. One of the most notable moves in the drive towards the automation of translation is the production of controlled languages. The move towards controlled language is also shadowed by a project to produce a simplified, readily understood version of global English. The chapter examines the implications of these developments and points to the often paradoxical and unpredictable outcomes of the development of supra-national or global *lingua francas*. The paradigm of controlled language and global English is situated in a tradition of Puritan translation in English closely allied to the notion of plain speaking. Less obvious, on occasion, are the costs of speaking plainly. In investigating how the notion of cost is invoked in debates around translation, it is argued that hidden or devolved costs mask the real nature of power relationships between languages, relationships that are deeply embedded in the engagement between translation and technology. This engagement is increasingly bound up with disintermediation, and the chapter explores the consequences for popular notions of translation of the emergence of online translation systems. One consequence is the increasing tendency to represent language in purely instrumentalist terms, that is, getting a message from point A to point B in the shortest possible period of time. What such instrumentalism might imply for science in particular is investigated as a way of challenging certain shibboleths around science communication in the digital age. If the instrumental view of language has become so dominant, this is related to a broader cultural pattern of the triumph of transitivity. Transitivity, the subordination of every activity to a specific, pre-defined end, is no stranger to translation. Novice expectations about there being one right way to do translation, or industry insistence on consistency and standardized outputs, have the transitive as an explicit horizon of expectation. The chapter explores an episode from Renaissance translation history and accounts of user interactions with translation technology to suggest that translation is in many respects anything but transitive in its practice and results.

A powerful ally of a strongly transitive or utilitarian view of translation in the digital age is the ideology of transparency: What You Get Is What You (always) See, and once you can see it, you can get it. In investigating the philosophical roots of this ideology in the nineteenth-century US Transcendentalist movement and twentieth-century US counter-culture, the chapter considers the consequences for contemporary translation practice of an ideology of transparency. Particular attention is paid to the way one understanding of transparency – transparency as an invitation to opacity – explains the contribution of digital technology to the growth of linguistic diversity. One of the areas of potential opacity is, of course, the true nature of the economic interests at play in the new digital economy and the extent to which translators are active or passive agents. This question of agency is situated in a distinction between digital authorship and digital interaction, and the chapter calls for a heightened degree of digital self-reflexivity in any emerging ethics of translation.

Chapter 3 is concerned with dominant representations of translation in the digital age. The notion of translation as an essential adjunct to the construction of a borderless world is a core concept in what the chapter refers to as 'messianic' theories of translation. In this view, translation, powerfully assisted by the digital toolkit, removes boundaries, abolishes frontiers, and ushers in a brave new world of communicative communion. However, it is claimed in the chapter that such messianic theories not only misrepresent obdurate political realities, but also fail to account in any adequate way for what translators actually do in the present and have done in the past. The notion of limits is introduced from an anthropological and philosophical perspective as a way into establishing how translators have allowed the internal and external experience of limits to structure their approach to translation, and how these experiences have, in turn, shaped the collective experience of language and culture. In positing the notion of limits, it is claimed that translation poses a challenge for extensive culture – the endless multiplication of goods, services, or ideas – and that more attention must be paid to the ways in which it is situated in intensive culture, in a culture of non-equivalence. This intensive culture is partly situated in an ecological concern with limits – in particular, the limits to growth – but it also relates to a representation of translation that has a long and enduring history: the idea of identicality. The notion that authorship consists of the exact execution of the author's wishes is central to the emergence of architectural individuality in the Renaissance period. The advent of mass industrial production gives renewed impetus to the regime of identicality where the notion of authenticity is predicated on sameness, from the acceptability of banknotes (forgeries try to be identical, but are not), to the saleability of Model Ts (reliable because the same). In tracing the history of changing understandings of literary translation into English in the twentieth century, the chapter looks at the varying fortunes of the semantic regime of identicality in translation. Inevitably, what emerges from this historical overview is the paradigm of variability, and this paradigm is linked to the work of translation in the age of digital reproduction. Digital reproduction allows for endless replication of difference, not endless replication of same. The digital object is structured around variability, not identicality. The chapter considers the implications for translation of these new forms of digital objects and how they do or do not relate to models predicated on extensive cultures. In particular, the question is asked as to whether translation can be considered as autographic or allographic, an activity that is primarily the work of a maker or artisan, or an activity that is routinely the unacknowledged work of others.

Chapter 4 explores the impacts of digital technology on translation practice. The underlying logic of the operations of a major translation provider is detailed to show the recurrent tension between local delivery and central control in the production and management of translation. The core concerns of this new translation economy in the digital age relate to volume, time, and cost, and the chapter investigates each of these notions as they impact on the practice of translation in the context of automation and semi-automation. Concerns around the direction of particular forms of translation activity, and particularly the existence of vastly different levels of access to IT services across the globe, have prompted the emergence of new forms of localization, and these are considered in terms of overall geopolitical tensions and corporate strategies. Underlying both the mass provision of translation by global translation providers and local initiatives to promote alternative forms of translation delivery are the shift to ubiquitous computing and the emergence of bidirectionality. Being able to access the internet from a smartphone, or being able to alter content on a website, has far-reaching implications for both the embedding of the digital in our daily lives and how the nature of what is digital is transformed. The chapter considers the implications for translation practice of the emergence of nomadic, interactive computing and details the emergence of new forms of translation production/reception and the translation fallout of crowdsourcing. A fundamental change in this context that is frequently ignored is changing norms of literacy. If translation has typically depended on a deep commitment to, and reverence for, the printed word, what happens when the experience of the printed word shifts from the page to the screen? The chapter asks whether we are moving to an age of post-print translation literacy and what might be the consequences for how translations are both produced and used. Treating the various changes to translation practice as an effect of the pre-eminence of information technology begs the question as to the nature of the technology. In exploring the emerging science of information and the centrality of the notion of convertibility to the digital, the chapter argues that it is information which is a subset of translation, and that it is more accurate to describe our contemporary moment as the translation age rather than the information age. It is as a way of describing specific sets of practices in the translation age that the chapter returns to the notion of transparency, this time to analyse the effects of identifiable practices. The notions of ethical, ostensible, and penal transparency are employed to show how, in everything from the construction of national identity to espionage, the fortunes of translation and the digital are inextricable.

Chapter 5 considers how we might respond to the new forms that translation is adopting in the digital age. The pioneering reflections on translation in the digital age of machine translation theorist and practitioner Alan Kay provide the introduction to a consideration of how two approaches to thinking about translation, 'massive' thinking and 'detailed' thinking, can help situate particular kinds of translation practice in the era of automation and semi-automation.

The strategic importance of detail in translation practice is located within the rising popularity of gist or indicative translation. Underlying both the 'massive' and 'detailed' approaches to translation, it is argued, are two different approaches to the question of the universal. The tension between easy universalism and difficult universalism is seen as bound up with projections of power and influence from which translation is not immune. In order to develop the implications of difficult universalism for translation thinking and practice, the notion of 'gap' is opposed to that of 'difference'. The idea of 'gap' avoids the reifying thrust of typicality that often underlies the invocation of difference, and favours not so much the celebration of identity as the cultivation of fecundity. In this view, translators look to languages and cultures not so much for values as for resources. Where these 'gaps' might be located is, of course, a source of endless conjecture, but it is argued that in translation practices in the digital age, one place to look is in the debates around quality and the pertinence or not of post-editing. These debates can, in turn, be situated within an emerging discourse around digital humanism. Digital humanism, which is an attempt to understand the fundamental changes that have occurred in contemporary culture and society with the advent of digital tools, is a movement of critical reflection, rather than a roadshow of cyber cheerleading. Central to this emergent movement is the philological perspective, the detailed engagement with the meanings and histories of languages and practices in the digitally informed world. How this perspective can be brought to bear on translation's relationship with technology is considered in the light of Ivan Illich's plea for tools of conviviality, for tools that will promote, rather than impede, human flourishing. One of the greatest enemies of this flourishing can, of course, be particular versions of consensual humanism that universalize particular cultural experiences and disguise exploitative relations of power. The chapter proposes a way of thinking about translation in human communities that assumes the permanence of conflict and the necessity to construct community, rather than to assume it. The contribution of translation to the construction of communities is described in a framework that challenges a conventional, genealogical unfolding of pre-set cultural attributes and proposes that the dynamic subversiveness of the company of strangers is the most radical promise of a self-aware translation praxis in our digital age.

The narrator in Somaya Ramadan's novel, *Leaves of Narcissus*, shares Andre Agassi's sense of uncertainty as she faces difficult choices at a particular moment in her life. The Egyptian novelist captures the sense of unknowability that ghosts all change, 'Beginnings, being beginnings, change constantly, change every time' (Ramadan 2002: 4). This, of course, is the danger that attends any attempt to describe a revolution when one is caught up in its midst. The beginnings change constantly, and there is the perpetual risk of being wrong-footed by events. Risk, however, is no excuse for renunciation. It is crucial that any attempt to consider translation in the contemporary moment must attend to the radically changed circumstances of its production and reception.

As new technologies evolve, they often give life to old ideas. In the expanding literature on the Web, one of the ideas that has been reintroduced to describe the nature of the Web is that of 'noosphere' (Blondeau and Allard 2007). This idea, first advanced by the French thinker Pierre Teilhard de Chardin, envisaged a continuous membrane of information encircling the globe which he called the 'noosphere' (Teilhard de Chardin 1966: 63). The Web is seen by many as the concretization of this noosphere. The presence of a global repository of information, instantly accessible and containing a constantly multiplying set of links to other sources of information, suggests that the Web be seen not in territorial terms, but as a kind of transcendent noosphere containing the collective intelligence of humanity (Vanbremeersch 2009: 22). Leaving aside the inevitable coefficient of exaggeration in any characterization of digital phenomena, the omnipresence of digital sources and ways of knowing in the daily lives of many inhabitants of the planet is inescapable. The working practices of translators have been changed beyond recognition in terms of the access to many different kinds of knowledge that are afforded by the infrastructure of the internet. The challenges are, of course, how to situate translation in that emergent noosphere and where to place it in the future reconfiguration of language, culture, and society in the digital sphere.

The digital sphere, like any other, is no stranger to politics. The use of social media during the Arab Spring has been widely commented upon and it is notable that when analysts began to consider the implications of what was happening, they began to turn to translation as a framework of explanation (Mehrez 2012). The political economy of translation in the digital age most obviously involves who gets digital access and on what terms, and what gets translated for whom and in what medium. At another level, the potential instantaneity and accessibility of digital media imply a greater acceleration of translation flows with potentially subversive effects, but equally the widespread dissemination of translations that strongly domesticate images of other polities and cultures to the dominant political, economic, and cultural agendas. Integral to the new digital order are the translation realities of millions of migrants who find themselves in that translation zone between life in a new language and continued digital interactivity with the language in their country of origin. The economic and the political are inevitable partners in any attempt to understand how, over time and in the present, translation has shaped and been shaped by the tools it uses. There is much to be confused about, but confusion as a prelude to enquiry is not an ignoble condition. If beginnings are constantly changing, there is no better place to begin than with change itself.

1 The house of translation

In the introduction to his treatise *On the Use of the Astrolabe*, the twelfth-century scholar and translator Adelard of Bath has some words of advice for his patron Prince Henry, the future King Henry II:

> You say that whoever dwells in a house is not worthy of its shelter if he is ignorant of its material and makeup, quantity and quality, position and peculiarity. Thus if one who was born and raised in the palace of the world should forbear after the age of discretion to know the reason for so marvelous a beauty, he is unworthy of it and, were it possible, ought to be cast out.
>
> (Lyons 2010: 128–29)

Adelard is instructing his young pupil in the use of an instrument that will radically change the fortunes of travellers from the Christian West. His treatise is itself the fruit of years of translating from Arabic and a demonstration of the technical superiority of the Arab world. What is notable is that the metaphors the scholar employs are those of the built environment: 'house', 'palace', 'material', 'makeup'. In other words, Adelard's defence of a new form of maritime technology is couched in the language of an existing technology, the technology of human construction, the house or the palace, which provides 'shelter'. For Adelard, understanding resides in knowing how the world works and that knowledge is inexpressible outside the language of artefacts. What his translations ultimately do is change the relationship between his readers and their world not so much through the words he writes, as through the new instrument he will cause them to use and understand. Human presence in the world can only be understood through and in the context of the made objects that mediate human existence.

Tools

So why are tools so fundamental to a sense of what it is to be human, and what possible significance can this have for how we understand translation? The archaeologist Timothy Taylor points out that there are many good reasons why human beings should not exist:

Our skulls are so large that we risk being stuck and dying even as we are struggling to be born. Helped out by a technical team – obstetrician, midwife, and a battery of bleeping machines – the unwieldy cranium is followed into the light by a pathetic excuse for a mammalian body, screaming, hairless and so muscularly feeble that it has no chance of supporting its head properly for months. How did a species in which basic reproduction is so easily fatal, and whose progeny need several years of adult support before they can dress themselves, not just evolve but become the dominant species on the planet?

(Taylor 2010: 4)

Not only have humans become the dominant species on the planet, but they inhabit almost every conceivable environment from mountain plateaux to (however temporarily) the sea floor. So how do these members of the animal kingdom, with their weak eyes, fragile backs, and infant helplessness, come to occupy a situation of such pre-eminence? One answer must reside in what Taylor terms the 'third system'. The first system comprises the system of physics and nonbiological chemistry, the second system is that of biology, and the third system is the set of material objects created and shaped by human beings (*ibid.*, 4–6). Evolution for humans is, in a sense, both biological and cultural. If we possess fire, tools, weapons, and clothes, we no longer need massive teeth, claws, and muscles, or a long, vegetable-absorbing gut. This permits humans to wrong foot conventional laws of natural selection which would dictate the inevitable disappearance of a notably fragile and vulnerable species of great ape.

What emerges from this reading of human evolution, the paradoxical survival of the weakest, is that third-system dependency leads to a particular symbiosis of the animate and inanimate. The trebling or quadrupling of human brain capacity which enabled the expansion and elaboration of the third system is itself the product of developments in the system itself. Changes in cooking, fermenting, and curing allowed for important gains in calorific value which enabled humans to absorb the high-energy, high-protein foods necessary to power large brains. These brains were and are perched on unusually short lengths of gut, a side-effect of the switch to upright walking (Wrangham 2007: 182–203). Thus, biology and *technē* interact in a manner central to human survival and development. It is the artificial realm that insulates us, cures and makes up for the deficiencies in our sight, metabolism, mobility, and memory. For this reason, when we speak about translation as a human activity, we need to take account of the intrinsic, and not simply extrinsic, involvement of *technē*. It is a question of ontology, rather than of utility. We evolve or are defined by the artefacts we use. The tools shape us as much as we shape them.

In assigning tools the importance they deserve in human evolution, it also necessary to contextualize tool use. Tools are used by human beings for specific purposes, and these purposes, from the provision of food to the transport of infants, are predominantly social. One of the difficulties faced by humans, once they were erect, was that they had to transport defenceless infants. These infants were born prematurely, in that they could not feed themselves, transport themselves, or defend themselves against predators without the assistance of adult humans. Bipedalism greatly enhanced human mobility, the distances that could be covered running or on foot, but the resultant pelvic modification meant that caring for the bipedal young demanded social cohesion so that the group could protect and defend the young who would transmit, in turn, these patterns of socialization (Coppens and Picq 2001). The need for social interaction is constant if survival is to be a possibility. The impulse towards social cohesion does not, however, imply that human societies are condemned to regimes of exclusive inwardness.

A constant of marriage arrangements in different human communities is that, if they do not always stipulate whom you should marry, they have strict rules about whom you should not (Héran 2009). Marriage rules are generally based on a scalar model going from, at one end, a too-great proximity (for example, the taboo on incest in many societies), to an excessive distance (marrying someone from a wholly alien culture) at the other. The complex interaction between kinship ties and spatial obligations (whether the couple will live with the family of the man or of the woman) means that the potential to extend the social exists in both group and spatial terms (Godelier 2004). Hence, the notion of what constitutes the social group is both extended by the nature of marriage arrangements and defined by them. Paradoxically, as Christian Grataloup argues, prohibition is the flip side of the perpetual need to create links, to generate social connectedness. Linking the prehistoric necessity of collective childcare to the complex grid of kinship possibilities, Grataloup argues that:

> Constant interaction is necessary between the members of the same group, precisely to reproduce on an ongoing basis the social link. Distance hinders these possibilities for interaction. If one member of the society is too far from the others, there is a danger that he or she will become wholly autonomous. The social is based on a whole web of links, a whole system of connections, kinship structures, languages, relations of production and power ... These interactions cannot tolerate distance or being over-stretched.
>
> (Grataloup 2011: 44–45)[1]

The risk in prioritizing the role of tools is to fall into the trap of a techno-determinism which ignores the profoundly social nature of humans' interaction with each other and the world. It is significant, however, from the point of view of translation, how that sociality has been characterized throughout human history. On the one hand, there is the search for group cohesion, the necessary trade-off between bipedal mobility and bipedal survival, and, on the other, the countless arrangements to extend and diversify the nature of what constitutes the social. Seeing translation as a kind of cultural kinship arrangement, a way of complexifying the constitutive relationships of a community, is one way of keeping in focus the abiding necessity of the 'social link' as a context for tool use, a link which, as we shall see in succeeding chapters, extends globally through the internet.

Entailment

One way of capturing this notion of tool dependence is to invoke the notion of entailment. A classic contemporary example of entailment is the modern car:

> A car needs wheels and fuel. These entail rubber plantations and oil wells, and complex manufacturing, refining, marketing and distribution processes. Once all the things that cars have to have to be cars are factored in – from metal, tarmac, and glass, through to traffic police, a licensing bureaucracy, test agencies and so on, each of which comes with its own primary and subsidiary systems of entailment – it is clear that the car can exist *only* within a modern globalized industrial system.
>
> (Taylor 2010: 51; his emphasis)

The difficulty with entailment is that it is implicit rather than explicit, and, for most of the time, it is not in fact clear to most people that a car can exist only within a modern globalized industrial system. The system is taken for granted, a naturalized given in the contemporary setting. In considering translation in the context of entailment, it is worth making a distinction between what might be termed primary entailment and secondary entailment. To illustrate the difference, we will look briefly at the history of one of the most famous translation artefacts, currently held in the British Museum in London, the Rosetta Stone.

The Rosetta Stone is a granodiorite stele from ancient Egypt inscribed with a decree issued at Memphis, Egypt, on behalf of King Ptolemy V. Three scripts are used in the decree, ancient Egyptian hieroglyphs, Egyptian demotic script, and ancient Greek. Designed to re-establish the rule of the Ptolemaic kings over Egypt, the stele was erected after the coronation of King Ptolemy V and was inscribed with a decree which established the divine cult of the new ruler. Though the texts in three scripts diverge, there are substantial similarities between them, similarities that enabled scholars such as Jean-François Champollion and Robert Young to begin to unravel the meanings of ancient Egyptian hieroglyphs. The decree ends with the instruction that a copy be placed in every temple, inscribed in the 'language of the gods' (hieroglyphs), the 'language of documents' (demotic), and the 'language of the Greeks', the language of the Ptolemaic government (Andrews 1985: 3–5). Though it is difficult to ascertain whether one of the texts was the standard version from which the other two were translated, the coexistence of the three scripts is material evidence of the translation zone that was Ptolemaic Egypt.

In the case of the Rosetta Stone, primary entailment is the system which allows the stele to be created and to exist in a meaningful context. There are the tools and processes of extraction which allow the rock to be extracted from a grandiorite quarry; the forms of carriage and locomotion that will allow a stele weighing more than 800 kilos (the Rosetta Stone, an incomplete stele, weighs 760 kilos; *ibid.*, 7) to be brought to a site; the built infrastructure (the temples) which house the steles; the artisans who will prepare the stone and carve the inscriptions on the surface of the stele. Implicit in the instruction that steles be placed in temples throughout the territory ruled by Ptolemy V is a whole technical infrastructure, a system of primary entailment, without which his decree would be null and void, invisible to everyone and understood by no one.

Secondary entailment is the manner in which the Rosetta Stone becomes integrated into a later process of decipherment and translation, a process that would revolutionize understanding of the ancient Egyptian world (Adkins and Adkins 2000; Ray 2007). By this we mean that later descriptions and analyses of life in ancient Egypt would be heavily dependent on the scholarship of Champollion, Young, and others, which provides the translation key to ancient Egyptian hieroglyphs, and whose work is distributed through the scholarly and print infrastructure of two competing empires, the French and the British. In other words, at both the original moment of the erection of Ptolemy V's decree and the subsequent translation of the texts carried on the stele, there are implicit systems of entailment that allow texts to function in multilingual contexts. Understanding the full force of the Ptolemaic decree entails the material manifestation of a decree in three scripts in particular sites and the existence of a professional class to translate the royal decree into the appropriate scripts, just as understanding ancient Egypt entails the physical dissemination of a translation enterprise undertaken by a scholarly class in nineteenth-century Europe. In both instances, translation emerges against the backdrop of entailment, and translation in turn becomes a form of entailment, something without which so much else cannot happen. In detailing the idiomatic use of the term 'Rosetta Stone' in English, the *Oxford English Dictionary* notes that it refers to a key to the process of decryption of encoded information, more particularly, when a small but representative sample is recognized as the clue to understanding a larger whole (Stevenson 2010: 786). When we examine the Rosetta Stone itself from the point of entailment, what is apparent is that the object itself, symbol of, and aid to, a culture of translation, is the clue to understanding a larger whole, the entire web of human–*technē* interaction presupposed by systems of entailment.

Central to the notion of entailment in this context is the control or mastery of distance. The domestication and selective breeding of certain animals such as horses and dromedaries had significant spatial consequences for the cultures that were able to avail themselves of these techniques. Indeed, such was the enduring importance of the spatial revolution brought about by the use of particular animals that, as David Edgerton has pointed out in the *The Shock of the Old: Technology and Global History since 1900* (2006: 71), Hitler invaded Russia with more horses than Napoleon. In later centuries, it was the invention of steam-powered machines that would revolutionize humans' relationship to space. A changing relationship to space is primarily about a changing relationship to proximity and distance. It becomes easier to go further. Going further is not, however, just about breeding the right horse or inventing the perfect machine. The mastery of distance implies an infrastructure which gives effective form to the possibility of a mode of transport, whether animal or human. Roads, bridges, ports – and later, railways, airports and information superhighways – are the essential components of systems of transportation. Covering distance becomes infinitely more problematic over a terrain with no road, or for a computer user with no access to a network. Implicit in the form of entailment represented by the infrastructure of transport are the twin components of organization and information. The emergence of a postal service in the Mongol Empire in the thirteenth and fourteenth centuries was heavily dependent on the existence of a more explicitly organized imperial administration. It was not enough to have the roads, the bridges, and the horses, it was also necessary to have a body which could organize a coherent, functioning network over great distances (Gazagnadou 1994). Organization is only effective, however, if you know what it is you are going to organize. It is necessary to know where the roads and bridges and ports are, if they exist, and, if they do not, where they need to be built, what the terrain is like, and who lives close by. Geographical, cultural, and political information is integral to the conquest of distance. When the Christian West embarks on a course of expansion, translators will be crucial to the acquisition of Arab cartographical knowledge which informed voyages of conquest and discovery (Lyons 2010). This knowledge was itself the product of the organizational and informational needs of an Islamic empire that at its height covered vast physical distances. The difficulty with mastering distance is that distance can exercise its own mastery. Herein lies an anxiety that has troubled translation and technology for centuries and is still very much part of contemporary debates on the internet, an anxiety that relates to what we might call the ethics of proximity.

Proximity

Valerius Maximus, the first-century CE Roman writer, noted that interpreters placed a distance between the Senate and the power of Greek rhetoric (in McElduff 2009: 145, n29). In seeking to master or overcome the distance between Latin and Greek, the interpreters created more distance between speakers and listeners, listeners who were thus distanced from the full force of the Greek rhetoric. Cicero shared Maximus' unease about the distance created by translation between the audience and the original utterance, but it is the historians Polybius and Livy who underline the fraught nature of translation as a means to overcome linguistic and cultural distance. Polybius in his *Histories* (20.9–10) and Livy in his *From the Founding of the City/Ab urbe condita* (36.28) speak of the calamitous consequences of the mistranslation of a word for the Greek Aetolians in 191 BCE. The Greek word *pistis* and the Latin *fides* taken out of context can mean more or less the same thing: faith or trust. When the Aetolians surrendered into the *fides* of the Roman people, they did not realize that in the specific context of conflict, this meant the unconditional surrender of all of one's people, goods, and lands. The distance between languages that had been overcome through the act of translation only revealed the much greater distance between two cultures or peoples in their understanding of what was entailed by particular words in specific contexts. In other words, what the Roman writers are exercised by, in an empire whose very existence is predicated on the centrality of organization and information, is whether the techniques and infrastructure of spatial compression do not need to be tempered by an ever vigilant ethics of proximity. Does translation whose existence attests to the presence of distance, to the emergence of a large, multilingual empire (Adams 2008), not also act as an unwitting litmus test for the pitfalls of estrangement? Does the attempt to overcome distance engender more distance, or is there something profoundly unsettling about techniques for mastering distance that endanger rather than enhance proximity? Does translation capture like no other practice the specific ethico-political consequences of technical advance and commercial expansion?

To answer these questions from a late medieval, rather than a classical Roman, perspective it is useful to consider a fourteenth-century Venetian translation of tenth-century Irish Latin text, the *Navigatio Sancti Brendani*. As Federico Italiano points out in his essay on the translation, *La navigazione di Sancta Brendani* is significant for a number of reasons:

> First of all, it is the encounter between the monastic Latin of northern Europe and the bubbling *lengua* of the Dogi, the Romance dialect spoken in the most prosperous harbour of the pre-Columbian Mediterranean. Second, it is the encounter between the language of a major maritime power – which, at least until the conquest of Constantinople by the Turks, ruled the trade in the eastern Mediterranean Sea – and a profoundly religious text, conceived mostly as a support for a monk's progress towards sanctity. Moreover, this translation represents the encounter between an east-oriented political and cultural entity, as Venice was at the beginning of the fourteenth century, with one of the first and most significant literary expressions of west-orientation in Christendom.
>
> (Italiano 2012: 7)

The *Navigatio* itself was, of course, an attempt to overcome distance: Irish distance from the Middle Eastern roots of anchoretic practice in Christianity (Thom 2006). By substituting the waves of the ocean for the wastes of the desert, the Irish were able to effect a geographical translation that legitimized an odyssey of exile and spiritual renewal in a very different setting. The East of early Christianity had to be translated into the West of later Christians. Part of this translation involved situating the journey of Brendan and his companions in the Old Irish narrative genre of the *immram* or odyssey tale. What is notable about the Venetian translation is that the differences which are detailed by Italiano are equally motivated by a desire to vanquish a particular kind of distance, but only in a sense by creating new forms of distancing. The Hiberno-Latin *Navigatio* is profoundly laconic about the earthly paradise that is the avowed destination of the monks' perilous journey. Getting there is all, and the description of the paradise is a matter of few lines. The author of *La navigazione*, on the other hand, devotes almost a fifth of the text to the description of the paradise island. The island is notable for the richness of its treasures and the exotic fulsomeness of its flora:

> Then we came closer to the wood, and there we found trees laden with precious stones, with leaves of silver and gold, and with gemstones on their branches. The other side of the trees seemed to be burning, and there came to our nostrils a fragrance so sweet that we almost fainted; it was like incense, aloes, musk, balsam, amber, rosemary, savin and roses, and like the scent of jasmine. But for all the flames we could not see any smoke. We went round to the side where the flames appeared to be, but we saw nothing but trees.
>
> (Davie 2005: 223)

The Venetian translator is aware of the potential distance between his audience and the tenth-century Irish text, so the purpose of his extensive interpolation is to bring his audience closer to his text. The way in which this is done is determined by the principal horizon of expectation of the Venetian world: trade.

Just as the paintings of Vittorio Carpaccio a century later will be replete with the mercantile technology of the Venetian Republic, the ships, arsenals, cranes, and ports, so the translator of *La navigazione* seeks to capture the imagination of readers through the earthly promise of foreign trade. The strong Eastern orientation of Venice is as much a matter of trading opportunity as aesthetic preference. If the Venetian Marco Polo's *Divisament dou monde* fuels what Italiano calls an 'east-oriented geopoetics' (Italiano 2012: 14), it is because trade in spices and other luxury goods from lands to the east of Venice provides a highly lucrative source of income for the Adriatic city-state. At the end of the Venetian translation, Brendan and his fellow brethren sail west to return home, in the completely opposite direction to the route indicated in the tenth-century *Navigatio*. This is the culminating moment of the shift from a 'west-oriented Atlantic geopoetics into an east-oriented, Mediterranean geopoetics' (*ibid.*, 1). Paradoxically, the Venetian translation brings the tale closer to its readers through the lure of the distant, the exotic. The translation reduces distance through the imaginative riches suggested by distance, the Eastern paradises of Venetian middle- and long-distance trade. In the late medieval period, the Venetians are quick to equip themselves with Arab navigational technology and through translation find the knowledge to use it (Crowley 2011). Whatever helps to overcome distance is to the advantage of the great maritime power of the Eastern Mediterranean. What is evident again is the convergence of an ethics of proximity (the familiar, fragrant trees in the domesticated island paradise) with the necessity of distance, the interval, the gap, the difference that must always be overcome, but which must always resist being overcome. As David Damrosch has noted with respect to the translation of poetry from ancient Egypt, 'they [the poems] achieve their full force as world literature when we translate them in such a way as to preserve both their immediacy and their distance from us, both their universality and their temporal and cultural specificity' (Damrosch 2003: 163–64). The infinitely flexible dyad of immediacy and distance gives meaning and purpose to the task not only of the translator, but of the trader and the artificer.

Trade

What the Rosetta Stone most obviously indicates is a prolonged Greek presence in Egypt, but what the translation–technology interrelation equally suggests is a much more profound reordering of geographies of influence that challenge Eurocentric biases in the ordering of historical accounts. When urban civiliz-ation developed in Mesopotamia, the fertile flood plain provided farmers with abundant crops but it did not provide many important, basic materials such as wood, stone, and metals. These materials had to be imported, mainly along the major rivers. What made these imports possible was the revolution in the technology of transport, with the development of 'metallurgy, the wheel, the pack-ass and sailing ships' (Childe 1964: 97). As the urban communities in Mesopotamia grew in size and complexity so did the extent and range of trade with merchant colonies established in towns like Kanesh in Anatolia in the second millennium BCE. As Gordon Childe notes, the cultural significance of this activity was immense. Trade became

> a more potent agency in the diffusion of culture than it is today. Free crafts-men might travel with the caravans seeking a market for their skill, while slaves would form part of the merchandise. These, together with the whole caravan or ship's company, must be accommodated in the home city. Foreign-ers in a strange land would demand the comforts of their own religion ... If cults were thus transmitted, useful arts and crafts could be transmitted just as easily. Trade promoted the pooling of human experience.
>
> (*Ibid.*, 105–06)

The pooling of experience is not going to happen if there is no mutual under-standing. What the logic of trade implies is the possibility of translation for the 'foreigners in a strange land', and it is this possibility which makes trade such a 'potent agency in the diffusion of culture'. Economic need in this instance con-joined to a technology of transport provides the context for a culture of trans-lation which permits a powerful 'pooling of human experience'. The fortunes of translation become inseparable from the technology (wheel, metallurgy, sailing ship) that makes long-distance trade possible. Long-distance trade by its nature makes the necessity of translation more deeply felt, in that it brings into contact speakers from non-cognate language groups, speakers who may, of course, come to influence these languages in their development. As Timothy Brook notes about Dutch trade in a much later period, first contacts give way to second contacts with predictable consequences:

> More people were in motion over longer distances and sojourning away from home for longer periods of time than at any other time in human

history. More people were engaging in transactions with people whose languages they did not know and whose cultures they had never experienced. At the same time, more people were learning languages and adjusting to unfamiliar customs.

(Brook 2008: 39)

Mesopotomia was not the only site of urban civilization. During the Bronze Age, from around 3000 BCE, Eurasia sees the development of a number of urban civilizations. These are civilizations in the technical sense of being urban cultures that depend upon advanced agriculture employing technology such as the wheel, the plough, and, in some instances, irrigation. Forms of urban living and the development of artisanal activities such as writing allow for new modes of communication, as well as new means of production. These urban societies are highly stratified and produce hierarchically differentiated cultural forms in the Red River Valley in China, in the Harappan culture of northern India, in Mesopotamia, in Egypt, and later in other parts of the Fertile Crescent of the Near East, as well as parts of Eastern Europe (Goody 2006: 29). What these societies share is a commitment to the development and use of existing and new technologies, an involvement in trade, and, by extension, cultural contact, which is only conceivable in any sustained sense through the agency of translation. Such was the importance of trade that Akkadian kings regularly intervened on behalf of merchants travelling abroad, and in Central America, among the Aztecs, refusal to trade served as a pretext for an attack (Adams 1966: 164).

Seeing translation, technology, and trade as a coherent triad of influence must inevitably challenge insular or schismatic notions of cultural and political evolution. Martin Bernal, in his trenchant critique of conventional accounts of the emergence of classical antiquity, *Black Athena*, is deeply sceptical of attempts to present the development of ancient Greek culture as being primarily the outcome of the invasion of Indo-European or Indo-Hittite speakers, what he refers to as the Aryan model (Bernal 1987: 1991). This reading involves the rejection or marginalization of Semitic or Afro-Asiatic influences from the Eastern Mediterranean. Hence, links to Phoenician and Egyptian civilization, and the effects of these civilizations on Greek language, script, and culture, have tended to be habitually downplayed. In Bernal's view, this Eurocentric bias is attributable to the rise of racism and anti-Semitism in late nineteenth-century Europe, but the social anthropologist Jack Goody sees this partial reading of history as dating from anxieties around the expansion of Islam in the seventh century, the successive defeats of the Crusaders, and the loss of Byzantium (Goody 2006: 61). There is a triple refusal at work in the ethnocentrism identified by Bernal and Goody: the failure to account for the importance of trade, the denial of the role and power of technology (both in terms of where it comes from and what it can do), and lastly, the elision of the possibility and potential significance of translation. In some instances, the paucity of written evidence makes the establishment of influence more problematic. The Phoenicians, although they had a written alphabet and therefore clearly kept records of various kinds, have left very few of these written records. The libraries of Carthage either disappeared or were destroyed after the destruction of the city by the Romans in 146 BCE. Evidence of the advanced knowledge of the Phoenicians in the area of agriculture is borne out by a later Latin translation of a Phoenician textbook on the subject (*ibid.*, 65). Titus Flavius Josephus, the first-century Romano-Jewish historian, noted that, 'among the nations in touch with the Greeks, it was the Phoenicians who made the largest use of writing both for recording affairs of life and for the commemoration of public events'. He also highlighted the external dimension to this practice of writing and recording by adding, 'for many years past the people of Tyre have kept public records, compiled and very carefully preserved by the state, of the memorable events in their internal history and in their relations with foreign nations' (quoted in Bernal 1991: 6).

It is difficult to say anything about 'foreign relations' if you do not know what you are relating to, and the very fact of giving meaning and form to contact implies the basic labour of translation. Exchanging the cedars of Lebanon with Egyptians for the building of boats (the Egyptians had no timber but knew how to build boats), or with the peoples of Israel for grain (the Israelis needed the wood for the temples and the Phoenicians needed the food to survive, since much of their land was covered in forests), the Phoenicians were in constant contact with speakers of different languages. Their search for the basic components of contemporary technologies, metals, led them to Carthage, Cadiz, and Cornwall, in the latter case in their quest for tin (Jidejian 1991). Translation would be necessary to enable trade to happen, and to make sense of what this trade involved or meant for the Phoenicians, but it also explains why it appears scarcely plausible to posit *sui generis* models of cultural evolution. What we might term the '3T' paradigm (Technology, Trade, Translation) of the interconnectedness of early urban cultures has a resonance for later cultural history. Peter Burke, for example, has shown how the Renaissance in Western Europe involved continuous interaction with Byzantium and Islam, both of which had their own 'renaissances' of Greek and Roman antiquity, and what characterized these interactions was the presence of translation, technology exchange, and trading relationships (Burke 1998, 2004; Burke and Po-chia Hsia 2007). Hence, the notion that the Renaissance was an exclusively Western European phenomenon is gainsayed by, among others, the persistent traffic of translation. Accounting for this traffic or applying the 3T paradigm helps to correct repeated geopolitical bias in the ordering of events or the explanation of transformation in languages, societies, and cultures.

Control

If trade, translation, and technology are marginalized in exclusivist readings of history, it is, in part, to do with the desire to control how the past is perceived. Presenting classical antiquity as a specifically Eurocentric development, or treating the Renaissance as a uniquely Western European phenomenon, answers to the geopolitical anxieties of the age. However, it is possible to argue that what translation brings to the fore is a more general issue of control that is not confined to any particular period or interpretation of history. Furthermore, it is nervousness around control which also characterizes reactions to the potential effects of technology and trade, a nervousness which is a recurrent feature of political and moral panics around the effects of both.

Official interpreters were a part of the ancient world, as borne out in papyri and military inscriptions (Hermann 1956: 25–59; Kurz 1986: 215–20; Calderini 1953: 341–46). Interpreters of Punic and Iberian languages in the Roman Senate are mentioned by Cicero in *De divinatione* (2.131.6), and interpreters are further mentioned in his *De finibus* (5.89). In a later text, the *Notitia dignitatum*, interpreter or *interpres* is listed as an established office in both the Eastern and Western empires of Rome (McElduff 2009: 144). Given the political, commercial, and military extent of the Roman Empire, an extension made possible in part by advances in Roman military technology (Dixon and Southern 1997), it is hardly surprising that the need was consistently felt to employ language intermediaries. Improved technology and expanding commercial horizons brought unprecedented opportunities for conquest and riches, but this expansion brought with it dilemmas over access and control, dilemmas that were articulated in prescriptive ideas as to what was the true and proper purpose of translation, and who should practise it.

Siobhán McElduff, in her analysis of the background to Cicero's famous declaration concerning his translations of orations by the Greek orators Aeschines and Demosthenes, 'I did not translate them as an interpreter, but as an orator' (*nec converti ut interpres, sed ut orator*), points out the sensitivities around class and status underlying Cicero's comments:

> Although a member of the elite might take it upon himself to act as an interpreter in special circumstances, it was not, on the whole, a high-status position in Rome, if only for the reason that a growing multilingual empire needed far more interpreters than the relatively tiny elite could ever provide, or would be willing to provide, in the case of low-status languages such as Celtic or Punic. So while the senator C. Acilius could interpret for the senate in 154 BCE (Aulus Gellus *Attic Nights*/*Noctae Atticae* 6.14.7–9), on the whole interpreters in the senate were anonymous figures called upon by senators as they were needed (*On Ends*/*De finibus* 5.89).
>
> (McElduff 2009: 136)

An expanding empire needed interpreters, but would the expansion of interpreting be the undoing of the empire? In his prosecution of the corrupt governor of Sicily, Verres, Cicero complained bitterly about the venality of Verres' interpreter, Aulus Valentius: 'There is in Sicily an interpreter called Aulus Valentius, whom that man [Verres] was accustomed to employ as an interpreter, not for help with Greek but with his thefts and outrages. This insignificant and needy interpreter suddenly became a tithe-gatherer' (*Against Verres*/*In Verrem* 2.3.84 (McElduff's translation)). The Roman dramatist Plautus, in his comedy *The*

Small Carthaginian/Poenulus (194/3 BCE), has a slave pretend to act as an interpreter between Punic and Latin for the Carthaginian Hanno, who, unbeknown
to the fraudulent interpreter, has a perfect command of both languages. That a
slave should act as interpreter is indicative of the highly uncertain social status
of interpreters, but the fact that he is both incompetent and deceptive confirms the
worst fears of Cicero and others that a little translation is a dangerous thing.

In his *De finibus/On Ends*, Cicero talks of Greek works appearing in shoddy
Latin translations, translations that have distorted Roman readers' view of
Greek philosophy (1.8). In the context of Epicurean philosophy, both he and his
correspondents identify the *interpretes* as the culprits (*Letters to his Friends/Ad
familiares* 15.19.2). A problem with the interpreters is that whereas they might,
at best, get to the second level of Roman schooling, the *schola grammatici* or
School of the Grammarian, they could never proceed to the final stage, the
rhetoris schola, where, under the tutelage of another Roman who had mastered
the art of rhetoric, they would finally be made ready for full participation in
public life. Needless to say, access to this third stage was predicated on being
admitted to the ruling elite. What is noteworthy about the second level of education, the *schola grammatici*, is that it is primarily about the mastering of the
technology of literacy, the close reading, parsing, and production of written
texts. Literacy and the simplicity of the Latin alphabet offer a democratization of
knowledge, and the effects are potentially far-reaching: 'one of the attacks on
these "interpreters" is that they use common or ordinary language (*vulgari ser-
mone* [*Academica* 1.4–5]) in their works rather than the sophisticated arguments
necessary for proper philosophical writing, and that their texts circulate
amongst the unlearned' (McElduff 2009: 142). The problems of control multiply,
because not only are people of the wrong social class engaged in translation,
but they are using the wrong kind of language, and the translations are being
read by the wrong kind of people. The translation needs of empire through the
technology of literacy are gradually subverting social and linguistic proprieties.
For Cicero, the recognition of the transformative potential of translation
detailed in *On the Orator/De oratore* is haunted by the nightmare of illicit dissemination, the unholy coupling of technology and translation in the uncontrolled
spread of text.

If we look at one of the iconic images of the emergence of translation in the
Western tradition, Peter Bruegel's *Tower of Babel* in the Kunsthistoriches
Museum, Vienna, tools are everywhere. Ladders, levers, pulleys, scaffolding,
and implements for cutting and shaping stone litter the construction site.
Arguably, the true common language here is technology itself, as the workers
make use of the assorted tools to build the tower to the heavens. In the biblical
account in Genesis, language is inseparable from technical potential, from the
potential to create, shape and transform: 'Behold, they are one people, and they have
all one language; and this is only the beginning of what they will do; and nothing
that they propose to do will now be impossible for them' (Genesis 11: 1–9).

What Bruegel's image makes manifest is that 'nothing that they propose to
do will now be impossible for them' because of the symbiotic relationship with

the third system whose evidence is everywhere in the painting of the sixteenth-century Dutch master. Furthermore, language itself – as it assumes the written form that ensures the endurance of the Genesis account and the emergence of the religions of the book which so captivate Adelard of Bath – becomes an especially potent tool. As James Gleick notes, when 'the word is instantiated in paper or stone, it takes on a separate existence as artifice. It is a product of tools, and it is a tool' (Gleick 2011: 30). The nineteenth-century British writer Samuel Butler, in attempting to define what it was about writing that so sharply distinguished it from the 'spoken symbol' that perishes instantly without material trace, opted for range and longevity:

> The written symbol extends infinitely, as regards time and space, the range within which one mind can communicate with another; it gives the writer's mind a life limited by the duration of ink, paper, and readers, as against that of his flesh and blood body.
>
> (Butler 1970: 198)

Implicit in Butler's understanding of writing is that this is a tool that transcends space and time. However, there is no transcendence without translation. For phonetically based languages like English, texts written in Old and Middle English are not readily intelligible to readers of Modern English and require forms of intralingual translation for those texts to be readily understandable (Steiner 1975). The infinite extension of the written symbol through time requires the good offices of the translator. Similarly, when the written symbol is considered in terms of spatial range, the default multilingualism of the planet means that there can be no extension in space without the work of the translator. The text needs translation to travel. So the afterlife of the text, dependent on elements of the third system, the artefacts of 'ink' and 'paper', relies also on the tool of language, and, by extension, translation, for its ability to reach 'readers' in a different time and space.

Medium

To develop a keener sense of how translation and technology are co-terminous in contemporary human culture, it is necessary to turn to the founding credo of media studies, as articulated by Marshall McLuhan. McLuhan famously argued that what mattered most about new media was not the content they carried but the medium itself (McLuhan 2001). Whereas a great deal of early debate had focused on television as a corrupter of youth because of the violent or 'decadent' nature of its content, McLuhan argued that the real message of television lay not in what it carried, but in what it was. The ability to beam images from around the globe into people's private homes within hours and eventually within microseconds of the events happening was infinitely more important in its effect (the creation of imagined global communities of spectatorship) than what was actually shown in these images. Footage of the *Apollo II* moon landing in private homes did much more to change the notion of what it was to inhabit the earth than to advance in any real sense popular understanding of what it might be to live on the moon.

Of course, television was only one of the many media throughout history where the medium itself was the most important message. Francis Bacon, writing in his *Novum Organum* in 1620, claimed that movable-type printing had so changed the world that 'no empire or sect seems to have exercised a greater power and influence on human affairs' (Bacon 1863: 178). The fruits of literacy, which had formerly been the preserve of a cultivated elite, were now made available to much larger numbers of people. According to one set of estimates, the number of books published in the half century after Gutenberg's invention was equal to the total output produced by European scribes during the previous one thousand years (Clapham 1957: 37). By the end of the fifteenth century, nearly 250 towns in Europe had print shops, and 12 million volumes had already appeared in print. Knowledge was miniaturized (no cumbersome codices), made portable, privatized (available to individuals of modest means and not just to institutions and the wealthy), and multiplied (more words on smaller pages in many more copies) by the new intellectual technology that was the printing press (Eisenstein 1980). As Nicholas Carr has pointed out, citing the examples of the map and the clock, intellectual technologies shape and articulate new worldviews:

> Every intellectual technology, to put it another way, embodies an intellectual ethic, a set of assumptions about how the mind works or should work. The map and the clock shared a similar ethic. Both placed a new stress on measurement and abstraction, on perceiving and defining forms and processes beyond those apparent to the senses.
>
> (Carr 2010: 45)

Seeing time as an objectively measurable quantity in a timepiece is a radically different experience from a subjective notion of time incorporated into a task which takes as long as it will take, but has no reference to 'external' time. A city dweller moving through streets familiar from birth will experience it very differently at a spatial and cognitive level from a tourist armed with a map. So if the medium is indeed the most important message to retain from human technical advances and our intellectual technologies – the tools that we employ to extend or support our mental powers – embody an intellectual ethic, what are we to conclude about the implications of these intellectual ethics for the development of our thinking about translation?

When Alister McGrath set about telling the story of the genesis of the most famous translation in the English language, the King James or Authorized Version of the Bible, he discusses Erasmus, Luther, early pioneers such as Wycliffe and Tyndale, and the Reformation insistence on the importance of the vernacular, but the very first chapter is devoted to 'Unknown to the Ancients: The New Technology' (McGrath 2001: 5–23). For McGrath, the new technology of

printing implied an intellectual ethic of mobility which would be hugely significant for the role of translation in religious and political history. In the early
sixteenth century, vernacular translations of the Bible were prohibited in
England, but as McGrath notes:

> it was one thing to block the production of such a Bible in England. What
> would happen if an English translation of the Bible were to be produced
> abroad, and smuggled into England? The very idea of such a Bible was
> deeply upsetting to the English elite at this time. The development of the
> technology of printing in Europe meant that there was a very real threat of
> someone producing such a Bible as a business venture, aiming to make
> money out of it. What could be done to stop this? As events proved, this
> much-feared development would not take place until the 1520s. As expected it
> proved formidably difficult to detect and prevent such an importation.
>
> (*Ibid.*, 22–23)

The intellectual ethic of mobility was not simply a matter of ideas that would
experience Butler's infinite extension in printed translation, but translation itself
had a recursive effect on the medium through which it was expressed, language.

In sixteenth-century England, as empire and commercial opportunity beckon,
the world's languages become a more vivid presence for the inhabitants of the
island. Contact ushers in a new self-consciousness. As Richard Mulcaster, a
London school headmaster observed in 1582, 'Forenners and strangers do
wonder at us, both for the uncertaintie in our writing, and the inconstancie in
our letters' (Mulcaster 1582: 12). The pressure to standardize spelling comes in
part from the new solidity of the printed word, unvarying in its presence on the
page, and from the comparative gaze of the scholars aware of the burgeoning of
vernaculars and translations from classical languages on the European continent.
When Robert Cawdrey produces the first dictionary of the English language, *A
Table Alphabeticall*, in 1604, he is heavily influenced by translation dictionaries
such as Thomas Thomas's 1587 *Dictionarium lingue Latine et Anglicanae*
(Simpson 2007).

The dictionary becomes the emblematic tool of the translator, but the technology
of printing that makes the tool a viable entity also ensures that its effects
become unpredictable. Cawdrey, for example, is alarmed at the prevalence of
borrowings from foreign languages, including Latin and Greek: 'Some men seek
so far for outlandish English, that they forget altogether their mothers language, so
that if some of their mothers were alive, they were not able to tell, or understand
what they say' (*ibid.*, 45). The technology that permits the rapid dissemination of
the English vernacular, that facilitates the creation of essential language tools
such as dictionaries, is also the medium that estranges the language from its
habitual users, leading the speakers away from the homely embrace of the
maternal to the siren songs of 'inkhorn' terms. Translation is not for the first
time Janus-faced, a custodian of language specificity (providing the template for
the first monolingual dictionary), and an incorrigible bearer of foreign, corrupting

influences, encouraging the 'counterfeyting' of 'the Kings English' (*ibid.*, 45). However, crucially, it is translation as a culture–technology hybrid that is unsettling, not the act of language transfer *per se*.

The anxieties the hybrid gives rise to are clearly articulated by Roger Ascham in *The Scholemaster* (1570), where he inveighs against the vogue for translations from Italian in late sixteenth-century England. Ascham complains that these 'translations were sold in every shop in London, commended by honest titles the soner to corrupt honest manners: dedicated over boldlie to virtuous and honourable personages, the easielier to begile simple and innocent wittes' (26 r–v). Ascham's solution to the problem was radical. The authorities should prevent publication of further translations from Italian, pointing to the fact that more of them had been 'set out in Printe within these fewe monethes, than have been sene in England many score yeare before' (28). Translation may involve a form of deception, the 'honest titles' in the target language masking dishonourable intent in the source language, but what are truly alarming are the viral effects of the technology. The effects are both spatial and temporal. The translations are no longer to be found in a handful of institutional libraries, they are now 'sold in every shop in London'. Through print, translations colonize the space of the everyday, menacing in their accessibility. It is not only where they are sold that is unsettling, but the numbers that are sold. The time of production and reception collapses from 'score yeare' to 'fewe monethes'. The sheer volume and speed of translation mean that Ascham feels it is time to react to save English virtue. The intensity of production abbreviates the time of response. Translation in symbiosis with Taylor's third system becomes a force with which to be reckoned.

The medium of printing thus becomes part of the message of translation. Ubiquitous, mobile, and accessible, the translated products of the printing press will provoke religious upheaval in country after country. A similar scenario will accompany the dissemination of the translated ideas of the eighteenth-century Enlightenment, nineteenth-century socialism, or twentieth-century liberalism (Delisle and Woodsworth 1995). In other words, when James S. Holmes in his celebrated 'map' of translation studies speaks of medium-restricted theories, he misses a crucial dimension of the relationship between medium and message in translation. For Holmes, medium-restricted theories can be subdivided into theories of translations performed by machines or performed by humans. Further subdivisions are possible depending on whether we are speaking of automated translation or of machine-assisted human translation. Other possible divisions follow whether the human translation is written or spoken, and whether the spoken translation or interpreting is consecutive or simultaneous (Holmes in Venuti 2004: 180–92). The notion of 'medium' is thus construed as a kind of classificatory aid, a way of expressing how contents are differently transmitted. However, it is arguable that 'medium-restriction' is more than a simple heuristic device, a convenient handle for defining content delivery. The definitional possibilities of medium affect translation in very profound ways in different media.

Imagined community

The relationship between translation and technology in the case of an emergent medium is captured in the case history of one translator deeply committed to the power of the printed word, Lady Jane Wilde:

> A week later, I am transferred here. Three more months go over and my mother dies. No one knew better than you how deeply I loved and honoured her. Her death was terrible to me; but I, once a lord of language, have no words in which to express my anguish and my shame. ... She and my father had bequeathed me a name they had made noble and honoured, not merely in literature, art, archaeology, and science, but in the public history of my own country, in its evolution as a nation. I had disgraced that name eternally.
>
> (Wilde 1973: 141)

Writing to Lord Alfred Douglas from the grim squalor of Reading Gaol, Oscar Wilde records in *De Profundis* the heartbreak of a loss magnified by his own bleak incarceration. Lady Jane Wilde died on 3 February 1896 and was buried in Kensal Green Cemetery two days later. A tiny crowd gathered for the funeral as Oscar was refused permission to attend, and Lady Wilde had explicitly requested in a letter that her funeral be private and that no one be asked to come. Her other son Willie was present as chief mourner, but in death as in life she would fall victim to his spendthrift indifference. He failed to make any arrangements with the cemetery, did not have any headstone erected, and after seven years, no fees having been paid, Lady Wilde's remains were removed to an unknown grave.

Almost half a century earlier, she had written to a correspondent in December 1848 that 'I should like to rage through life – this orthodox creeping is too tame for me – ah this wild rebellious nature of mine. I wish I could satiate it with Empires though a St Helena were the end' (Melville 1999: 53). The isolated ignominy of an unmarked London grave lacked the drama of St Helena, but much in the life and work of Lady Wilde speaks eloquently of her 'wild rebellious nature', a nature that would find an enduring form of expression in translations that would contribute in their own, specific way to the 'public history' of her native country, Ireland, a public history borne of the possibilities of print technology.

Jane Elgee was born in Dublin on 27 December 1821. Her father, Charles, was a solicitor and her grandfather, John, had risen to the position of archdeacon in the Church of Ireland. In later life, Jane was to claim that 'Elgee' was an Irish corruption of the Italian 'Algiati', and that 'Algiati' in turn was related to the family name of 'Alighieri'. Hence, an imaginary lineage ran from Dante Alighieri to Jane Elgee, a lineage highlighted by the adoption of an Italianate second name, 'Francesca', and her later *nom de plume*, Speranza. Her origins were somewhat more prosaic. Her great-grandfather, Charles Elgee, was a bricklayer from County Durham in England. He came to Ireland with his brother in the 1730s during a building boom and soon made his fortune. Wealth opened the way to social mobility, and the Elgees made their way into the solid professions of law and the Church (Melville 1999: 281–82). The first appearance of literary talent in the family came with the marriage of Jane's aunt, Henrietta, to the Reverend Charles Maturin. Maturin was deeply eccentric and often kept the shutters closed during the day so that he could give himself up to his passion for dancing. In addition to writing plays, he produced a number of tales of Gothic horror, the most famous of which, *Melmoth the Wanderer*, was published in 1820. When Oscar Wilde was released from prison, the pseudonym he adopted was taken from the hero of Maturin's novel, Sebastian Melmoth. Unusually for the family, Maturin was an Irish nationalist who had publicly denounced the Act of Union between Britain and Ireland (1800) in *The Wild Irish Boy* (1808). The Elgees were on the whole, however, staunchly Unionist, members of a respectable Protestant middle class in Ireland that was deeply committed to the link with the British Crown.

Languages rather than politics were to be Jane's first passion. She told a journalist from *Hearth and Home* four years before her death that 'I was always very fond of study, and of books. My favourite study was languages. I succeeded in mastering ten of the European languages. Till my eighteenth year I never wrote anything. All my time was given to study' (Melville 1999: 20). Horace Wyndham, one of the first biographers of Jane Wilde, noted rather archly that 'at an age when other little girls of her years were playing with dolls and looking at picture books this one was reading Latin and Greek "for pleasure". Taught by a succession of governesses and tutors, she also managed to acquire a sound knowledge of French, German and Italian' (Wyndham 1951: 14). The Wildes were no strangers to hyperbole, and the precise extent of Jane's language abilities remains a matter of conjecture. Due to the early death of her father, Jane's mother was not particularly affluent. She would not have been able to pay for a large number of governesses and private tutors. Though her translations that appear later in *The Nation* newspaper in the 1840s would mention Russian, Turkish, Spanish, German, Italian, and Portuguese originals, her actual language abilities (though still considerable) appear to have been confined to French, German, Italian, and the classical languages through the instruction of her uncle, a distinguished classicist, Richard Waddy Elgee (de Vere White 1967: 85). In later life, she would make determined efforts to learn Danish, Swedish, and Russian, but it is in translation from French and German that Jane Elgee made her principal mark as a translator.

In addition to a passion and talent for languages, Jane read voraciously, a fact borne out by the extraordinarily wide range of references of her later published works. The omnivorous interests of Jane have not always endeared her to a sceptical posterity. Horace Wyndham claimed, 'the trouble with Lady Wilde was that, where her output was concerned, she wandered (and often floundered) in too many fields. Poetry, philosophy, politics, history, biography, travel, criticism and fiction all engaged her pen' (Wyndham 1951: 162). If Sebastian

Melmoth's wanderings are obliquely associated with terror, Jane Elgee's excite her own biographer's disapproval. And yet it is a precondition of the practice of translation that the translator *wanders*. The translator wanders between languages, cultures, texts, bodies of knowledge. The essential nomadism of the translator's condition demands a creative restlessness that drives the translator's curiosity and enhances their ability (Cronin 2000). In this sense, the wide-ranging enquiries of Jane Elgee were a necessary prolegomenon to her later activity as literary translator. The nomadic ethic in translation has a further resonance in the specific area of gender. In an essay entitled 'The Bondage of Women', Jane Wilde inveighs against the social and economic subjugation of women. After a brief historical survey of the condition of women she observes, 'We have now traced the history of women from Paradise to the nineteenth century, and have heard nothing through the long roll of ages but the clank of their fetters' (Wilde 1893: 13). The dominant image is of the control of women's interests, desires, expression. Above all, her view of patriarchy is that it fears more than anything else the *mobility* of women, this dangerous, illicit, unchaperoned wandering from their assigned place in the social and economic order. Some women chose to break these fetters by engaging in the physical act of travelling, and Jane Wilde does indeed produce her own travel account in 1884 entitled *Driftwood from Scandinavia* (Wilde 1884). However, implicit in the act of translation itself is a movement, a rejection of fixity, the embrace of a world outside the familiar, the already known, the acceptable. It is perhaps no coincidence then that it is in the context of rebellion that Jane Elgee first comes to prominence as a translator.

In October 1842 a new weekly newspaper called *The Nation* was launched in Dublin. The newspaper espoused the political philosophy of Daniel O'Connell's Repeal Association, namely, it sought an end to the Act of Union which from 1 January 1801 united the parliaments of Ireland and Great Britain. The newspaper wanted an independent Irish parliament in Dublin and was committed to the development of a strong, separate cultural identity for the Irish. The founders of the newspaper were Charles Gavan Duffy, John Blake Dillon, and Thomas Osborne Davis. They were often referred to as the 'Young Ireland' group, as observers saw similarities between their aims and those of Heinrich Heine and the Young Germany movement in the 1830s and of the Young Italy movement led by Giuseppe Mazzini. The founders were committed to a non-sectarian, inclusive notion of Irishness, and the newspaper was an immediate success, being widely read in all parts of the country. *The Nation* was a classic example of the way a print culture, a new medium, became central to the definition of an imagined national community (Anderson 2006). Thomas Davis, the most intellectually capable of the three co-founders, died in 1845, and Oscar Wilde was later to claim that it was the impression made on his mother by the popular grief at Davis's funeral that led her to get involved in the newspaper (Ellmann 1987: 7). More probably, it was writings by Young Ireland propagandists, such as Richard D'Alton Williams, which gradually drew the spirited Jane Elgee to *The Nation* (Wyndham 1951: 23). She initially submitted both poetry of her own composition and translations to the newspaper, signing the poems and translations 'Speranza' and the covering letters 'John Fanshawe Ellis', instead of Jane Francesca Elgee.

Charles Gavan Duffy was keen to meet the author of the work and was instructed to come to a house at 34 Leeson Street, Dublin. A maid brought him into a room where he met George Smith, publisher to Trinity College Dublin and well known for his Unionist views. Gavan Duffy expressed his surprise at Smith being the author of the seditious verse, whereupon Smith left the room and returned with a 'tall girl on his arm, whose stately carriage and figure, flashing brown eyes, and features cast in an heroic mould, seemed fit for the genius of poetry, or the spirit of revolution' (Gavan Duffy 1883: 94). The very first poem by 'Speranza', published in the *Nation* on 21 February 1846, was a translation from the German entitled 'The Holy War'. The use of the pseudonym was obviously designed to protect Jane from the wrath of her family who were extremely hostile to the political programme of the *Nation*. An act of expediency became a byword for rebellion, and the name 'Speranza' was soon to become inseparable from the growing militancy of the Young Ireland movement.

The bulk of Speranza's translated verse was published in the *Nation* in 1846. The source languages for her translations were French, German, Italian, Spanish, Portuguese, and Russian. German was the dominant source language, and between 1846 and 1848 she produced seventeen separate translations from German. Alongside translating better-known figures like Machiavelli, Savanarola, Schiller, Lamartine, Camões and Ölenschläger, she translated anonymous folk material and unattributed poems by obscure minor poets. The predominance of German-language material was in keeping with translation tradition in nineteenth-century Ireland. Links between the British royal family and Germany, the prestige of German Romanticism, and the cultural impact of Prussian nationalism were all contributory, if at times contradictory, factors in continued Irish interest in German writing (O'Neill 1985). John Anster, the first English-language translator of Goethe's *Faust*, Charles Des Voeux, translator into English of Goethe's *Tasso*, and Anna Jameson, translator of popular plays by Princess Amalia of Saxony, were just some of the Irish translators working in the 1820s, 1830s, and 1840s who would have created a context for the reception for the translation work of Jane Elgee.

Many of Elgee's translations later appeared in the 1864 anthology of Speranza's original and translated verse (Wilde 1864). Significantly, the title given to the section containing the translations in this anthology is 'Wanderings through European Literature'. The 'wandering' is evident not only in the extremely eclectic choice of language and source-language authors (Machiavelli, Savanarola), but in her own political wandering from her Unionist family of origin. In effect, the translations frequently serve as propaganda vehicles for a nationalist sentiment that informs much of her poetic work for the *Nation*. A typical example is an unattributed poem from German entitled 'Our Fatherland' (Wilde 1864: 122–23):

Our Fatherland

Why pour the ruby wine,
For glad carousal, brothers mine,
In the sparkling glass that flashes
In your hand,
When, mourning, sits in dust and ashes
Why Why Our Fatherland?

The florid, emphatic nature of the writing with its lexical drama ('sparkling', 'flashes'), rigid juxtapositions ('glad carousal'/'mourning ... Fatherland') and rhetorical flourishes ('Why pour the ruby wine') typified much of the nationalist verse of the period, not only in Ireland, but in Italy, France, and Germany. In the period leading up to the Year of Revolutions, verse became a standard part of the arsenal of nationalist dissent. Paradoxically, though movements in France, Germany, Italy, and Ireland were animated by feelings of national distinctness and cultural separateness, what is apparent in the translation work of Jane Elgee, alias Speranza (and other contributors to the *Nation*, such as Denis Florence MacCarthy and James Clarence Mangan), is the existence of a form of nationalist internationalism. Poems translated from languages informed by similar political sentiments were put into circulation in different languages, all proclaiming their ineradicable difference. This circulation was possible because of the conjoined effects of print technology and journal and newspaper production. Standard readings of cultural nationalism often perceive the phenomenon to be one uniquely of closure, of a closed, sectarian inwardness. However, the translation activities of Jane Elgee in the context of the emerging medium of newsprint reveal local conflict as producing an opening out to conflicts elsewhere, expressed in other cultures and languages, even if the result is also the importation of doggerel into the pages of the *Nation*.

Translation through the technical medium of print contributes to the formation of specific, national sentiment, but its structuring principle points not to the uniqueness of Irish conditions, but to the potential universality of circumstances of oppression. There is a dual movement of construction of separate identity and dismantling of singularity at work in all translation in a nationalist context, and Elgee's translations are no exception. It is in the context of the technology of journal and newspaper production that this dual movement of translation comes to exercise its effects.

The year 1845 saw the beginning of the Great Famine in Ireland. The failure of the potato crop in three successive years, and the apparent indifference of the British administration to the plight of the Irish, had catastrophic consequences. Within the space of a decade, one million people had died, and one million had emigrated as a result of the famine. The famine deaths radicalized the Young Ireland movement, and particularly under the influence of John Mitchel many young nationalists were no longer calling for peaceful constitutional change, but for armed insurrection against the Crown administration in Ireland. A poem by

Jane Elgee that appeared in the 21 January 1847 issue of the *Nation* entitled 'The Stricken Land' (later republished as 'The Famine Year') expresses the increasing vehemence of her own writing (Wilde 1864):

> A ghastly, spectral army, before the great God we'll stand,
> And arraign ye as our murderers, the spoilers of our land.

The government eventually moved against the leaders of the Young Ireland movement, and the editor of the *Nation*, Charles Gavan Duffy, among others, was arrested on a charge of treason. While he was in prison, Jane Elgee wrote two inflammatory editorials for the newspaper, one for the 29 July 1848 issue entitled 'Jacta Alea Est', which began:

> The Irish Nation has at length decided. England has done us one good service at least. Her recent acts have taken away the last miserable pretext for passive submission. She has justified us before the world, and ennobled the timid, humble supplication of a degraded, insulted people, into the proud demand for independence by a resolved, prepared, and fearless Nation …
>
> Oh! for a hundred thousand muskets glittering brightly in the light of heaven, and the monumental barricades stretching across each of our noble streets, made desolate by England – circling around that doomed Castle [Dublin Castle, seat of British administration in Ireland], made infamous by England, where the foreign tyrant has held his council of treason and iniquity against our people and our country for seven hundred years.

The editorial provoked uproar, given the growing importance of the printed word and the wide circulation of the *Nation*, and the government immediately suppressed the newspaper. The editorial was added to the list of charges against Gavan Duffy, despite the fact he was already in prison when the editorial was published. In later years, melodramatic accounts of Jane Elgee's intervention in Gavan Duffy's trial were in wide circulation, notably that as the charge of writing the seditious lead article were read out, she stood up in court and denounced herself as the author of the piece. In reality, before Gavan Duffy's trial she went to the Solicitor General's office and declared herself to be the author (Melville 1999: 48–50). As a result, the Crown prosecution eventually dropped the charge from the indictment. Jane Elgee was not the only radical woman translator contributing to the *Nation*. When Oscar Wilde on his 1882 American tour included a lecture on 'The Irish Poets of 1848', one of the poets he explicitly mentioned was 'Eve', the pseudonym of Mary Anne Kelly (Ellmann 1987: 187). Like Jane Elgee, Mary Anne Kelly came from a staunch Unionist background, translated Lamartine, and would eventually go on to translate other French works, in her case principally the poetry of Pierre-Jean de Béranger (Webb 1997). Kelly, through her romantic involvement with Kevin Izod O'Doherty, another Young Irelander sentenced to ten years' transportation to Van Diemen's Land, remained close to nationalist circles for a number of years. This was not to be the case with Jane Elgee. The failure of an abortive rising in 1848 left her thoroughly disillusioned with nationalist politics in Ireland, and she began to move away from more direct political involvement.

Jane Wilde expressed opinions on a bewildering array of subjects, from political revolution to the appropriate form of dress for the literary lady, but translation, strangely, was not one of them. Her importance as a translator lies not in what she had to say about translation, but in what she translated, and in what contexts her translations appeared, most notably the power of a new medium to disseminate her translated work. Though not all her translations for the *Nation* were political, she clearly saw the potential of translation as propaganda. The political project, however, is not one of ethnocentric inwardness, but of opening up the Irish Question to other perspectives. By drawing attention to works expressing national sentiments in other languages, works that were made available through print culture, the effect of Wilde's translations was to broaden the intellectual and cultural basis of her nationalism. Though, in later years, she was to look more favourably on the connection with England, Jane Wilde was constantly aware of the provincializing effect on Irish life of political and economic power being located in London, rather than Dublin. She expresses her impatience with the disabling effects of cultural dependency in the opening pages of her 1884 travel account, *Driftwood to Scandinavia*. In these pages she describes the historic links between Ireland and Denmark and laments the sad decline of the present:

> But all relationship between Ireland and Denmark, through love or fighting, literature or commerce, has long since ended. Now not a Dane lives in Dublin. The race seems extinct; not a Danish teacher can be had, and no passenger ship leaves an Irish port direct for Copenhagen, nor indeed any other place, except the mails for England. We Irish only import coal and export cattle and live wholly dependent on another people for the means of transit, should we desire a dinner in Paris or a cup of coffee at Madrid; although centuries ago direct and constant intercourse was kept up, not only with Denmark, but also with France and Spain.
>
> (Wilde 1884: 9–10)

Wilde's translations were a means of maintaining 'direct and constant intercourse' between Ireland and the European continent, and it is significant that it is in her most politicized phase that her range of source languages is the widest. One of the avowed aims of the Young Irelanders was to promote a non-sectarian definition of Irish identity, hence the involvement of both Protestants and Catholics in the leadership of the movement. The women who wrote for the *Nation*, like Jane Elgee and Mary Anne Kelly, came from staunch Unionist backgrounds and shared this vision of Irishness that was not a hostage to religious affiliation. However, they broadened their notion of political emancipation by attempting to alter the 'means of transit' culturally through translation. Translation activity provided a means of both affirming cultural specificity (the explicit political content of a number of the translations) and opening up areas of commonality (the Irish case was not isolated, many more nations found themselves in a similar predicament in 1848) with other cultures and peoples. In the absence of the movement outwards, exacerbated by more essentialist notions of nationality, the Irish would be, as she puts it in her travel account, 'wholly dependent upon England for a latch-key, should we wish to leave our island prison' (Wilde 1884: 10). In both the affirmation of specificity and the opening up of areas of commonality, it is the intersection of translation and technology that allows for the unfolding of political possibility.

Differentiation

From the emergence of urban civilization to the dissemination of nationalist ideology in nineteenth-century Europe, it is apparent that what translation reveals again and again is not so much the world as puzzle (made of discrete pieces) as the world as network. However, it is not translation in isolation, as a transcendent Platonic idea, which gives it the reticular force that has characterized its role in human affairs. It is translation as an integral part of Taylor's third system that has provided an invaluable context and shape for its transformative effects in world cultures. Nonetheless, a question that arises out of this embeddedness is whether the very tools that make translation possible by their very nature overdetermine the effects of translation itself. Does the reproductive capacity of technology, the ability to use similar tools in very different settings, give shape to forms of globalization, for example, which are both reductive and homogenizing? I shall examine various responses to these questions in successive chapters, but here I would like to dwell for a moment on the historical dimension of the tension between homogenization and differentiation.

Around the second century CE, Apuleius composed his famous narrative *Metamorphoses*, known commonly as *The Golden Ass*. The hero Lucius, who has been changed into a donkey, travels around the Mediterranean coast where various adventures befall him. He eventually arrives in Egypt, where he meets the goddess Isis, who restores him to human form through a gift of roses. Apuleius begins his tale by offering 'to caress your ears into approval with a pretty whisper, if only you will not begrudge looking at Egyptian papyrus inscribed with the sharpness of the reed from the Nile' (1.3). What Apuleius is doing, in effect, is providing his reader with the technical background to the dissemination of the tale, the 'papyrus', the sharpened 'reed', the tool and material support without which the tale would not exist in a written, transmissible form. As a native speaker of Greek, Apuleius is apologetic about the quality of his Latin, but he sees his bilingualism as somehow appropriate to the story he wishes to tell: 'Now in fact this very changing of language corresponds to the type of writing we have undertaken, which is like the skill of a rider jumping from one horse to another. We are about to begin a Greekish story' (1.5). The horse, as was known to Apuleius, is of course the outcome of human efforts to domesticate space, and the ass, into which Lucius is transformed, is one of the most significant animals to interact with humans in the technical transformation of the world (Edgerton 2006: 108). So Apuleius' description of his translation task is bounded by the technology of spatial transformation. As Lucius' journey takes him from Rome to Greece to Egypt, he moves between different languages, traditions, and cultures. What his journey makes manifest, through his induction into the cult of Isis, whose rites he will practise on his return to Rome, is the nature of the world-network, the interpenetration of linguistic, religious, and cultural influences. The metamorphic figure of Lucius mirrors the translation process, but it also shows the hybridity implicit in the outcome, as Lucius reveals himself to be most human (he is restored to human form) when he is most deeply implicated in the culture of the foreign, Egyptian goddess. Lucius is transformed by his journey, not in the literal sense – for much of it he is a four-legged beast of burden – but in the sense that, although in the end he is restored to his former human self, he is a very different person, committed to a new set of beliefs.

The tale of Lucius is as much a tale of (transport and chirographic) technology as it is of translation. The outcome, however, is not more of same but more that is different. Apuleius' picaresque tale is, as the original title *Metamorphoses* suggests, all about transformation. Lucius' experience echoes the conclusions of the world systems theorist Immanuel Wallerstein, who claimed that 'the history of the world has been the very opposite of a trend towards cultural homogenization; it has rather been a trend towards cultural differentiation, or cultural elaboration or cultural complexity' (Wallerstein 1997: 96). One way of capturing that complexity has been to privilege space over time in the constructions of the global past and present. Whereas previously, a default evolutionism based on Western assumptions of cultural supremacy underwrote distinctions between 'developed', 'developing', and 'underdeveloped countries', the world is now divided along a spatial axis of North and South and East and West (Grataloup 2011: 34). The difficulty is, of course, that space is as compromised politically as time, and how national territories are defined or the notions of continents conceptualized is deeply implicated in sets of assumptions concerning politics, culture, and history. Where does Europe end and Asia begin? Where do Europe and Asia end and Africa begin? The great technical advances in the Fertile Crescent (domestication of plants and animals, emergence of cities, states, writing, the alphabet) spread as much to the Indus Valley, Central Asia, and beyond as they did along the Mediterranean. These developments would equally impact peoples and cultures on the eastern coast of Africa as along the trans-Sahara trade routes (*ibid.*, 101).

The controversy, for example, around Turkey's membership of the European Union reveals the sharpness of the political and cultural divisions that recruit geography as an alibi. What is immediately obvious from the translation history of Turkey is that attempts at dichotomous definition, at defining Turkey as 'European' or 'Asian', are largely meaningless. Not only the multilingual and multicultural Ottoman Empire but more recently the Turkish nation-state has been a continual crossroads of linguistic, cultural, political, and religious influences transiting through the porous zone of translation (Susam-Sarajeva 2006; Tahir Gürçaglar 2008). The continuous efforts to impose boundaries, whether geographical or religious, are endlessly frustrated by the translation record which attests to the permanent presence of liminal openness in a plethora of different cultures and circumstances. Is there a fundamental conflict, however, between the porousness of boundaries as detailed in translation histories, and the processes of differentiation as new identities emerge from linguistic and cultural contact through translation? Does difference not, by definition, involve the rejection of similarity, a refusal to see what is shared in favour of what makes one different?

An insight into this question of differentiation, which echoes a number of the historical episodes referred to in this chapter, is provided by the *New York Times*' reaction to the discovery of cuneiform tablets in the ruins of Nineveh. A few days after his discovery of the tablets, George Smith telegraphed news of it to a British newspaper, the *Daily Telegraph*. The anonymous author of the *New York Times* article is captivated by the differences between the two forms of communication:

> It is hardly possible to conceive of two more opposite literary productions than the modern newspaper and the crumbling and mysterious records found among the ruins of antiquity. A telegraph dispatch and a cuneiform inscription are both composed of letters, and are alike *media* for the transmission of intelligence; and yet how immeasurably different are the ideas of life, time, and space which the mention of the two suggests. The one is gray with the dust and mist of the past, the other fresh and throbbing with the life of the present. One is fading out of all practical suggestiveness, the other deals with nothing else.
>
> (Cited in Damrosch 2003: 54–55; original emphasis)

The *New York Times* writer is correct to see both the clay tablet and modern newsprint as media for the transmission of intelligence, but the ideas of life, time, and space are not so 'immeasurably different' as the writer suggests. Practical necessity, possibilities of communication over time and space, shifts between languages and cultures, questions of technical infrastructure (ovens for clay tablets, printing presses) are issues as pressing in the Assyrian kingdom of Ashurbanipal as in the emergent media infrastructures of the nineteenth century. The aim of the *Daily Telegraph* was to make a difference in how its readers viewed the world, just as Ashurbanipal wanted his great library to make a difference in how he dealt with his subjects and their worlds. In both the 'telegraph dispatch' and the 'cuneiform inscription' we find potent factors of diversification, making the nature of trade and government, or information and communication, immeasurably more complex. Both the Assyrian ruler and the British newspaper had recourse to translation and technology, whether to make administration viable or news available. The differences that ensued, however, revealed not so much what separated the two civilizations, standing at a great remove in time, but rather what they had in common. Ghosting both periods is the third system, the material objects invented by human beings that acquire their full sense in the deeply socialized world of human interaction. Adelard's Palace of the World may have had many mansions, but they all remain tellingly interconnected, and it is these interconnections in late modernity that will be the subject of the following chapters.

2 Plain speaking

One of the core questions faced by translation in the digital age is how one of the tools that humans use to communicate, language, is influenced by the other tools that they use. If time, critical mass, and cost are factors informing the organization of translation as an activity, what happens to language itself in the new regimes of translation? Beginning with cost, it is currently estimated that it costs $200 to write, review, and publish a new page of documentation. The cost rises to $1,200 if the page is translated into the 23 official and working languages of the European Union (Wignall 2009). The notion of cost is bound with the polysemous nature of language. The more that is said in one language, the more it costs to say it in other languages. As the Business Development Director of Software and Documentation Localization (SDL) phrases it, 'the multiplicity of ways in which we can say the same thing means that we have to review and approve everything that is written. With no way to see in advance what is the "correct" way to say something, writers are continually and unwittingly creating new material' (Wignall 2009). So one new sentence in the original language generates twenty-three new ones, for example, in an EU context. This new material is referred to as 'accidental content' and a reduction in the generation of this accidental content, it is argued, can generate significant savings. However, the rationale for combating the proliferation of 'accidental content' is not just financial. Too much content of this type 'reduces clarity, quality and ultimately ease of use. In extreme cases, it may even impact safety if content is sufficiently inconsistent and confusing' (*ibid.*). The duty of clarity and care come to the rescue of cost in this scenario.

The use of versions of a controlled natural language (CNL) is held to be one way of avoiding the expensive and dangerous chaos of novelty. CNLs in English generally use specific sets of grammatical and style rules, a restricted vocabulary, limited sentence lengths, determiners, and the active rather than passive voice to generate content. This makes texts easier to translate but it also means that more translations can be reused as the likelihood of 'accidental content' being generated in the source language is diminished. The less that is being said, the more often it can be said (in other languages), at no extra cost. Procedural information (e.g. removing and replacing the casing on a PC), warnings and cautions, component level reuse (e.g. documentation relating to similar engines and gearboxes reused across different model ranges) all lend themselves to the type of content reuse which is viewed as an important element of the economies of scale of large-scale translation projects.

Lingua franca

However, it is useful to reflect more broadly on how natural language, and not simply specific corporate CNLs, become an object of control in an era of global communication, and how actual practices resist specific ideologies of control.

Martin Schell, the managing director of the company globalenglish.com, sees global rights as carrying global responsibilities:

> Our company focuses on promoting and refining the use of English as a tool for global communication. We feel that native speakers of English need to become more responsible about the global role of our language. This means speaking and writing English more clearly so that it can be understood throughout the world.
>
> (Schell 2008)

Speaking and writing English as a *lingua franca* involves simplifying syntax by reducing subordinate clauses and modifier phrases, minimizing the total number of compound nouns, verbs, adjectives, and adverbs, and expressing an action as a verb rather than a gerund. The global English of Schell, like the controlled natural languages of SDL, is deemed to be simpler, safer, and more economic. In addition, however, it is presented as more culturally sensitive. Whereas it might be assumed that the particular complexity or 'thickness' of a language constitutes its richness, and that cultural sensitivity in translation involves capturing and respecting that thickness, Schell's global English paradigm is strikingly different. The more English is shorn of its difference, the more it is sensitive to difference. Responsible intercultural communication for the English native speaker is to be always-already translated, to imagine what it is like to experience English as a translated subject. Removing, not preserving, 'accidental content' is the only way to avoid the accidents of misunderstanding, real or imagined.

Ironically, the rhetoric of transparency finds support in the 'Fight the FOG' campaign started by translators of the European Commission Translation Service in 1998. FOG is an acronym for a number of expressions such as 'farrago of Gallicisms', 'frequency of gobbledygook' and 'full of garbage' (Taviano 2010: 44). The campaign was prompted by a concern that the English increasingly being used as a *lingua franca* in EU institutions was characterized by wordiness, imprecision, and clumsiness. In effect, what the campaign acknowledged was that many of the source documents produced by the EU in English were themselves previously translated, in that they had been compiled by multilingual groups who did not have English as their first language. The collaborative and interactive capacities of information technology, in addition to the reduced time necessary for the physical production and virtual delivery of documents, both facilitate and accelerate the creation of these multi-authored documents. In the increasing prevalence in the European Union of English as a *lingua franca* (see Phillipson 2003), it would appear that, just as there is technical convergence in terms of norms of exchange and interoperability (e.g. internet protocols), there is a similar convergence at linguistic level in terms of a common language of exchange and communication. One operating system. One language. Is English, then, the 'Perfect Language' that Umberto Eco's scholars have striven for over centuries (Eco 2010), the Language of Eden that communicates its meanings with perfect clarity, its communicativeness a perfect parallel to the instantaneous connectivity of global IT?

Stefania Taviano, in her study of the translation of English as a *lingua franca*, notes that, in the case of many EU documents in English, what tends to characterize these documents is convoluted syntax (overuse of relative clauses, embedded and subordinate clauses), use of uncommon collocations, Eurojargon, adjectives/past participles in a post-modifier position, and extensive use of nominalization (Taviano 2010: 27). She notes further that:

> Noun phrases tend to be post-modified by a prepositional phrase with an embedded non-finite verb phrase, as in the case of 'the establishment of a mechanism of structured cooperation with the Member States using methods that have been tried and tested under the Open Method of Coordination was welcomed by many respondents'.
>
> (*Ibid.*, 29)

English as a *lingua franca* in the corpus she examined was not a language of incisive immediacy, but was, rather, complex, prolix, and, in places, impenetrable. It was the existence of these hybrid, tacitly multilingual texts that led Anthony Pym to characterize translators not as agents of hybridization, but as practitioners of dehybridization:

> Contemporary professional non-literary translation in Europe is an agent of dehybridization for the simple reason that source-text generation processes are increasingly multilingual, whereas translation outputs are normally monolingual. Translations in general are agents of dehybridization in the sense that they create and project the illusion of the non-hybrid text.
>
> (Pym 2001: 11)

In an experiment that Taviano carried out with her students (mainly native speakers of Spanish and Italian), she found that they considered the translation of the long and complex sentences from English into Italian and Spanish to be relatively straightforward. The hybridized texts, due to the presence of syntactic structures common to Romance languages, had already done the work of dehybridization for the translators. It was the rendition of terse, more succinct prose that proved more problematic (Taviano 2010: 76–77). The tacit translation present in the production of the documents, in a sense, facilitated the task of explicit translation in their translation into other languages. What is striking, as Taviano points out, is that the widespread use of English 'seems to contradict the view ... according to which we should be witnessing the use of a reduced and simplified international language for the sake of global intelligibility and limited translated costs' (*ibid.*, 40). English may be coming to dominate the institutions of the European Union, but there is no simple or obvious correlation between greater usage and greater simplicity. More means more.

Arturo Tosi, in his study of the translation of EU green and white papers into Italian, concluded that the translations led to the production of a hybrid: Euro-Italian. The translators, in other words, were engaged not so much in a process of dehybridization as one of parallel hybridization of the target language (Tosi 2007). The Italian translations were characterized by relatively high levels of lexical ambiguity, a marked lack of coherence and cohesion due to a tendency to follow the patterning of the source text, and a repeated preference for maintaining more or less the same word count as the English original. What further amplified these trends was the recourse to translation memory systems that stored previous translations and databases which encouraged the use of previous translations. The multiplier effect of translation technology, as noted in Tosi's study, gives the lie to the more utopian visions of language instrumentalism that characterize particular presentations of translation tools. If English-language dominance of information technology (Microsoft, Apple, Google, Facebook) has, in part, favoured the widespread dissemination of English, it does not necessarily follow that the fate of English as a *lingua franca* for translation is as a language devoid of 'accidental content' or dramatically simplified for the purposes of instantaneous, global communication. On the contrary, the greater incidence of non-native-speaker production of text in English can lead to a collaborative hybridization of the text to facilitate collective production and understanding of the text. The epidemiological effects of digital technology are expressed through the use of translation memories and terminology databases which further the dissemination of new translated varieties of this hybridized English.

Plain speaking

The idea that 'speaking and writing English more clearly so that it can be understood throughout the world' carries with it the assumption that the rhetorical and cultural preferences of one language community can be mapped onto a code of universal communication. In other words, the idea that the use of plain, unadorned speech is the ideal and most effective way to communicate is rooted in the theocratic ideology of Reformation English. An important impulse for the translation of the Bible into vernacular languages was, of course, the notion that in this way the Word of God could be communicated directly to the community of the faithful. No more hiding behind the borrowed prestige of a dead language or dependence on the unreliable mediation of a corrupt clergy, the Word of God would be made directly accessible to Everyman and

Everywoman (McGrath 2002). In a further Puritan elaboration of the ideology of directness and immediacy, great emphasis is placed on plain speaking, the simple, unfussy statement of unadorned truth, and there is a widespread suspicion of all forms of figurative speech, which made Elizabethan and Jacobean theatre a particular object of opprobrium (Cronin 2005: 13–24). The idea of plain speaking is a rhetorical preference that is linked to a particular set of religious and cultural dispositions, and there is no reason to assume that it can be the expression, or must found an idea, of universal intelligibility. Indeed, in Pascal Mercier's novel *Perlmann's Silence*, the assumptions that it might are what irritate the German linguist Philip Perlmann in his reactions to the language usage of his American colleague Brian Millar:

> The voice formed the words in a completely undetached way. Its tone didn't just show that this was the speaker's mother tongue; the tone wasn't only an expression of the self-evidence with which the language was at the speaker's disposal. There was more at stake: the tone contained ... the message that this was the only language that truly deserved to be taken seriously. *Self-righteous, you understand, his penetratingly sonorous voice is self-righteous. He speaks as if the others were to blame and very much to be pitied for the fact that they, too, don't speak East Coast American, this Yankee language.*
>
> (Mercier 2011: 42; his emphasis)

Perlmann is expressing these opinions to his partner Agnes who is somewhat sceptical of his sweeping generalizations about speakers of American English. However, what Perlmann fails to observe as a linguist is that circulation deterritorializes a language, and that the technology of circulation is not an indifferent factor in the mutation of the language. That is to say, the greater the incidence of English-language usage by non-native speakers, the more probable are the translation effects in English of second-language usage, as is borne out by the development of a particular English-language variety in the European Union. What gives more permanent presence to these translation effects is that they are in turn captured in translation into different European languages, leading to the kind of hybridization described by Tosi in the case of Italian. An important link in this process of replication is the technology of translation and terminological memory. The technology acts as a powerful multiplier of mutation. In this respect, it is no different from the print technology of Reformation Europe where the conjoined effects of vernacular translation and print dissemination led to the emergence of markedly different varieties of language, German being a case in point (Sanders 2010). As James Gleick argues:

> The revolution of Protestantism hinged more on Bible reading than on any point of doctrine – print overcoming script; the codex supplanting the scroll; and the vernacular replacing the ancient languages. Before print, scripture was not truly fixed. All forms of knowledge achieved stability and

permanence, not because paper was more durable than papyrus but because there were many more copies.

(Gleick 2011: 400)

Stability, permanence, reliability are dependent on the power of duplication. Readers can discuss texts and know that they are referring to the same version wherever they find themselves once they have the same printed edition. This capacity to reproduce the same endlessly implies, of course, the powerful consolidating effects of mechanical or technical reproduction. However, what is also apparent is that there are no predictable outcomes in terms of the translation fortunes of global English or the effects of English as a *lingua franca* in translation in a digital age.

One potential translation scenario is the chaste utopia of Schell's global English or the minimalist functionalism of SDL's controlled natural language. Such developments would appear to dovetail with a digital logic of frictionless, instantaneous convertibility, simplified, monosemic speech circulating even more rapidly along information superhighways. English as a language then would not only reflect the predominantly Anglophone corporate dominance of the internet but would also become the preferred language of digital communication through the promotion of highly controlled and specific varieties of the language. Of course, the fundamental impulse for this development is translational. The optimal version of the language is optimal translatability. The easier it is to translate the original document, the more successfully 'global' the language of composition, with ease of translation as the implicit parameter for global intelligibility and acceptance. In this scenario, English as cybertongue is always already translated.

There is, however, another potential path of translation development involving English. Nigel Reeves, in assessing future directions for the evolution of translation, outlined two broad categories of translation activity:

> The first might be called spontaneous translation, done on the spot, often from International English, or direct composition in English by business people, civil servants, scientists, and secretaries, a kind of internalized translation that removes the need for the translator as middleman. The second will be specialist translation in technical, professional, legal, political and cultural domains, including the related studies of summarizing and information transfer.

(Reeves 2002: 28)

Implicit in Reeves's distinction is an opposition between English as the source language of global communication that disavows the fact of translation (removing the need for the 'middleman' or, more often, middlewoman) and English as a source and target language for translation that explicitly recognizes translation as a constituent part of the cultural identity of particular groups of speakers of the language. This distinction mirrors a familiar one between English as a language of global communication and English as the 'basis for constructing cultural identities' (Graddol 2001: 27). The division in turn maps onto a ready differentiation between the automatic or semi-automatic translation of text for 'Global Information Management (GIM) solutions' (Wignall 2009), and highly particularized forms of translation, involving substantial human input, such as new renditions of Dostoevsky's novels into English. However, such translation polarities, with their attendant machine/human opposition, tend to mask the reality of a global *lingua franca* evolving into distinctive hybrid varieties which are not necessarily simpler or less complex, but are nonetheless distinct. EU English is not the mother tongue of any citizen of the European Union, but it is the recognizable *lingua franca* of the discourse community of its speakers. What gives the language its force is the cyborg interface of humans (translators) and technology (translation memories) which reproduces for the digital age the disseminatory effects of the printed copy in the time of Gutenberg and Caxton. The 'internalized translation' that Reeves speaks of complicates the notion of a reduced pidgin that would serve as the perfect parallel for the binary reductionism of the digital. As a language such as English is more widely disseminated through information technology, it does not follow that Schell's global English is the inevitable medium of realization, as opposed to a horizon of rhetorical expectation (see also Crystal 2006). On the contrary, the replicative effects of the technology do not so much eliminate the translator as middleman as turn potentially every middleman into a translator with access to their own virtual printing press. This is not to assume that power is evenly distributed throughout discourse communities, but it is to acknowledge that the effects of circulation in translation are neither predictable nor homogeneous.

Cost

The historian and cultural commentator Tony Judt noted in a work published shortly before his death that there was something profoundly wrong about the way people lived their lives in the contemporary world:

> For thirty years we have made a virtue out of the pursuit of material self-interest: indeed, this very pursuit now constitutes whatever remains of our sense of collective purpose. We know what things cost but we have no idea what they are worth.
>
> (Judt 2010: 1)

Even if the 'we' in Judt's claim needs to be qualified and refers to particular parts of the planet where material self-interest can be distinguished from physical survival, he diagnoses a recurrent and habitual concern with cost as the ultimate arbiter of what is of value in many contemporary societies subject to the dictates and constraints of the market economy. Indeed, it is frequently the costs associated with translation which become a core argument in attempts to remove translation altogether from societies and impose a *lingua franca*. For example, one commentator on the translation situation in the United Kingdom said:

> It's a shocking figure: more than £100m was spent in the past year on translating and interpreting for British residents who don't speak English. In the name of multiculturalism, one Home Office-funded centre alone provides these services in 76 languages … The financial cost is bad enough, but there is a wider problem about the confused signals we are sending to immigrant communities. We are telling them they don't have to learn English, let alone integrate.
>
> (Rahman 2006)

What is noteworthy is the way the idea of cost itself is constructed. Costs are always a cost to someone, and it is that someone who goes on to define what a cost is, but strictly, of course, in their terms. Implicit in Rahman's argument is the contention that, if everyone learned English, the unnecessary costs associated with translation would disappear. This is a variation on an argument that is articulated in critiques of the foundational multilingualism of supranational bodies such as the European Union. Large sums of money, it is argued, currently being spent on translation and interpreting services would be saved if the sole working language of the EU was a vehicular language like English (see van Parijs 2004: 13–32). What these arguments centred on cost fail to make apparent is the equally onerous costs of having to resort to a *lingua franca*. If one takes the example of English, vast sums of money are spent by governments around the globe to teach the language to their citizens (Grin 2004: 189–202). This is a cost borne not by English speakers themselves but by those who do not speak the language and feel the necessity to learn it. In addition, the circulation of cultural goods such as music, cinema, literature in English does not automatically have to bear the translation costs that are almost axiomatic for non-Anglophone cultures which seek global circulation of their own cultural goods. In a sense, what is at play here is a practice of what might be termed *transferred* or *devolved cost*, which is characteristic of the redefinition of consumption in digital contexts. In a practice that originated with low-cost airline operators, passengers are invited or, in the case of some airlines, obliged to print out their boarding passes in advance. This entails the passenger having access to the equipment (computer and printer) and internet connection which allow him or her to enter the necessary details and print out the pass. Both the equipment and the connection are a cost to the passenger or to the entity that has made them available to the passenger. There is the further opportunity cost of the time spent accessing the site, filling in the details and printing out the pass. During this time the passenger could have been doing something else. In short, what were formerly production costs for the airline, paying someone to prepare and print out your boarding pass, now become consumption costs for the passenger.

Digital technology allows the transfer of the cost from the producer to the consumer. The labour is done by the passenger, not the airline operator, so that the surplus value accrues not to the passenger but to the airline. When the argument is advanced that the use of a *lingua franca* eliminates translation costs, what one has, in effect, is another form of transferred cost. Whether as consumers of the *lingua franca* or potential producers of the language, those who do not speak it must bear the often considerable costs of acquisition. These costs include not only the monies actually spent on formal education, but also the opportunity costs of learning the language, that is, the time that could have been spent pursuing another potentially lucrative activity. Thus, while much has been said in the context of translation about how digital technology can reduce translation costs, little thought has been given to the notion of cost itself and how it is construed and by whom. Translation is always a 'cost' to the dominant language, but the dominant language is supposedly cost free. The costs disappear from view, discreetly transferred to the speakers of the non-dominant idioms. What translation, or the demand for translation, makes apparent is the nature or existence of this embedded cost for the non-native speakers of a global *lingua franca*. If there is no need to translate, this is because one of the parties has spent considerable time and/or money dispensing with that need.

Disintermediation

The making invisible of the language labour encoded in the use of a global language is partly facilitated by the phenomenon of *disintermediation* which is a striking feature of economic and social practice in the digital age. As the British writer and economic commentator John Lanchester remarks, 'Every time you deal with a phone menu or interactive voicemail service, you're donating your surplus value to the people you're dealing with' (Lanchester 2012: 8). When you withdraw money from an ATM or book a flight on the internet, you are doing the job of an absent human agent. The agent who formerly booked the flight or the bank teller who handed you your money, the intermediary, is no longer there. Digital technology allows for the disintermediation, and you now do the work. In effect, what disintermediation tends to favour is an ideology of convenience that masks the nature of the real costs involved.

There is another dimension to disintermediation which has to do not so much with the cost as with the nature of what is being mediated. In a Google search of sites in another language, alongside the results of the search, there is, in square brackets, the lapidary phrase, 'Translate this page'. By clicking on the translation option, the results can, of course, be highly uneven, and much occasional humour at gatherings of translators is devoted to providing ever more egregious examples of what comes out at the other end of online machine translation systems. The jokes may be entertaining but they are not always particularly instructive. What is revealing about Google Translate is not the limits to what it can do, but the unlimited nature of what it says about what it means to translate. What we have, in effect, is another form of disintermediation: in this instance, the translator as intermediary is nowhere to be seen. The labour of translation is made invisible, and the only ostensible labour is the greater or lesser degree of post-editing on the part of the user, as they try to make sense of the translated passages. However, there is another dimension to this phenomenon of translation disintermediation which relates to how the activity of translation itself comes to be perceived.

Knowledge is fundamentally a matter of distinctions. We understand some-thing by reference to something else – the ways in which a lemon, for example, is similar to an orange, and the ways in which it is different. Of course, what we choose to compare something with will determine what aspects of it will be to the fore and what will be marginalized. So, as Iain McGilchrist has argued, comparing a football match with a trip to a betting shop will bring out some aspects of the experience, while comparing it with going to a place of religious worship will bring out others:

> The model we choose to understand something determines what we find. If it is the case that our understanding is an *effect* of the metaphors we choose, it is also true that it is a *cause*: our understanding itself guides the choice of metaphor by which we understand it. The chosen metaphor is both cause and effect of the relationship. Thus how we think about ourselves and our relationship to the world is already revealed in the metaphors we unconsciously choose to talk about it. That choice further entrenches our partial view of the subject.
>
> (McGilchrist 2009: 97; his emphasis)

If we assume that the universe is mechanical and take the machine as our model, we will find, not surprisingly, that the body and the brain are particular kinds of machines. As McGilchrist observes, 'To a man with a hammer everything begins to look like a nail' (*ibid.*, 98). So if we assume that the mind is a kind of computer, our notion of memory changes, as Nicholas Carr has pointed out. We begin to think of memory as a static repository of pieces of information, potentially infi-nitely extendable, its effectiveness determined only by our memory capacity. The fact that human memory transforms and alters the information that it contains and is fundamentally a dynamic and metamorphic process is masked by the dominant, computational metaphor (Carr 2010: 110–11). Whereas a file in a folder will, if uncorrupted, remain exactly the same if we retrieve it a year, two years, or ten years later, memories of events in our lives often change substantially over time. As we experience more and more, memories are added to our existing store, and earlier memories are altered or reconfigured by these new additions. Such is the prestige and power of the digital that a certain, almost inevitable metaphorical leakage occurs so that humans increasingly tend to think of their own memories as similar to the memories in the hard drives of their computers.

An analogous development potentially affects the activity of translation as a result of the emergence of online machine translation. The disembodied, instantaneous execution of the translation task implies that translation is an agentless, automatic function that can be realized in no time at all, and that translation is fundamentally a matching or substitutive operation, the text changing as the language is translated, but the layout remaining the same. Hitting the 'Translate' button or the 'Translate this page' link is more than a keystroke, it is a paradigm shift. Irrespective of the results, what is implied in the form of disintermediation at work is the representation of translation as a form of instantaneous language transfer akin to the automated sub-routines of digital processing. Saint Jerome in his study gives way to the silicon chip. Implicit in this representation, of course, is a particular notion of what language is in globalized forms of exchange. The purpose of language here is primarily instrumental. Its function is as an instrument of communication and the quicker the better. As Eric Schmidt, the Chief Executive Officer of Google argued, presenting Conversation Mode, an oral translation application for Google Translate, 'Never underestimate the importance of fast' (Schmidt 2010).

Science

In order to understand what happens to languages in periods of global change, Wismann and Judet de la Combe have set up a distinction between what they call a 'service language' (*langue de service*) and a 'culture language' (*langue de culture*) (Judet de la Combe and Wismann 2004: 33–35). The service language is a language in the restricted sense of something used to convey information of an instrumental nature from one speaker to another, typically a language like English used at international meetings of experts on climate change or air traffic regulation. Language, of course, does many things, not all of which involve communication in the narrow sense of information transfer. As Claude Hagège has pointed out:

> Whatever may be the case, whether or not the dominant language is the one in which he or she dreams, this capacity of languages to function as a support for thoughts, imagination and dreams completely overshadows, without of course suppressing it, the instrumental function of communication in language.[1]

(Hagège 2012: 180)

Each language has a triple form of distinctness. Firstly, each language has a separate and distinct set of linguistic structures and by extension, to a greater or lesser extent, different linguistic representations of reality. Secondly, each language community has a specific set of social practices that are articulated through language. Thirdly, each language community is a discourse community or set of discourse communities that expresses history, culture, and belief systems through the discourses that have evolved within the community (Hagège 1985: 352). The idiomatic, symbolic, and collective fields of reference account for the particular semantic density and historical specificity of each group of speakers. It is this density and specificity that Judet de la Combe and Wismann try to capture in their notion of a culture language. The difficulty, however, with the term 'culture language' is that it suggests that language as a factor of differentiation is largely concerned with areas of high culture, and that science and technology, for example, lie mainly in the realms of a service language. From this perspective, putting a Rilke poem into an online translation system would be inviting trouble, but feeding in the operating instructions for a combine harvester would not seem particularly anomalous. The culture language and the service language would have different translational outcomes. This is a false dichotomy in that what is at stake in scientific and technical translation is arguably as important as what is at play in literary translation, though their fortunes are rarely associated.

Laurent Lafforgue, the winner of the Field's Medal for Mathematics in 2002, claimed that, contrary to popular opinion, French mathematicians continued to publish in French not because French mathematics was so strong but because writing and publishing in French added to the originality and creativity of French mathematics:

> At a psychological level, choosing French is a sign of a combative spirit, the opposite of the notion of abandonment or renunciation. Of course, a combative spirit is no guarantee of success, but it is necessary. As the Chinese proverb says, the only battles we are sure to lose are those we fail to wage. On the moral plane, that is to say, at the level of values, which are even more important, the choice of French, or rather a distant attitude with respect to the currently dominant language in the world, means that we consider research itself more important than communicating the results. In other words, love of truth takes precedence over vanity. This does not mean not trying to communicate with others. Science is a collective enterprise that has been pursued down through the centuries, and even the most solitary researcher is wholly dependent on what he or she has learned and continues to receive every day. Nevertheless, refusing to attach excessive importance to immediate communication is to be reminded of the meaning of scientific research.[2]
>
> (Lafforgue 2005: 32)

Scientific history has borne out Lafforgue's contention that writing about science in a language other than English is no obstacle to discovery. Mendel, Planck, and Einstein wrote in German, Marconi wrote in Italian, and Carnot wrote in French. The period from the end of the nineteenth century to the beginning of the Second World War was characterized by a notable degree of multilingualism in scientific research, and it was rich in innovation in a multiplicity of disciplines (for German examples, see Watson 2011). If scientific research is about, among other things, curiosity, complexity, innovation, risk and creativity, it is difficult to see how it can be left outside the purview of culture language, as these are attributes of our ability to function effectively in the symbolic richness and historical depth of a particular language. Scientific activity is part of the culture of a community, and the cultural richness of science is enhanced, rather than diminished, by the cultural plurality of languages if only because, for example, everybody does not end up reading the exact same articles in the exact same language.

The incorporation of science into a notion of culture language is implicit in the very existence of scientific or technical translation, as much as in the practice of literary translation. What translation as a practice is articulating is a notion that the value of any field of enquiry or cultural practice is greatly enhanced by the expressive and hermeneutic resources of a speech community. Allowing scientists to write in their mother tongue is as important a part of the cultural ecology of humanity as allowing sonnets to be composed or novels to be written in the many idioms of the globe. Translation allows this to happen while simultaneously ensuring that the developments in a particular ecological niche inform the other idioms of the globe. In this context, it is possible to argue that translation is crucial to the emergence of *speciation* as opposed to *specialization*. Speciation is a term which refers to the development of particular species usually as the result of certain isolating factors. Specialization is the tendency of research in modern science to fragment into smaller and smaller sub-disciplines. The linguist Claude Hagège has pointed to the intense creativity of ancient Greece, Renaissance Italy, and the Germany of the Holy Roman Empire (mid-sixteenth–late eighteenth-century) as based on the marked fragmentation of the political entities to be found in these periods. The city states or principalities were both separate and in regular contact, so new ideas could be explored in relative isolation before the stimulating and beneficial contact with other cultures (Hagège 2012: 132–33). In other words, particular historical exempla point to the possibility of speciation as the precondition and expression of polycultural and polylingual plurality which is opposed to the prevalence and danger of monocultural and monolingual specialization, the endless elaboration of dominant models in a dominant language in a state of repressive equilibrium.

Transitivity

In a sense, the paradigm of purposive instrumentality that underlies representations of online translation services relates to a more general conception of translation that is tenacious and deeply held. In an article reviewing plans by the US military to develop new translation devices, Adam Rawnsley notes:

> The US military has tried out all sorts of gizmos on the battlefield. But devices like the Phraselator and the Voice Response Translator are limited.
>
> They can't translate just any words you'd like to say. Instead, they spit out a few key phrases and words in local languages likely to be useful on the battlefield.
>
> The blunt phrase exchanges can't produce the kind of complex communication that the Defense Department would like soldiers to be able to engage in.
>
> (Rawnsley 2011)

The aim of the Broad Operational Language Translation (BOLT) research initiative is to use visual, tactile, and language inputs, so that the robot can hypothesize and perform automated reasoning in the acquired language. Implicit in Rawnsley's comments on the translation devices developed to date by the Defense Advanced Research Projects Agency is the notion that 'blunt phrase exchanges' and the spitting out of a few 'key phrases and words' do not constitute 'complex communication' or represent language use in the real world. Translation that is underpinned by a paradigm of purposive instrumentality is doomed to the pidgin speak of command and control. That translation should be seen in such terms is hardly surprising, as one of the most difficult myths around translation is what we might call the myth of translation transitivity. Transitivity here is used in the grammatical sense of a verb taking an object. In order to understand more clearly what I mean by the term 'translation transitivity' it is important to look at different representations of human labour or production. In his unfinished magnum opus *Dialectics of Nature*, Friedrich Engels claimed that humans differed from other animals in that the works of the former were determined by an 'aim laid down in advance' (Engels 1934: 34). He claimed that 'The further removed men are from animals, the more their effect on nature assumes the character of premeditated, planned action directed towards definite preconceived ends' (*ibid.*, 178).

Seeing translation in these terms is hardly unusual. It is a standard trope of functionalist theories of translation that translations have definite, preconceived ends (to persuade, entertain, instruct), and that what the translator must do is to orient or plan her actions to bring about these ends. In other words, translation has a particular object. If I am translating medical instructions for the use of a nasal spray, I do not normally have as a desired outcome that the translation should read like a set of instructions for changing a tyre or an exhortation to join the Church of Scientology. The transitive vision of translation underlies the instructions of the British Army officer Colonel Lancey to his translator/interpreter Owen in Brian Friel's play *Translations* (1981): 'Do your job. Translate' (Friel 1981: 61). Lancey wants Owen to inform the civilian population of planned evictions by the Army in reprisal for the abduction of a fellow officer and he is not interested in any of Owen's humanitarian qualifications of his planned action. The difficulty with the transitive representation of human production is that it only offers a partial account of what happens when humans engage in an activity. As Tim Ingold has pointed out, not only are the materials with which someone works transformed by the process of labour, but the labourer himself or herself is transformed by the process, and this sum of transformations is what might otherwise be referred to as experience. As the person works, latent potentialities of action and perception are developed. The productive process is not limited to the finalities of any particular project but carries on through, without beginning or end, punctuated by the forms, whether material or ideal, that it brings into beginning. As Ingold argues, production 'must be understood *intransitively*, not as a transitive relation of image to object' (Ingold 1986: 321, author's emphasis). So the verb 'to produce' would be more akin to other intransitive verbs such as 'to hope', 'to flourish', and 'to dwell', rather than being ranged alongside such transitive verbs as 'to plan', 'to make', and 'to build'. The privileging of ongoing process over final form means that we end up with a substantively different notion of what it is to produce:

> Once we dispense with the prior representation of an end to be achieved as a necessary condition for production, and focus instead on the purposive will or intentionality that inheres in the action itself – in its capacity literally to *pro-duce*, to draw out or bring forth potentials in the person of the producer and the surrounding world – then there are no longer grounds to restrict the ranks of producers to human beings alone. Producers, both human and non-human, do not so much transform the world, impressing their preconceived designs upon the material substrate of nature, as play their part from within in the world's transformation of itself.
>
> (Ingold 2011: 6, author's emphasis)

The transitive representations of translation both radically oversimplify the notion of what it is to translate and fail to account for the marked plurality of translations. The fixation on prior representation of ends also leads to a more general failure to account for the manner in which translation, in Ingold's sense, *pro-duces* or draws out and brings forth potentials in the person of the producer and the surrounding world.

   The history of translation is littered with examples of translations whose impact greatly exceeded the original transitive purpose, the stated end of the translation. One such case is the translations of the writings of Hermes Trismegistus, an apocryphal author believed in the Renaissance period to be an Egyptian priest–philosopher whose birth predated that of Plato, and who allegedly anticipated in his writings a number of key Christian concepts. The works themselves were later discovered to have been written in the second or third century CE. Around 1460, a Greek manuscript turned up in Florence, brought there from Macedonia by a monk. The corpus contained an incomplete copy (thirteen of the fourteen treatises) of the *Corpus Hermeticium* attributed to the sage and practitioner of astral magic, Hermes Trismegistus. The monk who brought the manuscript was in the employ of the Florentine nobleman Cosimo de' Medici. Marsilio Ficino, a scholar and translator in the household of Cosimo, was immediately ordered to set about translating the work of Trismegistus into Latin. What is especially significant is that Ficino was to embark on a translation of Plato's work, as he tells us in his dedication of his Plotinus commentaries to Lorenzo de' Medici, but was told to cease all other activity until he had finished his Trismegistus translations: 'mihi Mercurium primo Termaximum, mox Platonem mandavit interpretandum' (cited in Yates 2002: 14). As the historian Frances Yates notes:

> It is an extraordinary situation. There are the complete works of Plato, waiting, and they must wait whilst Ficino quickly translates Hermes, probably because Cosimo wants to read him before he dies. What a testimony is this to the mysterious reputation of the Thrice Great One! ... Egypt was before

Greece; Hermes was earlier than Plato. Renaissance respect for the old, the primary, the far-away, as nearest to divine truth, demanded that the *Corpus Hermeticum* should be translated before Plato's *Republic* or *Symposium*, and so this was in fact the first translation Ficino made.

(*Ibid.*, 14)

Thus, the aim of Ficino's enterprise was to translate for a patron close to death the esoteric writings of a scholar believed to have hailed from ancient Egypt. Ficino was profoundly affected by his translations of Trismegistus and went on to develop his own version of 'natural magic' (*ibid.*, 66–89). In other words, as he works on his renowned translations of Plato into Latin, he begins to conceive of similarities between ideas he finds in Plato and the hermetic speculations on astral magic. The translation of the *Corpus Hermeticum*, *pro-duces* a new form of thinking for Ficino, it 'draw[s] out or bring[s] forth potentials in the person of the producer' in the form of *De vita coelitus comparanda*, the third book of his *Libri de vita*, first published in 1489. In this book he expounds a number of his ideas around natural magic and his evolving Neoplatonic theories. The effects of Ficino's hermetic translations were considerable and influenced everything from Renaissance painting and decorative arts to the philosophical and theological speculations of Giovanni Pico della Mirandola and Giordano Bruno. In this respect, the translation 'brings forth potentials' not only in the person of the producer, but in 'the surrounding world'. As the translator is transformed by his translation, so, too, is the world that surrounds him and survives him.

It might be argued, however, that this intransitive excess is solely confined to works of high art or of perceived philosophical or theological originality. The vast majority of translators, labouring in the pragmatic vineyards of the commercial, technical, and medical, are always working to a 'prior representation of an end to be achieved' and must remain object/output-focused in their activities. At one level, of course, this is patently not the case. Much to the chagrin of novice translators, there are no translation recipes. There may be certain general trends in the stylistic organization of languages that are useful to bear in mind for translators and that explain the continued interest in contrastive stylistics in translation studies, particularly in the Francophone world. Certain writers on translation, notably Peter Newmark, offer translators advice on how they might approach particular translation difficulties, such as the translation of figurative language (Newmark 1981, 1993, 1996). However, these stylistic trends or heuristic tips can in no way be construed as prescriptive algorithms that will each time ensure an accurate or acceptable translation of a particular text. The discrediting of the 'fair copy' approach in translation pedagogy, where students aspire to produce a translation which will match the perfect rendition of the instructor, is not only motivated by a move away from magisterial to collaborative forms of education, but is also based on the perfectly reasonable observation that it is possible to have more than one acceptable translation of a particular text. The end to be achieved can be expressed in terms of functional generalities (the nurse should successfully administer the medication, not break into song), but the actual process of the translation, the 'purposive will or intentionality that inheres in the action' of translation cannot be reduced to a narrow-gauge transitivity. Latent potentialities of action and perception are revealed to the translator because, if they were not, there could be no such thing as translator education or translator experience. Solutions would always, already be there. Continuing translation over time is the triumph of ongoing process over final form, a form of pro-duction that partakes of the world's transformation of itself, in every-thing from the spread of Hollywood cinema to the exponential rise in mobile phone usage.

There is another level at which the tyranny of transitivity in understandings of translation is challenged and that is by translation technology itself or, rather, by the way this technology interacts with human users. Maeve Olohan, in a study of how translators interacted with translation memory software, notes how the reactions were anything but predictable. In order to understand what was happening, she employs an idea from Andrew Pickering, the 'mangle of practice':

> The mangling process is 'temporally emergent', by which Pickering means that the contours of human and material agency are impossible to predict in advance; they emerge in the course of scientific practice, just as the mangled laundry will assume a different and unpredictable shape as it emerges from the mangle. It is not possible to predict in advance where resistances will be encountered and what will play a constitutive role in the development of science and technology, or any course of events.
>
> (Olohan 2011: 345)

Because the majority of translators who use translation memory (TM) software do not receive formal training in its use, they are self-taught. In this context, online technical support forums take on a particular importance. In tracking a discussion thread on one of the forums devoted to a new version of a TM tool produced by SDL – *SDL Trados Studio 2009* – Olohan shows how the users and the software engage in a 'dance of agency' (*ibid.*, 344). The users identify particular problems or resistances in the software and either attempt various strategies of accommodation or reject the software outright. What is note-worthy is that, in the discussions between translators, there is no sense of the interaction with the technology as scripted by the transitive objectives of the software. In other words, the translators both point to the shortcomings of the software and reveal how certain previously unsuspected potentials in the TM software are realized by their engagement with it. In both instances, then, there is a kind of intransitive excess, where both the human agency of the translator and the material agency of the software 'draw out or bring forth potentials in the person of the producer and the surrounding world', the surrounding world in this instance being the software. That is to say, in pro-ducing a translation using the new version of the software, they reveal the transitive deficit of the software (the things it purports to do, but cannot) and the intransitive growth of the translators who discover new ways of working beyond 'the prior representation of an end to be achieved'.

In her work on translators, technologies, and new electronic networks of practice, Iulia Mihalache argues similarly that there is, in the interaction between translators and new digital technologies, constantly a tension between prior representations of ends and the actual nature of production in translation. Technology suppliers focus primarily on strategies for implementing the technology at local and international levels and finding ways of automating the translation process, whereas 'professional translators seem to be more concerned with their technological needs, the long-term and short-term advantages that they could gain, and the technical and practice-related obstacles they might encounter while using specific technologies' (Mihalache 2008: 62–63). In the dance of agency between the translators and the suppliers, the activities of both parties are in a sense in excess of the transitive expectations of the other. It is partly for this reason that Mihalache proposes shifting the focus in translation research from the '*information* society' of translators who work with technology to speed up the processing and storage of data to 'the *interaction* society of translators, considered in their continuous and mobile interaction through geographic cultures and spaces by means of new technologies' (*ibid.*, 62; her emphasis). This interaction society of translators is the surrounding environment that both shapes and is shaped by the ongoing process of production that plays a part in the world's transformation of itself. As the writer and professional translator Geoffrey Samuelsson-Brown argues, translation is a 'system' involving three sets of elements: inputs, translation processes, and outputs. These include not only human agents, but also concrete or abstract objects such as texts, practical and intellectual skills, experience, technologies, and return on investment (Samuelsson-Brown 2006: 39):

> The interaction between these human and non-human agents shows that the construction of knowledge and of translator identities is a dynamic, conflict-provoking process where ideas about what translation is (declarative knowledge) and how it should be done (procedural knowledge) migrate, transform themselves and are negotiated and constantly reinterpreted.
>
> (Mihalache 2008: 65)

It is precisely the 'dynamic, conflict-provoking process' which means that 'to translate' as an intransitive verb is always in excess of 'to translate' as a transitive verb. This is not only because of unforeseen outcomes – as in the Ficino translations, or the specific dance of agency with translation technology, or the interactional evolution of electronic networks of practice – but relates more directly to the distinctions evoked earlier between different kinds or uses of language. For the user of a language, it is possible to argue that there are two components: a system and a corpus. The system comprises the rules or systemic regularities traditionally captured in grammars that allow a user to speak and/or write a language competently. The system by itself is inadequate, however, if not complemented by a corpus. The corpus is the entirety of the spoken speech or written texts in the language that the user has encountered since birth. It includes proverbs, clichés, quotes, 'commonsense' judgements or opinions held within families or more generally within a specific society, the whole gamut of verbal expression to which users are exposed from an early age (Rastier 2007: 426). Corpus studies have, of course, been a feature of translation research for more than two decades, and corpora are central to the operation of many online translation systems such as Google Translate, but here I want to situate the notion of corpus in a different translation context, a context that is central to contemporary representations of the digital world.

Transparency

Don Tapscott, in his study of the generation of young people who have grown up with the internet from a very early age, notes the following eight characteristics of what he calls the Net Geners:

> They prize freedom and freedom of choice. They want to customize things, make them their own. They're natural collaborators, who enjoy a conversation not a lecture. They'll scrutinize you and your organization. They insist on integrity. They want to have fun, even at work and school. Speed is normal. Innovation is part of life.
>
> (Tapscott 2009: 6–7)

Implicit in Tapscott's description of the Net Geners is their commitment to transparency. Hence the insistence on scrutiny and intregrity, the sense that recurs throughout his study of the internet as a means by which what was previously the privileged knowledge of the few becomes the collective knowledge of the many. The notion finds political expression in the German Pirates Party who, despite the vagueness of their political platform, have scored significant electoral successes in recent years. Their one clear strength, however, in the words of Melissa Eddy, a *New York Times* journalist, is that they know 'how to rally voters around the idea of increased transparency and direct voter participation through technology and the Internet' (Eddy 2012: A6). When Eric Schmidt, the CEO of Google, speaks of the future of 'augmented humanity', he speaks not only of the 35 billion devices that are connected to the internet at any one time, and of the potential of cloud computing, but says repeatedly that the internet will provide us 'with everything we need to know'. He sees search engines as not merely providing knowledge but anticipating requests for knowledge, so that, imagining a stroll through Berlin, his handheld device will act as a voluble guide saying over and over, 'Did you know? Did you know?' (Schmidt 2010). The epistemic drive of the internet makes the foreign city transparent to the late modern *flâneur*.

What Schmidt is articulating is a form of digital utopianism which has long been part of the public pronouncements on the internet by apostles of the digital such as Bill Gates, Steve Jobs, and Nicholas Negroponte (see Breton 2000). In order to answer the question 'Did you know?' about historical features of a non-Anglophone city, you need access at some point to translated information. So translation must be a part of that epistemic ideal of transparency. Otherwise, there are multiple zones of exclusion, and, of course, in everything from good business practice to espionage, translation is seen as removing the veil of opacity that conceals the truth, whether that takes the form of a commercial opportunity or a security risk. Indeed, the constant move towards he automation of translation, and the ubiquitous presence of online translation options, is arguably part of the vision of a global knowledge community animated by resurgent democratic ideals of liberality and transparency. These ideals, in turn, mean that the digital is invested with a political significance that goes beyond the narrowly instrumentalist notion of dependent tool use.

In this context, it is worth briefly considering the philosophical origins of the US counter-culture that was highly formative in much of the thinking around the possibilities of the digital generally, and of the internet in particular, before returning to the question of how ideals of transparency impinge on translation in the digital age. A central current of influence on the Beat Generation and the Hippies in the US in the late 1950s and 1960s was the transcendentalist philosophy of Ralph Waldo Emerson and Henry David Thoreau (Braunstein and Doyle 2001). Transcendentalist thinking is based on a belief in the spiritual unity of the world, an attempt to bring together faith and reason. What is an essential task for each human being is the necessity to go beyond the falsity of appearances and surfaces and discover the inner, divine truth of self. In this exploration of self, however, each individual discovers what is universal in the self. In other words, it is when the individual is most honest, most authentic to himself or herself, when the façades of half-truths and delusions are torn away, that he or she comes closest to the truth of others (Gura 2008). Emerson and Thoreau were ardent advocates of individualism, freedom of conscience, and expression because to be true to oneself is to be true to others. In this respect, traditional divisions between the public and the private no longer obtain. Drawing on a familiar Puritan trope, the spotless or sinless soul has nothing to hide. The voice of truth is the voice of those who are true to themselves. Engaging in genuine dialogue with others is one authentic voice engaging with another.

Movement is essential to this conception of self. Migration is a rupture with the moribund cultures of the Old World, given over to an inordinate preoccupation with surfaces and appearances. The New World is the unknown territory staked out by those pioneers of the self who favour the unsettling risk of authenticity over the inauthentic solace of the familiar. As Magali Bessonne has pointed out, there is a clear genealogy going from transcendentalism, to counter-cultural thinking, to the ideology of the internet. Discussing the marked profession of anti-conformity in transcendentalist thinking, she claims:

> Four major aspects present in this critique of conformism in the name of a
> genuine democracy based on individualism are relayed by the counter-cultural

movement and subsequently by the ideology of the internet: the refusal to conform to dominant norms; the exaltation of movement; the fundamental importance of voice and conversation; the challenge to the social categorization of public and private.[3]

(Bessonne 2011: 149)

In Tapscott's description of Net Geners, we find a clear echo of the transcendentalist precepts that fed their way into the counter-cultural movement, the movement that shaped the horizon of expectation of the Baby Boomers, the parents, in Tapscott's terminology, of the Net Geners. Thus, the cult of anti-conformism and individualism is made manifest in 'freedom and freedom of choice' and the desire 'to customize things' and 'make them their own'. The premium placed on voice as an authentic mode of expression is encapsulated in the claim that Net Geners 'enjoy a conversation not a lecture'. The celebration of movement is captured in the slogan 'Speed is normal', and the belief that the public and the private are not separate categories is expressed in the claim that 'They'll scrutinize you [private] and your organization [public]'. The insistence on 'integrity' is a recurrent reminder of a core value of transcendentalist thinking. The decline of intimacy on the internet, as characterized by aspects of Facebook usage and the perceived erosion of the barriers between the public and the private, needs to be situated in a specific philosophical tradition with an identifiable lineage, rather than seen as the unfortunate misapplication of a particular kind of technology (Turkle 2011).

If we consider the role translation played in the European Reformation in making scripture 'transparent' to believers, it is clear how the Puritan substrate of transcendentalism plays out in the ideology of transparency that is part of the localization industry: 'The localization and language industry helps companies, governments and not-for-profit organizations create global content for audiences of any culture and who speak any language' (GALA 2012). There is, however, a fundamental paradox at play here which makes the relationship of translation to an ideology of transparency more than problematic. On the one hand, creating global content that can be understood by anyone anywhere feeds into a notion of transparent immediacy on the internet. Language and cultural differences (and the technical problems that ensue) are so many surface impediments that must be cast aside. On the other hand, that notion of transparency must be contested if the work of the localization industry is to make any sense. It is because languages and cultures are to a greater or lesser degree opaque to each other and therefore not transparent that translation comes into existence in the first place. Too much visibility or transparency, and the translator becomes invisible. Not enough transparency, and it is the absence of translation that becomes visible. Thus, both the desirability and feasibility of translation become bound up with the highly charged notion of transparency in the digital age. One way of exploring this relationship is to consider how new technical environments condition the social development of humans and what the implications are for language and, by extension, translation.

Nicholas Ostler, a linguist and historian of language, has commented on the close affinity between language and technical change:

> The invention and take-up of logographic writing systems (Sumerian cuneiform, Egyptian hieroglyphs, Chinese characters, Mayan glyphs) made possible the logistics of large-scale agricultural empires; the radical simplification that came with alphabetic scripts disrupted ancient social hierarchies and produced the more open and mercantile societies of the Phoenicians, Greeks, Sogdians, and Arabs; printing overthrew the grip of the Roman church (and Latin) on the cities of Europe; oceangoing ships (directed with magnetic compasses and exactly drawn portolan charts) allowed European ways of war and agriculture to spread beyond the bounds of a single continent, and with them have spread European languages, whether as mother tongues of settlers or as lingua-francas of cosmopolitan powers.
>
> (Ostler 2011: 249–50)

Language is both a cause and beneficiary of particular technical developments with widespread social consequences. By implication, periods of radical technical change do not leave languages unscathed. Although it has become something of a truism to claim that one of the reasons for the hegemony of English in late modernity is its close association with US technology (Crystal 2003: 14–15), it is less often observed that the technology itself is not uniformly predictable in its social and linguistic fallout. Between 2000 and 2009, the fastest-growing languages on the internet in terms of users were Arabic (twentyfold increase), Chinese (twelvefold), Portuguese (ninefold), Spanish (sevenfold), and French (sixfold). In that same period, English merely trebled its number of users. The smaller languages in the world, with respect to internet usage, are growing at a faster rate than the larger ones. The top ten languages grew their user base 4.6 times in the decade, but all the others grew sixfold. By the end of the decade, English had as many users as the next two languages (Chinese and Spanish) combined, but it now accounts for only a quarter of the online community, a proportion that continues to fall with each passing year (Internet World Stats by Language 2012). What these developments point to is a notion of transparency that promotes, rather than eliminates, diversity. For example, Ostler claims that 'the long-term tendency is for information-technology developments to lessen the inaccessibility of the world's languages, to break down language barriers, but without abolishing the languages that cause them' (Ostler 2011: 263). In this view, the availability of cheap and ubiquitous digital technology would remove the need for a global *lingua franca* as the 'frustrations of the language barrier may be overcome without any universal shared medium beyond the compatible software' (*ibid.*, 261). Fundamental to this conception of the demise of a global *lingua franca* is a serviceable model of machine translation. The shift from rule-based machine translation approaches to a greater reliance on machine intelligence, enabling inference engines to derive their own rules from exposure to very large amounts of translation equivalence data and the greater use of statistical matching, has indeed meant an exponential growth in MT usage in our age (Wilks 2008; Koehn 2009). The oft-repeated complaints about the inadequacy of MT, and the frequent recitation of online translation howlers, miss the more important point about complex interactions between technology, language, and society. The internet statistics indicate that technology is supporting, not decimating, language diversity. The potential role for MT, as outlined by Ostler, is not based on the notion that the only acceptable form of MT output is perfect idiomatic expression of meaning in the target language. Apart from the fact that, as Maria Tymoczko (2007) has pointed out, any notion of total capture of meaning in translation is deeply problematic, the needs of users can differ greatly, and an imperfect translation may be perfectly adequate in certain circumstances. More to the point, current developments in information technology indicate the potential move to a form of transparency that relies paradoxically on opacity for its democratic promise.

If 'information-technology developments' are 'to lessen the inaccessibility of the world's languages' and 'break down language barriers', then the role for translation is clearly presented as one that, in line with transcendentalist precepts, increases the transparency of the other and opens up the private domains of languages and cultures to the public gaze of the online and offline world. Conversely, the greater availability of electronic resources for different languages and the increased diversification of online translation services (Google Translate provided translation for six languages in 2001, but for sixty-three by 2012), even if there are still very significant differences between the resources and services available in different languages, point to the elaboration and consolidation of language difference. Digital technology and translation, in this respect, play a role that is strikingly similar to the role played by mechanical printing and translation centuries earlier. The revolution in mobility represented by the construction of oceangoing caravels in the fifteenth to seventeenth century is matched in the late nineteenth and twentieth centuries by the emergence of locomotives, automobiles, and aircraft. The communications *aggiornamento* of the printing press and publishing industry is paralleled by developments in telecommunications and computing in late modernity, and, as Ostler argues, multilingual language technologies 'correspond to the grammatization of Europe's national languages, which saw each of them monumentalized with its own grammar and dictionary' (Ostler 2011: 265). The drive towards transparency, in the move towards online translation services, can in fact generate the counter-movement of language and cultural opacity, as the complexification of electronic resources reveals languages to be distinct entities whose worlds of meaning need to be endlessly renegotiated. This is where the extensivity of information technology allied to translation becomes the potential agent or carrier of the intensive culture of language and cultural difference.

Power

One of the primary motives for advancing an ideal of transparency has always been a suspicion about the activities of the powerful. From Luther's denunciation of the occult manoeuvres of Latin-speaking clergy to the worldwide dissemination of classified diplomatic and security information by WikiLeaks, transparency has long been a watchword of those contesting established truths. When we examine the notion of transparency in the digital age, the question of power inevitably arises. This question relates not only to the cyber-stratification of languages, the fact that some languages are more richly endowed with electronic resources than others, but more fundamentally to the nature and value of communication in digital settings and to the exact role of the translator working in a digital environment.

A basic way of describing what happens when information is transferred electronically is that there is an exchange of information. In an information economy where a fundamental unit of operation is a piece of information, each item of information has potential exchange value. The less the division between the private and the public, the greater the amount of information about individual feelings, tastes, preferences that is available for potential exchange. The facts that eight out of every ten internet users are members of a social network and that over 200 million people tweet on a regular basis indicate the informational value of these new forms of digital interactivity (Belot 2012: 1). The stock market valuations of firms like Google and Facebook are in large part driven by the 'big data' they have at their disposal, data that are provided free of charge by their users and then made available for commercial uses by the firms in question, generally in ways that are unknown to the users who are unable or reluctant to work their way through pages and pages of terms and conditions of use. In this respect, there is extremely limited transparency, as the exchange value of freely provided information in market economies provides a powerful disincentive to maximum disclosure. Translation is a part of the value-creation process in this economy of information exchange, as is made apparent in the remarks by Erick Schonfeld in an article for a new technology site, TechCrunch:

> Facebook has long relied on its own users to help translate the site into more than 65 different languages. Now, Facebook wants to unleash its army of volunteer translators on other sites and apps across the web. Any site or app that use Facebook Connect can now tap into the Facebook Community to get help in translating their site into any language that Facebook translations supports ... The Internet is a global platform, which makes translation a must for sites both large and small. But the effort it takes to translate a site into many languages is expensive and time-consuming. Getting the users to do the heavy lifting is appealing. Even if the translations aren't top notch off the bat, they will improve over time if enough people who speak a particular language care enough about a site to fix it.
>
> (Schonfeld 2009)

What we have here is an instance of the devolved costs which I mentioned earlier, where the costs of providing information, this time in translation, are devolved or transferred to the users of the information rather than borne by the service providers. The users become not only a free source of commercial information, but they further evolve into a free source of commercially valuable translation services. What is rarely transparent in the communitarian or utopian rhetoric around social networks is how transparency itself becomes a prime site of commercial opportunity for private interests. The more data the networks contain about personal tastes, preferences, opinions, the more valuable the data are to everyone from supermarket chains to state security agencies. Translation as a further enabler of the process of transparency adds value to the 'big data' thus accumulated. It is for this reason that a politics of translation in a digital age has to contend with power in a different guise. That is to say, one of the responsibilities of translators and translation critics is to make manifest the invisible, devolved translation costs of the new social media. This critique, however, must be incorporated into a wider movement to prevent the privatized exploitation of information in an exchange economy. Whether through global, transnational regulatory frameworks or legitimate forms of cyber activism, it is necessary to protect information as a public good, all the more so in an informational economy where information becomes the principal unit of exchange.

In considering the question of translation and power in the digital age, there is a further dimension to contemporary information technology that needs to be reckoned with in any future politics of translation. This is the question of split agency in the era of digital reproduction. In the digital or parametric design of objects, there are two levels of authorship. At one level, the primary author is the designer of the generic object or objectile – the program or series or generation notation that generates other objects – and at another, a secondary author specifies the generic object in order to design individual end products. In a sense, the secondary author is to the primary author what the player in the video game is to the video game's designer. The players may invent (author) their own stories, but they are playing by rules and in an environment designed by someone else. Janet Murray described the player in the digital video game as an 'interactor', rather than an author, an interactor who exerts only a limited and ancillary form of agency. Mario Carpo indicates the nature of the choice represented by split agency:

> Open-endedness, variability, interactivity, and participation are the technological quintessence of the digital age. They are here to stay. And soon designers will have to choose. They may design objects, and then be digital interactors. Or they may design objectiles, and then be digital authors. The latter choice is more arduous by far, but its rewards are greater.
>
> (Carpo 2011: 126)

The dilemma is familiar to translators who are faced with the question of whether they are to be digital interactors or digital authors in the future.

Tim Foster is responsible for Software Globalization at Sun Microsystems, which has an annual translation throughput of around 40 million words, and he describes Sun's vision of translation technology as follows: 'Ultimately, we would like to improve the process to the level of getting translations "out of the wall", that is, in the same way you access your bank account using an ATM, we would like to translate software by simply plugging the source files into a translation system and receiving the results immediately' (Foster 2010). In order to arrive at this stage, it was necessary to work on the Translation Editor, the main interface translators use to translate files for Sun. As Foster notes, 'While developing the editor, we sought feedback from our translation vendors and feel confident that it feeds the needs of these users. As with any end-user-focused application, the editor had to be simple and intuitive. It is easy to configure and provides all of the features that a translator would expect' (*ibid.*). In the representation of the development of the Translation Editor, there is a form of limited authorship accorded to translators or translation companies through the reference to feedback and the inclusion of supplementary features in the Editor, such as format checking, translation status markers, TM match navigation, and easier navigation. If the Sun Translation Editor is a kind of objectile that allows for the production of a wide variety of translation objects or texts, the question is whether the translator is increasingly cast in the role of interactor or author. If 'out-of-the-wall' immediacy is the translation *telos* of Sun Microsystems, then what are the possibilities for designing the rules of a game, rather than playing by the rules of a game designed by others, no matter how 'simple and intuitive' these rules are? Do translators find themselves inevitably and ultimately condemned to a form of limited and ancillary agency?

To some extent, the dilemma of split agency relates at a more fundamental level to the relationship between knowledge and power that Giorgio Agamben has captured in the notion of 'apparatus'. For Agamben, the apparatus is anything which has the capacity to capture, orient, determine, intercept, model, or control the gestures, conduct, opinions, or discourse of living beings. Thus, the apparatus is to be understood not only in the Foucauldian sense of prisons, confessional boxes, factories, and hospitals, but also as the pen, writing, literature, philosophy, agriculture, the cigarette, computers, mobile phones, and indeed language itself (Agamben 2009: 10). He sees a fundamental dichotomy between living beings and the apparatuses to which they are subject, a division between the ontology of creatures and what he calls the *oikonomia* or organized system of the apparatuses which determine and govern their lives. Agamben argues that each apparatus traditionally brought with it its own form of subjectivity. An apparatus only became effective when one willingly complied to its demands and took on the role of the model prisoner or the good student, otherwise the only way the apparatus could be enforced was through pure violence. In our present era, however, Agamben argues that what we are increasingly experiencing through various kinds of political and technological apparatuses is a form of desubjectivization (*ibid.*, 22). In other words, rather than the apparatus giving rise to a new form of subjectivity, it leads to the loss of subjectivity or the reduction of the subjective to larval or spectral forms. Hence, the increasing difficulty of thinking of contemporary politics in terms of traditional subjectivities and identities such as the working class, bourgeoisie, and so on or the eclipse of major policy differences between parties of the Left and Right, so that politics becomes a mere matter of technical governance. The much-vaunted era of the individual becomes the age of the vanishing subject. The diminished agency of Murray's interactor gives way to the full desubjectivization of Agamben's creature, caught in a web of apparatuses that preclude any possibility of subjective identity.

Daniel Gouadec, in his postface to *Translation as a Profession*, offers a futuristic vision of translation desubjectivization in the form of a dystopian vignette. The translator of the (not too distant) future sits in a chair and responds to the automated translation offered to him. His agency is reduced to accepting or refusing the system's suggestions except on those happy occasions when there are no suggestions and he can dictate his own translation:

> What the translator does not know, of course, is that there is no real deadline. There is no 'client' at all, either. And no one is going to read or listen to his translation ever ... What he is actually doing is taking part in a test designed by the pluridisciplinary research team to pit their latest pet algorithims (written for the *WTE, or World Translation Engine*) against a good old human translator.
>
> (Gouadec 2007: 370)

The subjectivity of the translator is pure illusion. The translation has already been done in micro-seconds by the *WTE*, and the interruptions in the suggestions were purely for the scientists' entertainment. Agamben's analysis has the advantage of situating any present or future crisis in translation agency within a wider political crisis of subjectivity in market or state capitalist economies. As a counter-move to the decimation of subjectivity, Agamben argues for the notion of 'profanation' which he defines, following the ancient Roman jurist Gaius Trebatius Testa, as the act of returning to the use of human beings anything which is religious or sacred (Agamben 2009: 43). Profanation of the apparatus and the restoration of a form of subjectivity, just like the access to digital authorship, is indeed, in Carpo's words, an 'arduous' process. Part of the process involves a properly material understanding of translation, both as it has manifested itself in the past and in the forms it takes in the present. That understanding also implies, as is repeatedly emphasized throughout this volume, the embedding of translation critique in contemporary forms of political economy. A new form of translation subjectivity not only involves revealing the ungovernable in language or culture, the multiple resistances of meaning and place, as we shall see in the next chapter, but means making advanced digital reflexivity a core component of understanding what it is to translate and use translation in the twenty-first century.

3   Translating limits

Almost 400 years ago, an English cleric and scholar wondered how he would cope. His days were invaded with news from elsewhere:

> I hear news every day, and those ordinary rumours of war, plagues, fires, inundations, thefts, murders, massacres, meteors, comets, spectrums, prodigies, apparitions, of towns taken, cities besieged in France, Germany, Turkey, Persia, Poland, & c. daily musters and preparations, and such like, which these tempestuous times afford, battles fought, so many men slain, monomachies, shipwrecks, piracies and sea-fights, peace, leagues, stratagems, and fresh alarms ... New books every day, pamphlets, currantoes, stories, whole catalogues of volumes of all sorts, new paradoxes, opinions, schisms, heresies, controversies in philosophy and religion, & c.
>
> (Burton 1927: 14)

Robert Burton, author of *The Anatomy of Melancholy* (1621), who in his lifetime had amassed one of the world's largest private libraries of 1,700 volumes, was not unhappy. He was simply astonished. His only difficulty was how to keep up with all that was being written and reported. Of course, his wonder had its intermediaries. To know what towns have been taken or cities besieged in 'France, Germany, Turkey, Persia, Poland', someone has to translate the news for the speakers of a minority language on the periphery of Europe. The 'New books every day' and the 'whole catalogues of volumes of all sorts' contain a great many translations. Indeed, so prevalent was the practice of translation in the Tudor and Stuart periods that one scholar, Robert Cawdrey, author of the first monolingual dictionary in the English language, *A Table Alphabeticall* (1604), was convinced that the English would soon forget what language they spoke: 'Some men seek so far outlandish English, that they forget altogether their mothers language, so that if some of their mothers were alive, they were not able to tell or understand what they say' (cited in Simpson 2007: 41).

Messianic theories

As Burton's world expands and his library grows apace, translation is everywhere in the emergence of proto-global information networks. It is this presence of translation in the expansion and opening up of civilizations that leads to the development of what we might call messianic theories of translation. The extraordinary thousand-year history of Indian–Chinese cultural exchange through the translation of Buddhist scriptures – starting with the Eastern Han Dynasty and the Three Kingdoms period (148–265 CE), continuing through the Jin Dynasty and the Northern and Southern Dynasties (265–589), and culminating with the Sui Dynasty, the Tang Dynasty, and the Northern Song Dynasty (589–1100) – points to the profoundly transformative effects of translation on a people's culture and beliefs (Zhong 2003).

The immense contribution of Arab-speaking peoples through inwards and outwards translation in a bewildering variety of areas, from architecture to cartography, pharmacy, poetry, and veterinary science, is well recorded (Lyons 2010). The creative engagement of the Ummayad and Abbasid Caliphates, and the pioneering roles of figures like al-Mansur, al-Ma'mun, and Huynayn Ibn-Ishaq point to the crucial catalytic effect of translation in the evolution of cultures and languages. As a result of the demonstrable contribution of translation to the opening up and enrichment of cultures, there is a clearly understandable tendency to invest translation with messianic or redemptive qualities. That is to say, in a world riven with dissension, border disputes, persistent racism, and ethnic violence, translation would appear to offer the possibility of mutual understanding, a vision of harmony, a tantalizing glimpse of a world where conflict would be but a distant memory. This millenarian promise is echoed in the names of organizations, books, and online journals devoted to literary translation in particular: Literature across Frontiers, Words without Borders, Literature without Borders, and so on. The first principle of the PEN Charter adopted at its congress in Brussels in 1927, on the initiative of John Galsworthy, was 'Literature knows no frontiers and must remain common currency among people in spite of political or international upheavals' (Rotondo 2011). A commonplace image of translators is as bridge-builders, as prophetic figures in the coming of a global, cultural Parousia. The prodigious expansion in information diffusion with the arrival of the interactive Web seems to provide the necessary material infrastructure for the realization of the messianic promise of translation. Facebook, as of September 2011, had 870 million users worldwide with an average of 130 friends per user, Twitter had 256 million users, YouTube was adding on average 48 hours of video footage every minute, and LinkedIn had 100 million users and rising (Cano 2011: 22–23). However, the question that might be asked is whether the messianic conceptualization of translation is the most appropriate, or even the most desirable, in a global age.

The dismantling of tariffs barriers, the deregulation of financial markets, the collapse of the Soviet bloc, the spread of the internet, and the rise of satellite television are often depicted as contributory factors in the emergence of a 'flat earth' where borders are more honoured in the breach than in the observance, and where limits of any kind are seen as the doleful remains of backward-looking protectionism (Friedman 2006). The political reality of the planet, however, is at variance with the frontierless enthusiasm of the flat-earthers. Since 1991, particularly in Europe and Eurasia, 27,000 kilometres of new borders have been created, and 10,000 more kilometres of walls, divisions, and partitions between territories are planned over the next decade (Debray 2010: 19). There are now almost four times as many nation-states represented at the Union Nations as there were at the first meetings of the General Assembly held in London in January 1946. A striking feature of cities across the globe is the rise of gated communities, CCTV, and private security companies, and there seems to be no limit to the appetite for social and economic demarcation (Sennett 1993; Förster, Jesuit, and Smeeding 2003). Do these realities simply indicate that we have to try harder in preaching the frontierless doctrine of messianic translation, or do they, on the contrary, force us to reconsider how to think about translation and borders in a globalized world?

In order to think about the notion of limits, it is worth briefly considering a philosophical and anthropological perspective on the question, before considering in greater detail the implications for translation. The French anthropologist André Leroi-Gourhan argued that the principle of socialization has always consisted of 'imposing order, from a particular standpoint, on the surrounding world'[1] (Leroi-Gourhan 1965: 150). A significant shift in human development occurred over 30,000 years ago with the strict delimitation between waste and living space. A way of organizing one's environment and defining who lived where was to separate detritus from human habitation. Keeping your house in order was keeping your house together. The distinctions that many of the major world religions make between what is pure and what is impure, and the huge investment humans make, in even the most difficult and trying circumstances, to maintain a modicum of cleanliness and order in their homes, point to a fundamental link between spatial cohesion, sense of self, and delimitation (Kaufmann 2011: 19–46). For the German philosopher Ludwig Feuerbach, the Roman deity Terminus stood at the entrance to the world. He argues that a fundamental condition of human existence was self-limitation. No being can exist unless it exists as determined in some way. He goes on to argue, 'The incarnation of the species with all its plenitude into one individuality would be an absolute miracle, a violent suspension of all the laws and principles of reality; it would, indeed, be the end of the world' (Feuerbach 1839). The absence of limits in Feuerbach's vision is cataclysmic. Where there are no limits, there is no distinct being. A world without borders, in effect, is no longer a world. It is an undifferentiated void, without ground or figure, a black hole from which nothing emerges. Thus, limits, boundaries, borders are seen from these different anthropological and philosophical standpoints in two different centuries as constitutive of self, community, and reality. If this is the case, then where do we situate translation within thinking about limits?

Translation and limits

When Marcel Proust embarked on his translation of John Ruskin's *The Bible of Amiens* (1897), he undertook to visit as many of the sites associated with

Ruskin's writings as he was physically able (Tadié 1996: 431–45). In a sense, he gave physical reality to the movement that underlines all translation, the passage from one language, one culture, to another. Proust's pilgrimages to the cathedrals of northern France or to the hallowed Stones of Venice captured the nomadic impulse that brings the translator to the foreign lands of the text and language to be translated. As I have argued elsewhere, it is possible to see all travel writing as a form of translation and all translation as a form of travel writing (Cronin 2000). What travel involves, of course, is an exercise in self-definition. It is when the traveller goes elsewhere that they become aware not only of where they are and where they are going, but also, crucially, where they have come from.

It is a commonplace of that permanent form of travel which is exile that a sense of identity is never more cruelly felt than when you are away from your place of birth or origin. In this context, there is the story of James Joyce being visited by an old friend, Hanna Sheefy-Skeffington. It was on a visit to Paris that the great revolutionary, feminist, and social activist went to see Joyce, who had been at University College Dublin with her brother, Eugene Sheehy, between 1898 and 1902. Joyce subjected Sheehy-Skeffington to a relentless and seemingly endless interrogation on the minutiae of Dublin life until, in her brother's account of the conversation,

> Half-dazed with his cascade of enquiries, she at length said to him:
> 'Mr   Joyce, you pretend to be a cosmopolitan, but how is it that all your thoughts are about Dublin, and almost everything that you have written deals with it and its inhabitants?'
> 'Mrs   Skeffington!' he replied, with a rather whimsical smile, 'there was an English queen who said that when she died the word "Calais" would be written on her heart. "Dublin" will be found on mine.'
> (O'Connor 2004: 38)

For students embarking on a course of translation, the initial draw can be the voyage outwards, the lure of the foreign, the delights of difference. However, what makes translation different from foreign language learning is that it is the journey home that proves to be the most revealing. The student of translation soon realizes, and this is as true of translating Joyce as it is of translating manuals for agricultural machinery, that the genuinely strange and unexplored territory is their mother tongue. In other words, there is a sense in which translation becomes a dual experience of limits in language and culture.

There is the external experience of limits, which is the recognition of irreducible differences in the structure and lexicon of two languages. It was these irreducible differences that greatly exercised the minds of translation scholars who were strongly influenced by the linguistics paradigm, such as Roman Jakobson, Vinay and Darbelnet, and J.C. Catford. A standard example is the use of the formal and informal second person (*tu/vous, tu/Usted, du/Sie*) in many European languages, and the difficulty of rendering the nuances of this usage into modern English, which has only one form of the second person singular, *you*. The difficulty of translation resides in having to contend with these limits and finding satisfactory or creative ways of dealing with them.

The internal experience of limits is the acknowledgement by translators of the limitations to their knowledge of their native language. As they translate a text from a foreign language, they frequently have to ask themselves the question that David Bellos includes in one of his chapter headings in his recent work on translation: 'Is Your Language Really Yours?' (Bellos 2011: 57). The internal experience of limits is subjective, whereas the external experience is objective, but the internal experience is no less real for this. Marcel Proust would spend several years testing and reworking his personal knowledge of French before he felt properly able to offer a satisfactory rendition of Ruskin's work in the Frenchman's native language. He presents the recognition of limits and the desire to transcend them as the inescapable path to self-knowledge: 'This voluntary servitude is the beginning of freedom. There is no better way of becoming aware of what one feels oneself than to try to recreate within oneself what a master felt. In this major task, it is our own thought, as well as his, that we are bringing to light'[2] (cited in Tadié 1996: 439). The dual axis of external and internal delimitation in the translation experience of the individual translator is matched at a collective level by the role of translators and translation in the construction of national vernaculars.

One of the main influences on the language that Proust had to translate was the English of the King James Bible that was mentioned in Chapter 1. The so-called Authorized Version of the Bible published in 1611, and translated by a team of translators led by Myles Coverdale, would have a profound impact on writing in English for many centuries after its initial appearance (McGrath 2002). An important precedent for Coverdale and his fellow translators was, of course, Martin Luther's translation of the Bible into German which often earned for Luther the sobriquet 'Father of the German Language'. In his famous 'Open Letter on Translating' (1530), Luther defends his insertion of the word *allein* where the word *solum* did not exist in the Latin or Greek text of Romans 3:

> In all these phrases, this is a German usage, even though it is not the Latin or Greek usage. It is the nature of the German language to add *allein* in order that *nicht* or *kein* may be clearer and more complete. To be sure, I can also say, 'The farmer brings grain and *kein* money,' but the words '*kein* money' do not sound as full and clear as if I were to say, 'The farmer brings *allein* grain and *kein* money.' Here the word *allein* helps the word *kein* so much that it becomes a completely clear German expression. We do not have to ask the literal Latin how we are to speak German, as these donkeys do. Rather we must ask the mother in the home, the children on the street, the common man in the marketplace. We must be guided by their language,

by the way they speak, and do our translating accordingly. Then they will understand it and recognize that we are speaking German to them.[3]

(Luther 1909: 640)

Here, Luther is confronting the external limits to the German language, the differences that he identifies between Latin and German grammatical usage. It is these differences which guide his choice of language in translating the New Testament passage. It is the juxtaposition of the Greek, Latin, and German languages which makes the specificity of the German language emerge. His 'Open Letter' is an attempt to marshal the external, objective evidence of language delimitation to justify the detail of the German text he has produced, and in so doing to lay the foundations of the modern German vernacular language.

At another level, however, what Luther is expressing in his 'Open Letter' is the translator's internal experience of the limits to his knowledge of his native language. Self-knowledge is no knowledge. It is not by remaining sequestered in his or her study that the translator will answer to the demands of the task. The translator must move, go out into the world, 'ask the mother in the home, the children on the street, the common man in the marketplace'. The Translation Zone is not a Comfort Zone. When Luther speaks of the translation of the Old Testament, on which he collaborated with Philip Melanchthon and Matthew Aurogallus of the University of Wittenberg, he notes that, on occasion, it took them up to four days to translate three lines:

> Now that it has been translated into German and completed, all can read and criticize it. The reader can now run his eyes over three or four pages without stumbling once, never knowing what rocks and clods had once lain where he now travels as over a smoothly planed board. We had to sweat and toil there before we got those boulders and clods out of the way, so that one could go along so nicely. The ploughing goes well in a field that has been cleared. But nobody wants the task of digging out the rocks and stumps. There is no such thing as earning the world's thanks.[4]
>
> (Luther 1909: 642)

The 'sweat and toil' of the translators is the difficulties for translators working into their mother tongue. Digging out 'the rocks and stumps' is the arduous exploration of a terrain that is suddenly rendered unfamiliar by the demands of the text to be translated. The fields of language that have to be 'cleared' are the fields that are part of their landscape from infancy. The internal and external experiences of limits are, however, porous. Translators shape as much as they are shaped by the limits of language and culture. Luther will give form to a new kind of German. He will influence in a profound and enduring way the German that will be spoken and later written by the mother in the home, the children in the street and the common man in the marketplace (Sanders 2010). In other words, in exploring the subjective limits to his knowledge of German, he will set new limits to the configuration of the 'smoothly planed board'. It is precisely these new limits that will make his German recognizably different.

Extensive and intensive culture

What have these experiences of limits to say to us about translation in an age which is dominated by images not of limits, but of flux and ceaseless movement? As the British sociologist Scott Lash observes:

> Contemporary culture, today's capitalism – our global information society – is ever expanding, is ever more *extensive*. There are Starbuck's and McDonald's – indeed many Starbucks and many McDonalds – in not just London, Paris and Berlin, but in seemingly every district of Shanghai and Beijing, Delhi and Bombay, Johannesburg and Lagos, Dubai and Abu Dhabi, São Paulo and Mexico City, and also increasingly in Chongqing and Wuhan, in Bangalore and Madras, in Nairobi and Cairo, Buenos Aires and Bogotá.
>
> (Lash 2010: 1, author's emphasis)

Capitalism, society, culture, and politics are thus increasingly extensive. Another dominant image used to capture the present moment is that of flux (Urry 1999). In notions of extensivity and flux, limits are, of course, notable by their absence, or if they do appear, it is increasingly as a way of benchmarking a past that is irrevocably past. Translation as a global language industry would appear to partake of this culture of extensivity and fluidity. As Iulia Mihalache notes in a discussion of the interaction in a technologized space between translators, technologies, and electronic networks of practice: 'translators are prompted to develop a kind of managerial cognition that enables them to target clients, strategic groups and companies worldwide' (Mihalache 2008: 56). Translation, in this representation, is what makes globalization a reality. It partakes of the culture of fluid extensivity. It allows the channels of global exchange to keep on flowing so that, if nothing else, the Starbuck's customers, wherever they are, know what to order, and the staff know what to give them. Scott Lash goes on to make a distinction, however, which suggests that limits may not always be off-limits when discussing translation and globalization. He argues that 'Extensive culture is a culture of the same: a culture of *equivalence*; while intensive culture is a culture of *difference*, of *inequivalence* (Lash 2010: 3; his emphasis).

Both extensive and intensive cultures are to be found in late modernity. Extensive culture is best captured by the Big Mac, whose value rests on its interchangeability. It is precisely because it is the same standard product wherever one goes that one can be assured of its dependability. Intensive culture is expressed in popular terms by the cult of the brand. It is precisely because the watch or the pair of trainers or the particular consumer product is not supposed to be like any other watch, or pair of trainers, or product that the brand acquires its reputation or aura. But, of course, the idea of intensive culture goes much deeper than the strategic cynicism of branded products and relates to a desire for human singularity. The resistance to a culture of the same, a culture of equivalence, lies in the fear that if everything in a market society becomes interchangeable, then even human beings and their bodies become goods like any other goods, to be traded like any other commercial product. What Régis Debray calls the tension between the 'technocosm' (the physical and virtual infrastructure of global circulation) and the 'ethnocosm' (the space of individual and collective self-definition and belonging) is another way of formulating the tension between extensive and intensive cultures in a global and digital age (Debray 2010: 57).

The tension between a culture of extensivity and a culture of intensivity is articulated in translation by two competing representations of the act of translating. Both cultures find forms of expression that determine how translators and translation come to be seen in processes of globalization. Translation and extensive culture are noticeably paired in the world of translation applications for smartphones. A readily available application for the iPhone is called 'Word Lens'. The description of the app claims that you can 'Instantly translate printed words from one language to another with your built-in video camera in real time ... Use Word Lens on vacation, business travel, and just for fun' (Quest Visual 2012). Word Lens becomes World Lens. There's more to the picture than meets the eye. Sightseeing becomes a form of simultaneous translation and seeing is not so much believing as decoding. The designers do add some nervous caveats to the utopian promise of the product:

- best used on clearly printed text (e.g. signs, menus)
- does NOT recognize handwriting or stylized fonts
- it's not perfect but you can get the general meaning!

(Quest Visual 2012)

However, implicit in Word Lens is the notion that language can be subsumed to an extensive culture, a culture of the same, where language is a matter of instantaneous equivalence flashed up on the screen of an iPhone. Unfortunately, for the designers, their idiomatic nervousness is justified. In the product description, they give an example of usage where one is shown a sign in French, 'Danger! Par fortes marées', and this is translated into English as, 'Danger! By strong tides'. One does indeed get the general meaning, but there is an almost comic, poetic archaism in the literal rendering of the sign, 'By strong tides I walked, lonely as an April cloud ...' The lack of idiomaticity in the translation is a casualty of a culture of approximation, but what is significant for the purposes of the analysis here is that Word Lens, in common with many other translation apps, offers the user a vision (literally, in the case of Word Lens) of a borderless world of instantaneous language access. The range of languages may be severely limited for many of the apps, but the implicit logic is one of potentially endless extensivity.

The embedding of translation in intensive culture emerges when one looks more closely at particular translation flows in late modernity. In a report on literary translation from Arabic, Hebrew, and Turkish into English from 1990–2010 in the United Kingdom and Ireland, the authors noted the marked resistance to translation in the Anglophone world. Although the British and Irish publishing industry was one of the most productive in Europe, with an average annual output of 120,000–130,000 titles, only 1.5–2 per cent of the titles (around 2,500) were translations, and of these, only a fraction were literary translations. In contrast, in countries like the Czech Republic, Finland, Estonia, and Slovenia, around 20–30 per cent of all new titles published between 1990 and 2005 were translations, while the figures for Germany and France ranged between 10 and 15 per cent over the same period (Büchler, Guthrie, Donahaye, and Tekgül 2011: 7). The situation with respect to the wider Euro-Mediterranean region, although somewhat improved in the second decade of the study, was scarcely more reassuring. In the first years of the 1990s, the average number of published titles translated from Arabic, Hebrew, and Turkish was between two and eight per year. In the 2000s, the average rose to between 10 and 16, with 26 translations from Arabic published in 2009, 7 from Turkish, and 8 from Hebrew (*ibid.*, 8). The authors of the report further note that translation choices from the three languages are strongly overdetermined:

> There are still not enough translations published from the three languages, and, with some exceptions, interest in books coming from the Arabic, Turkish and Hebrew speaking world is determined by socio-political factors rather than by the desire to explore the literary culture of the Middle East and North Africa for its own merits, with the result that books from this region are often approached primarily as a source of socio-political commentary or documentary, rather than as literary works per se.
>
> (*Ibid.*, 8)

What emerges from the analysis of literary translation in this period is the extent to which a culture of difference, a culture of 'inequivalence' to use Lash's term, is very much to the fore in the Anglophone world's relationship with the non-Anglophone world. There is a sense in which the dominant presence of English in the global technocosm, and the accompanying discourse of universal connectivity, contrasts sharply with the resistance of the Anglophone ethnocosm (despite its multiple internal differentiations) to engagement with literature in translation.

Even when translations do appear, as the authors point out, it can often have more to do with immediate socio-political interests, so that translation is more to do with an instrumentalized narcissism than with a disinterested involvement with the wider world. As one translator, Marilyn Booth, notes with respect to translation from Arabic, there is the 'longstanding focus on asking for sociology instead of literature' (*ibid.*, 69). Insufficient funding, lack of training opportunities, media indifference, poor pay, and absence of academic recognition for translated work are among the limits to the growth of translation from Arabic, Hebrew, and Turkish into English that are identified by the translation practitioners in the report. In other words, what tends to define this practice of translation is the obdurate reality of limits in the putative flat earth of globalizing fantasy. Luther reminded his readers that facing up to the presence of 'inequivalence' was hard work. The Arabic translator Jonathan Wright, for his part, notes that 'there's a big difference between reading a newspaper, negotiating a business deal and reading pre-Islamic poetry. Arabic is such a vast body of material, with clear distinctions chronologically and in registers, that students and teachers have to set priorities' (*ibid.*, 73). In this view, the culture of translation cannot be anything other than intensive because the translator is constantly attempting to cope with the seemingly intractable differences of languages and cultures. Overcoming the differences does not so much annul them, as confirm their existence.

If we consider the difference between translation in extensive culture and translation in intensive culture, one striking dissimilarity relates to time. Grappling with the intricacies of pre-Islamic poetry and tapping a smartphone belong to different orders of time. The consequence is that, if time is money in a globalized real-time economy, spending more time means spending more money, and this entails lower return on investment. The near instantaneity of online connectivity reinforces a sense of a 24/7 culture of instant delivery. The Arabic translator Catherine Cobham captures the consequences of this dilemma when she notes:

> Bad pay keeps standards down, making people rush, cram, work when tired; it also means that work gets farmed out to translators who are not really ready to take it on yet. I think literary translators should be paid more. A lot of the faults as they are in translations as they are now may stem from people doing them too quickly because they aren't paid much and can't afford to spend the necessary amount of time on them.
>
> (*Ibid.*, 74)

Limits to growth

A foundational text in the birth of the modern ecology movement was the publication in 1972 of a report commissioned by the Club of Rome that was tellingly entitled *The Limits to Growth*. The authors of the report examined the implications of the mismatch between a growing world population and the finite resources of Planet Earth (Meadows, Meadows, Randers, and Behrens 1972). Part of the contention of the ecology movement was that it was vital to protect the diversity of flora and fauna on the planet (bio-diversity) and the different natural environments and landscapes in which living beings and inanimate objects reside (geo-diversity). Are there limits to translation growth? Is there a sense in which we need to insitute a notion of what Paul Virilio has called 'chrono-diversity' (Virilio 2010: 27), alongside the by now familiar notions of bio-diversity and geo-diversity? By this is meant the need to protect different rhythms, different experiences of time, in order to protect and maintain human flourishing. In a 24/7 culture dominated by the near instantaneity of text messaging and emails, the sense of being overwhelmed, of being engulfed in the kinetic inferno, is easily reached. Acknowledging chrono-diversity in translation practice is recognizing that there are very real limits to achievement and accomplishment within specific timeframes and that different kinds of translation require radically different levels of investment in time. A world without limits of time is a world where time for anything is sorely limited. The real limits to growth, as the authors of the famous 1972 report readily admitted, are the absence of limits. Nothing grows in a landscape of endless depletion.

If the rhetoric around translation has gravitated to the messianic hopefulness of a borderless world, it has hardly been surprising. Dictatorships are famously suspicious of translators. The culturalization of limits can be used to justify the worst forms of virulent xenophobia, and the border can be much more a site of exclusion than a place of passage. This understandable wariness, however, leads to a frequent inability to recognize what actually happens when we engage in translation and what are the real dilemmas faced by translators in a global and digital age. It is also fatal to misconstrue the promise of limits. The impulse to move, to travel anywhere, is driven by the desire to go beyond familiar horizons, to breach the limits of a familiar world. Without limits, the sense of curiosity, excitement, achievement would be meaningless. This is the famous, destructive boredom of the delinquent. Having, for whatever reason, no internalized sense of limits, the delinquent out of despair desperately seeks to provoke surrounding society into imposing limits through harmful or reckless behaviour. In the geopolitical context, as Régis Debray observes, people who believe they know everything and claim to be at home wherever they are on the planet are generally much to be feared (Debray 2010: 81). This is the implicit message of Ovid's famous declaration in his *Fastes*, 'Other peoples were given a specific territory: the world and the city of Rome are the same thing'[5] (II, 683–84). Part of the necessary humility of translators is to know the limits to one's understanding of a culture or a language or a people. A lifetime is rarely enough to take in the fractal immensity of even one language pair. Although translators have been much criticized in recent years for a culture of excessive humility, for concealing themselves throughout history in an apologetic rhetoric of submissiveness, is this stance not to be much preferred to the imperial hubris of the subject who imagines no bounds to his or her knowledge and power?

From this perspective, it may be more helpful to resituate translation within a world of limits, borders, and divisions and see its emancipative power not in a messianic abolition of limits but in a rhythmic engagement with the forces of globalization in our age. In other words, translation is a profoundly ambiguous operation. It juxtaposes phases of openness (taking in ideas, texts, expressions from elsewhere) with phases of closure (the definitional labour of deciding what can and cannot be said in a text or language). Examples of this labour are omnipresent in online discussion forums where translators and non-translators alike will discuss at length the appropriate rendition of a particular word or expression in a language. In a WordReference.com language forum, the request for a French translation of 'cream cheese' generated twenty-five separate posts (WordReference.com 2005: 1–2). One post claimed that 'crème de fromage' existed in French and also 'crème de gruyère', but another senior member,

'Claude123', responded, 'No, no, no, Cream Cheese is a North American reality; it has nothing to do with Fromage fondu. In Quebec the "Comité intergouvernemental de terminologie de l'industrie laitière" has adopted Fromage à la crème as an equivalent.' This post prompted a response from another senior member, 'Rodger', 'Sorry Claude123, it's a french [*sic*] reality! Called Saint Moret.' A debate ensues about the appropriateness of 'fromage frais' as a translation, with further references to the Office de la langue française, a contribution from a senior member, 'williamtmiller', who works for a French cheese company where 'cream cheese' is translated as 'Fromage Frais Fondu' or 'Fromage Frais à Tartiner', and a discussion as to whether Saint Moret really tastes like cream cheese. What is apparent in the range and intensity of the discussion is that the participants are both testing and defining the limits of what can be said in French to capture a culinary reality that originated in the United States in 1872 as an attempt to recreate the French cheese Neufchâtel. The attempted cultural translation of a French food product leads over a hundred years later to a polemical effort to retranslate the product, this time linguistically, back into French.

In negotiating the rhythms of closure and openness in languages and cultures, translators both filter and infiltrate the target language and culture. In this respect, it might be opportune to move away from an image that has often been used to capture the task of the translator, that of the bridge. Translation as a bridge between cultures, translators as bridge-builders, these metaphors are commonplaces of irenic pronouncements on the global importance of translation. However, it may be more useful to look under the bridge and see what is swirling down below. James Joyce opened his hymn to the polyphonic possibilities of modern urban life with this downward gaze:

> riverrun, past Eve and Adam's, from swerve of shore to bend of bay, brings us by a commodius vicus of recirculation back to Howth Castle and Environs,
> Sir Tristram, violer d'amores, fr'over the short sea, had passencore rearrived from North Armorica on this side the scraggy isthmus of Asia Minor to wielderfight his penisolate war
>
> (Joyce 1939: 1)

The river that runs through *Finnegans Wake* carries with it the multitude of languages and cultures that have passed through the city and into the mind and writings of the artist. Without the river, there are no banks and no bridges. It is the river that defines the banks, brings the bridges into being. Rivers both define and ignore boundaries. They gather materials from both banks and bring materials to both banks. If the great civilizations of translation have grown up around rivers – the Nile, the Tigris, the Euphrates – is this not a reminder that translation is better understood not as suspended in the air, but as caught up in the living currents of language and cultures that continue to flow through the landscapes of our dwelling places? The riverrun of translation both divides and unites us, and if, in Heraclitus' words, no man steps in the same river twice, that is because both the river and the man are themselves in endless recirculation, in an endless state of perpetual retranslation.

Identicality

What happens in that process of recirculation is a subject which greatly pre-occupies Christa Malone, the heroine of John Crowley's novel *The Translator*. In one of her early meetings with the Russian poet she will eventually translate, Christa, or Kit as she is more generally known, wonders how much she has actually understood from their conversation:

> She had understood all that he had said, with no way of knowing what he meant. It was as though he himself existed here in this town in this state of translation, ambiguous, slightly wrong, too highly colored or wrongly nuanced. Within him was the original, which no one could read.
>
> (Crowley 2003: 59)

Part of their conversation had centred on an English-language translation of one of Innokenti Isayevich Falin's poems. Falin claimed that the original poem and the translation may have been *about* the same things, but they were not *saying* the same things. He wondered aloud to Kit whether an English translation that, unlike the Russian original, had no rhymes or identifiable metre could really be said to be the same poem as the one he had written. Kit does what she can to defend the translator's art but is handicapped by a lack of experience and a more general failure to reflect on what it is that translators do, and both of these conditions will change as the novel progresses. The core issue for Falin in his critique of the translator's rendition of his poem is the problematic relationship between authorship and identity. When he says that the translation in English is 'not my poem' (*ibid.*, 57), he is denying authorship of the translation because he feels that it has in various ways betrayed or falsified the identity of the Russian original. Kit, when she wants to reflect on their exchange, uses the familiar binary of authentic original and translation as travesty ('slightly wrong', 'too highly colored', 'wrongly nuanced').

Underlying this all-too-common antinomy is a problem that greatly exercised thinkers in the early modern period, and whose resolution profoundly affected the fortunes of culture in Europe and elsewhere for many centuries thereafter. If it was an avowed aim of Renaissance humanist scholars to go back to the texts of classical antiquity, they were faced with a recurring dilemma: what texts? Centuries of manuscript copying had the inevitable con-sequence of omission, mistranscription, interpolation, and variation. Part of the philological enterprise of Renaissance humanism was to reconstruct a satisfac-tory version of the 'original', or to approximate as much to a putative original as the availability of texts or the state of scholarship would permit (Cerquigini 1989). The wider concern that is articulated in this move is that of stabilizing identity. Extracting an identifiable original from a plethora of variants meant by extension locating an identifiable authorial voice in a chorus of competing versions. Elusive fluidity gives way to recognizable stability.

For the fifteenth-century Italian polymath Leon Battista Alberti, this stability was as much a project for the future as a predicament for the past. How would he ensure that the buildings he designed would be the buildings that would eventually be built? He addressed the vexed question of variability through the development of architectural design. By developing a specific system of notation, his aim was to ensure that the design of the building and the building itself would be identical. Furthermore, such a system would clearly identify Alberti as author of the building. Although others would build the building, they were simply following his instructions to the letter or, more commonly, to the number. Alberti's preference for drawings over models meant, of course, that he had to render a three-dimensional reality using a two-dimensional system. As Mario Carpo points out:

> Consequently, a building and its design can only be *notationally* identical: their identicality depends on a notational system that determines how to translate one into the other. When this condition of *notational identicality* is satisfied, the author of the drawing becomes the author of the building, and the architect can claim some form of ownership over a building which in most cases he does not in fact own, and which he certainly did not build – indeed, which he may never even have touched.
>
> (Carpo 2011: 23; his emphasis)

Alberti's notion of authorship presupposes identicality, and his idea of identicality presupposes translatability. It is the advent of printing, contemporary with the activities of Alberti, that will provide the regime of identicality with a powerful impetus. It now becomes possible to produce countless numbers of identical copies of the same text. The Industrial Revolution and the later introduction of assembly-line production allows for the mass production of standardized goods. More costs less. The Albertian engagement with identicality as a firm basis for individual, authorial identity becomes the matrix for modernity as printing presses and production lines proclaim the triumph of identicality over variability. Carpo argues that the influence of this matrix has been profound:

> In the course of the last five centuries, the power of exactly repeatable, mechanical imprints has gradually shaped a visual environment where identicality is the norm, similarity insignificant, and the cultural expectation of identical copies ultimately affects the functions and values of all signs. Under this semantic regime of modernity, only signs that are visually identical have identical meanings. This is the way modern logos, emblems and trademarks work. They are recorded and protected by copyright laws, which register an original and all identical copies of it.
>
> (*Ibid.*, 24)

As was noted earlier, Alberti's design theory is only operative if there is a translation practice to sustain it. Identicality in this instance depends on how successfully the notational system translates two-dimensional into three-dimensional realities, plans into buildings. The more successful the translation, the greater the semblance of identicality. Consequently, what the 'semantic regime of modernity' implies is that the only legitimate form of translation is that which promotes identicality. Only under conditions of identicality can authorship be clearly identified. Thus, Falin decides to disown the translation in Crowley's fiction. The Russian poem and the English translation can in no way be considered identical, so any notion of his being the author of the poem that appears in the English-language anthology is, in his view, absurd. If the combined effects of the Albertian theory of authorship, the emergence of printing, and the standardized outputs of mass production gave sameness and identicality pride of place in the development of modernity, where would translation situate itself in the context of this paradigm, and how is this changing in the age of digital, as opposed to mechanical, reproduction? One way of assessing the impact of modernism's semantic regime is to consider briefly the changing norms governing the practice of English-language literary translation in the twentieth century.

Translation and the rise of the reader

In Karl Breul's 1913 introduction to an English translation of Goethe's *Dichtung und Wahreit*, he makes mention of the revised translation by Minna Steele Smith. The translation is based on an earlier one by John Oxenford, 'but the scholarly translator [Steele Smith] has throughout referred to the latest German editions and commentaries, and has improved the English text, not merely in style, but in clearness and correctness' (Breul 1913: xxiii). Steele Smith in her 'Translator's Preface' expresses her hope that 'at least an accurate rendering of the original has been given'. The emphasis on scholarship, accuracy, and, to a lesser extent, clarity is an important norm in translation in the opening decades of the twentieth century. The normative expectations of scholarly translation from the latter half of the nineteenth century continue to be articulated. A.T. Murray, in his presentation of *The Iliad* for the Loeb Classical Library in 1924, offered a cogent but nuanced expression of the dominant norm of source-text-oriented fidelity: 'He [the translator] has endeavoured to give a version that in some measure retains the flowing ease and simple directness of Homer's style, and that has due regard to the emphasis attaching to the original: and to make use of a diction that, while elevated, is, he trusts, not stilted. To attain to the nobility of Homer's manner may well be beyond the possibilities of modern English prose' (Murray 1924: vii). Murray was still concerned that the Homeric style in English be suitably 'elevated', but not 'stilted'. However, in expressing Chryses' plea for the return of his daughter as follows, 'but my dear child do ye set free for me, and accept the ransom out of awe for the son of Zeus, Apollo, that smitheth afar' (*ibid.*, 5), it was clear that the definition of what was 'elevated' and what was 'stilted' was a matter for debate. It is important to situate the norm of source-text-oriented fidelity in the educational context of the opening decades of the twentieth century. The primary experience of translation for the majority of those producing, commenting on, and reading translations, in an era before widespread literacy and access to education was gained in the class-room, where translation into and from Latin and/or ancient Greek was *de rigueur*. Examples from translations of the classics were likely to be more per-suasive by dint of familiarity. Indeed, even when modern languages co-opted translation into the curriculum, they were largely to borrow methods used in teaching translation for the classical languages, though this would change in the latter half of the twentieth century when the communicative approach dismissed translation as a valid form of language instruction.

Curricular changes in the English-speaking world since mid-century have tended to obscure the extraordinary tenacity of the classical languages in the education of elites (Waquet 1998) and to conceal the important pedagogic imperative in much thinking about literary translation in the early half of the twentieth century. T.F. Higham, in his introduction to the *Oxford Book of Greek Verse in Translation* (1936), explicitly acknowledges the classroom dimension in his defence of the practice of translation: 'No disparagement can obscure the essential value of an art which alone can mediate between past and present, or between living men of different speech. In every school and college it is taught and practised; and if practice must be guided by example, a book of this kind, at least in its intention, has a plausible excuse' (Higham 1936: xxxiii). The result was a way of thinking about translation that was preoccupied with source-text scholarship, was strongly prescriptive and evaluative in its outlook, and which saw translation primarily as a way of getting to know the source text better. It is possible to argue further, however, that what is also at work here is a move in the direction of identicality as a way of asserting the primacy of authentic, expressive authorship. Goethe and Homer emerge as the true 'designers' here, and the closer the construction of the translation to the design of the original, the clearer the sense of distinct authorship.

For Stephen MacKenna, a translator of Plotinus, the underlying assumption guiding a highly prestigious collection of classical texts and their translations, the Loeb series, was a static concept of the target language which in effect undermined its claim to accuracy. Not only, as he saw it, was the language used vastly impoverished through multiple exclusions of words and idioms, but the '"literal English" turns out to be (1) Liddell & Scott English or (2) a bastard English, a horrible mixture of Elizabethan, Jacobean, fairytale-ese, Biblicism and modern slang (not slang of word but, what is worse, of phrase or construction)' (Dodds 1936: 155–56). Philological literalism obscured rather than revealed authorial presence. Stilted or archaic language was certainly to be found in volumes in the series, but the evidence of many of the translations is that there was a degree of self-reflexivity among the scholar-translators and they were not as obtuse as MacKenna suggested. James George Frazier, for example, in his translation of Apollodorus' *Library* for the Loeb series, is quick to defend his translation on the grounds that it is the original writer, not the translator, who is to blame for any ungainliness of style: 'But with all his [Apollodorus'] sim-plicity and his directness he is not an elegant writer. In particular, the accu-mulation of participles, to which he is partial, loads and clogs the march of his sentences' (Frazier 1921: xvi). It is the designer, not the maker, who should be held account for any construction flaws. When W.A. Oldfather reviewed previous English translations of Epictetus in his prefatory remarks to a new translation in the same series, he spoke of 'a vigorous and idiomatic reproduction' by Elizabeth Carter, 'a learned and exact rendition' by George Long, and a 'most fluent and graceful version' by P.E. Mathesen, and acknowledged that the translation he had produced was indebted to all three, and this was reflected in the translation (Oldfather 1926: xxxvii). Though the dominant norm was one of close fidelity to source-text language and to a notion of appropriate (parti-cularly poetic) diction, the scholarly translations were by no means all beholden to the 'literal English' so decried by MacKenna.

It would be wrong, however, to see the translators in the early decades of the twentieth century as wholly in thrall to a source-text-oriented literalism, and here we will see the articulation of a current of thinking that will take on an added resonance in the digital age. In 1901, A.C Bradley in his Oxford lecture on 'Poetry for Poetry's Sake' claimed that any translation of poetry 'is not really the old meaning in a fresh dress. It is a new product, something like the poem, though, if one chooses to say so, more like it in the aspect of meaning than in the aspect of form' (Bradley 1901: 23–24). Bradley would find an ally in J.S. Phillimore (1919), who quoted Edward FitzGerald's dictum, 'Better a live spar-row than a dead [sic] eagle', and argued that a poetic translation in English must exist as a convincing poetic creation in its own right, independently of the demands of scholarship. To this extent, it must become the 'new product' that brings the original to life. The poet Robert Bridges, for his part, was hostile to the dominant notion that translations of Greek verse should read like well-written conventional English verse, which indeed was the case with many of the poems to appear twenty years later in the Higham anthology. In his view, the reader should expect the unexpected: 'A reader of Homer is like a man in a dream, who enters into a strange world of beauty unlike that which every day besets him' (Bridges 1916: 142).

What Bradley, Phillimore, Murray, and Bridges had in common, however, despite their apparent divergences, was a concern with literary translation paying due attention to the source-language literary tradition. In other words, although the means to realize the translation might have been radically different, the purpose was first and foremost to convey the foreign, source-language literature to the English reader. Thus, the focus of critics of scholarly literalism was less on the effects on English language and literature than on what disservice was being done to foreign literatures in translation. E.S. Bates indeed presented the class of professional academic translators (though he allowed many honourable excep-tions) as predominantly the spoiled children of another age, and 'the liberties these men allowed themselves amaze anyone who now examines what they did and said: their perversions, omissions, re-writings' (Bates 1943: 11). If 'Grammarians and

Academics' (*ibid.*, 13) plague literary translation, it is because they ignore the higher Romantic calling of lived experience ('Life'), which alone confers authority on a translation through a more creative fidelity to the original. Bates, therefore, saw these professional academic translators as being, in a sense, akin to the monastic copyists of the pre-print age, adrift in the uncertain waters of unreliability and variability despite their scholarly protestations to the contrary.

Ezra Pound is, of course, the writer most associated with what is conventionally understood to be modernist thinking on translation, though his own views on the subject were more complex than is often believed. Pound refers in his essay on his translations of Guido Calvacanti to the type of translation where the '"translater" is definitely making a new poem' and where the translation 'falls simply in the domain of original writing' (Venuti 2004: 33). In other words, the translated text was not to be viewed primarily in terms of its relationship with the foreign or source text (though for Pound this relationship should never be lost sight of) but was to be accorded an autonomy of its own. In addition, the text itself was to be judged not primarily, as before, in terms of its fidelity or adequacy to the source text, but as part of the literature of the target language. Translations as independent texts could now be evaluated as texts in their own right in the English language. When T.S. Eliot argued that the 'work of translation is to make something foreign, or remote in time, live with our own life' (Eliot 1928: 98), the life to which he referred was not just the contemporary world of the reader, but was increasingly taken to mean, in a particular kind of modernist poetics, the life of the text itself. As the text led its own life in the English language, the question that could be asked was: on whose terms?

One of the effects of Pound's hostility to metaphysical abstractions, and his embrace of imagism and subsequently of vorticism, was that he committed himself in his poetry and prose writing to a precise vernacular that sought to do away with the fussy elaborations of Victorian and Edwardian language. Indeed, part of Pound's fascination with Chinese ideograms was their apparent rootedness in the world of clearly imagined details and particulars. Implicit in elements of Pound's translation practice was a notion that translation would live on in the modern age if it spoke the language of the everyday, rather than the mannered speech of polite letters. Another dimension to the literary experience of modernism that would greatly influence dominant norms for translating poetry was the general embrace of free verse and the increasing unpopularity of rhyme and metre.

It was not the more radical translation experiments of Pound that would invite imitation in the post-war period, however, but a more general modernist commitment to the production of translations in English that were closely attuned to the dominant norms of the contemporary written and spoken language. E.V. Rieu, the founding editor of Penguin Classics in 1944, expressed what was to be the guiding norm of his translations in a preface to a translation of the *Odyssey* first published in 1946: 'This version of the *Odyssey* is, in its intention at any rate, a genuine translation, not a paraphrase or a retold tale. At the same time, and within the rules I have set myself, I have done my best to make

Homer easy reading for those unfamiliar with the Greek world' (Rieu 1946: 9).
He defended his decision to make Homer available in mid-twentieth-century
English prose on the grounds that 'Too faithful a rendering defeats its own
purpose; and if we put Homer straight into English words, neither meaning nor
manner survives' (*ibid.*, 18). Desmond Lee, in his 1955 preface to the translation
of Plato's *Republic*, explicitly refers to his translation brief: 'Dr Rieu's
instructions to me were to aim at the "general reader". Though this is not a
very definite description, it clearly relegates to the background any use [of the
translation] for more strictly academic purposes' (Lee 1955: 9). The emergence
of an emphasis on the reader was the single most striking feature of translation
norms in the period after the Second World War. If previously translation
norms had largely been determined by the nature of the source language or the
prestige of the source-language author, now the emphasis was on the making
available of translations that were readily accessible to the educated layperson.
J.M. Cohen, a prolific and widely published translator of Spanish and French
literature, gave vivid expression to the centrality of the reader in his 1950
translation of *Don Quixote*:

> There is no doubt at all that the book improves as it progresses; the second
> part, published some ten years after the first, is by far and away the richer
> and the subtler. It is also more of a unity. For such digressions as there are
> do not take the form of separate tales, but are incorporated in the main
> body of the story. These digressions certainly offer an obstacle to the present-
> day reader; and my advice to anyone who finds himself bogged down by
> the goatherd's tale in the twelfth chapter is to skip it judiciously.
>
> (Cohen 1950: 17)

Cohen's intimate complicity with the reader would seem at one level to be at
variance with Rieu's own strong admonition that 'the most heinous crime that
a translator can commit' is to 'interpose the veil of his own personality between
his original and the reader' (Rieu 1946: 21). However, Cohen's solicitude was
occasioned by the overriding norm of readability and the recurrent desire to
make translations in English as palatable as possible to the language and tastes
of the English-language-reading public. What is striking is that the orientation
towards the reader and the preference for unmarked language are justified in terms
of bringing the reader closer to the original author. By bringing the author
closer to the reader, the fiction of identicality is strengthened. The author
speaks directly and plainly to readers in their own language. There are no veils
to conceal the expressive purity of the original.

Indeed, one way of articulating and defending a norm of target-oriented fluency
was to offer a reading of translation history with a clear teleology. William
Atkinson, in his account of previous translations of the *Lusiads*, set up an
opposition between the 'boldness' or looseness of the 1776 translation by
Mickle, on the one hand, and the overweening fidelity of Burton's 1870 translation,
on the other. Atkinson's verdict on Burton was damning: 'The interests of the

modern reader were nowhere consulted, and the upshot was as could have been foreseen: his version, the most ambitious of all and the most firmly rooted in scholarship, fell from the press stillborn, unreadable' (Atkinson 1952: 33). Atkinson presented his prose translation as the happy union of accuracy and readability. In other words, previous translations are presented as either too literal, and therefore unreadable, or as too readable, and therefore inaccurate. Only in the modern age is there a viable compromise between fidelity and accessibility, though paradoxically it is the putative general reader who powerfully determines the conditions of identicality.

In the post-1945 period, among the push factors for a normative turn towards target-language-oriented translation, and prose rather than verse translation, were the commitment of the welfare state to education for all, rising rates of literacy throughout the English-speaking world, the continued expansion of paperback publishing, the launch of readily available series like Penguin Classics, and the gradual democratization of speech habits through the influence of the broadcast media. Archaism was explicitly shunned and Philip Vellacott in his 1953 translation of plays by Euripides states, 'In general, I have eschewed archaic diction' (Vellacott 1953: 24). There was, of course, an alternative current in the Poundian approach to translation – the 'interpretative' translations (Venuti 2004: 33) of poets like Guido Calvacanti and Arnaut Daniel, where Pound deliberately mixed different archaic forms of the English language to restore for the English-language reader a sense of the foreignness of the source-language text. A similar strategy was used by Samuel Beckett in his translations of contemporary French-language poets (Shields 2000: 59–89). In the archaizing strategy employed by Pound, it was again the desire to bring the reader closer to the foreign text that made the poet–translator search out the marginal, the neglected, and the forgotten in the domestic resources of the target language. It was not the tradition of interpretative translations, but what Pound referred to in the Guido essay as 'the other sort' (Venuti 2004: 33) – autonomous, fluent, and formally unfettered – that would, however, act as the dominant paradigm for translation in the second half of the twentieth century. What is significant is that both the 'interpretive' translations and 'the other sort' establish as their *telos* a notion of identicality: that the reader will experience the text as an original, in the full force of its expressive design.

If the archaic was avoided as a baleful reminder of the dead hand of the 'grammarian', the scholarly apparatus of the 'academic' as translator became equally suspect. Una Ellis-Fermor, in the introduction to her 1950 translations of plays by Ibsen, detailed the choice that the translator must make and signalled the abandonment of a norm of thick translation prevalent in the earlier decades of the century: 'We perhaps do Ibsen's art more injury by checking the flow of his dialogue to explain what he is at than by substituting an inadequate translation of the original for a conscientious translation. If we have to choose between the run of the dialogue and the accurate presentation of one of its component sentences, the interests of the dialogue as a whole must win' (Ellis-Fermor 1950: 20). In discussing the difficulties of translating the Norwegian *du* and *de* into

English, Ellis-Fermor argued that to leave *du*, the familiar form of address in the original Norwegian, would require a reference number and footnote, which would 'kill the dialogue for the majority of modern readers' (*ibid.*, 20). Though translations would still, of course, continue to be published with footnotes, the norm was increasingly not to use them at all, or to keep them to a bare minimum. Even in those forms of translation practice where footnotes and annotations were previously the norm, the tendency was to plead extreme necessity when they did appear, as Jeffrey Rusten does in his translation of Theophrastus' *Characters* for the Loeb Classical Library: 'Many allusions in the *Characters* to the daily life of Athens require explanation; so when necessary I have not hesitated to annotate the translation more (on 16, "Superstition", *much* more) than may be customary for a Loeb volume' (Rusten, Cunningham and Knox 1993: vii; his emphasis).

There was by no means unanimity on the desirability of target-language-oriented, readability norms, and the most vocal dissenter in the 1950s was Vladimir Nabokov. In an essay published in the *Partisan Review*, he was scathing about reviewers who praise a translation because it 'reads smoothly', and who in their ignorance of the source language and text praise as 'readable' an 'imitation only because the drudge or the rhymester has substituted easy platitudes for the breathtaking intricacies of the text' (Nabokov 1955: 127). His conviction that form and content were indissociable in the work of Pushkin led him to argue famously, 'The clumsiest literal translation is a thousand times more useful than the prettiest paraphrase' (*ibid.*, 127). He expanded on this observation later in his essay, arguing, 'The person who desires to turn a literary masterpiece into another language has only one duty to perform, and this is to reproduce with absolute exactitude the whole text, and nothing but the text' (*ibid.*, 134). The notion of 'literal translation' was in Nabokov's view tautological, since anything else was not a translation, but an imitation or a parody. What Nabokov demonstrated in scholarly detail was the indebtedness of Pushkin to French writers, major and minor, which must somehow be rendered in translation, and the considerable complexity of Russian metre. The fact that English lacks the same metrical resources forces the translator to abandon any hope of producing a rhymed version. The absence was to be compensated for by describing in 'a series of footnotes the modulations and the rhymes of the texts as well as all its associations and special features' (*ibid.*, 143). Nabokov, indeed, wanted his practice for the *Onegin* to become more general, and he declared, 'I want translations with copious footnotes, footnotes reaching up like skyscrapers to the top of this or that page so as to leave only the gleam of textual line between commentary and eternity' (*ibid.*, 143). At one level, the norm articulated by Nabokov was a return to the richly annotated, scholarly tradition of the earlier half of the century, with its overriding concern for the source text, but there is no sense in which Nabokov was seeking, in the translation of the *Onegin*, an 'elevated' or exalted diction for Pushkin, even if many readers of the translation, most famously Edmund Wilson, found it unreadable. What is notable is that the focus of Nabokov's ire is the masking of Pushkin's genius as a result of poor translation that again does an injustice to distinctive authorship through an almost deliberate shunning of identicality.

A new context for the normative practices that emerged in the 1940s and 1950s was provided by the translation workshops which came to be a feature of the American academy in the 1960s. The establishment of the pioneering translation workshop in the University of Iowa in 1964, and the creation of the National Translation Center in the University of Texas at Austin in 1965, provided a forum for the practice and discussion of translation that echoed and complemented the decisive shifts that had already taken place with respect to literary translation in the post-war Anglophone world. The work of I.A. Richards and the subsequent development of New Criticism motivated the drive for close reading and analysis of texts, with an assumption of a unified meaning that could be transferred into another language. Even if Richards later recognized that translation shows just how problematic the establishment of meaning can be, he none the less believed that, with a suitable curtailment of ambition and the right educational training, texts could be carried across from one language to the other (Richards 1953: 247–62). In his thinking, Richards was partially influenced by the post-war vogue for information theory pioneered by Claude Shannon, Norbert Wiener, and John von Neumann, and as a result he presented translation as essentially an elaborate process of encoding and decoding.

Frederic Will, who was associated with the University of Iowa translation workshop from its beginnings, claimed in *Literature Inside Out* (1966) that the universality of human experience provides the conditions of possibility for translation, although he acknowledged that linguistic and cultural dissimilarities can make for difficulty in translation, and render the notion of unified, transferable meaning problematic. It was a metaphysical belief that there was in a sense something beyond language that allowed for meanings to be carried across cultures. In putting this argument forward, Will gave expression to an important tenet of translation in the period, namely that if loss was an intrinsic part of translation, the 'message' or essential 'story' could be communicated. Identicality might be an impossible ideal, but it still remains as a kind of horizon of expectation of modernist translation practice. Will's later collection, *The Knife in the Stone* (1973), was less sanguine about notions of unified texts and meanings. However, Will looked to Chomsky and the notion of deep structures, however imperfectly understood, to provide him with a justification for his own transcendental vision of meanings that lie behind words, beneath the surfaces of the literary work. It was the inherent wholeness of literature itself as a unitary ideal that opened the door to translatability. Will used the writings of the communications theorist Donald MacKay to show that the literary translation of Pound and, by extension, all literary translation, through a merging of the specific cultural goals of the writer and the translator, produced a new cultural configuration which could engender change in the poetics of the receiving culture. The ready association of literary translation with the counter-cultural movement in the English-speaking world in the 1950s, 1960s, and 1970s by Robert Bly, Ted Hughes, Paul Engle, and others seemed to bear out in part the validity of Will's assumption that translation could make things happen (Hughes 1983: Engle and Engle 1976). However, it was Will's appropriation of the Poundian tradition (or, rather, his version of it) that would indeed make things happen in poetry translation in ways that were not so much subversive of dominant norms as a contributory factor to their continued existence. Will saw much of previous thinking about literary translation as overly concerned with questions of exact or even approximate equivalence, a subjection to the tyranny of textual meaning, whereas what constituted the most vital element of a poem, in Will's view, was its basic energy or 'thrust'. If the normative thrust in the period was a concern with getting a message across into the other language or culture, then Will's kinetic take on the act of translation was in keeping with the prevailing notions of what constituted acceptable translation. Good translation was translation that released energy into another text in another language.

The difficulty for theorists and indeed critical commentators on translation was that the 'thrust' appeared to resist definition, and therefore could potentially be recruited as an alibi for just about any translation a translator might care to produce. The implicit theoretical assumptions of the translation workshop and the selective readings of what Pound said about and did with translation provided support for a highly normative approach to literary translation, in which a sober, unadorned style corresponding to the literary taste of the educated Anglophone reading public becomes an almost canonical style for the translation of many different kinds of literary text into English in the late modern period. As with any normative trend, however, there were moves in the opposite direction. When the translation of *The Brothers Karamazov* by Richard Pevear and Larissa Volokhonsky appeared in 1990, the translator duo stressed the importance of scrupulously close attention being paid to the Russian text so that the full extent of Dostoevsky's writerly range could be captured in the translation, and when their translation of *Demons* was published in 1995, the volume had copious notes detailing political and cultural references and violating the general trend in trade publishing to keep notes to an absolute minimum, if not exclude them altogether (Remnick 2005: 35–49). A similar desire to convey the complexity of the original is expressed in William Butcher's 1998 translations of Jules Verne's *Around the World in Eighty Days* and *Twenty Thousand Leagues under the Sea*. Butcher argues in the case of both texts that his desire is to have Verne recognized as a serious writer with stylistic concerns, and that many previous translations have sacrificed the intricacies of Verne's language to a normative notion of reader-oriented fluency (O'Driscoll 2011).

Variability

It is possible to read the repeatedly expressed anxieties about norms for literary translation into English in the twentieth century as part of a more general crisis for translation in modernity. Under the semantic regime of identicality that will motivate so many areas of modernist practice with a consequent commitment to authorial primacy, it is hardly surprising that translation will be repeatedly dogged by charges of inaccuracy, loss, betrayal, and misrepresentation. From basic workshop practice to the repeated translations of the same poem or poems by different translators, it is clear that any notion of identicality is extremely problematic for translators. Reading the multiple translations of Eugenio Montale's 'Dora Markus' and 'L'Anguilla' gathered together in Marco Sonzogni's anthology, *Corno inglese*, it is abundantly clear that constant variability is the dominant semantic regime of translation practice (Sonzogni 2009). Not only are the translations not 'identical' to the original, they are, of course, not identical to each other. Variability is the signature tune of the translator's art. What is more, it is the very variable nature of translation practice that places it at the centre of the profound changes in the culture of the digital age.

In the age of mechanical reproduction, a metal plate that is used to make one print will result in a very expensive print. In the age of digital reproduction, a laser printer can print one hundred copies of the same page or one hundred different pages at no extra cost per page. As Mario Carpo notes:

> The same principle applies to all kinds of mechanical imprints, as well as to all processes where the identical repetition of the same sequence of actions, whether manual or mechanical, are used to generate economies of scale. Under certain conditions, digital technologies can now deliver serial variations at no extra cost, and generate economies of scale while mass-producing series in which all items are different – but different within limits.
>
> (Carpo 2011: 99)

This new form of production, known as 'nonstandard seriality' (*ibid.*, 41), implies that economies of scale are largely irrelevant in digital production processes. Industrial mass production depended on mechanical matrixes, moulds, and casts where the upfront costs had to be covered by using them as often as possible, but with the elimination of mechanical matrixes, digital fabrication tools can produce variations at no extra cost. In Carpo's words, 'in a digital production process, standardization is no longer a money-saver. Likewise, customization is no longer a money-waster' (*ibid.*, 41). Content customization has, of course, become a primary source of profitability in digital environments, as companies like Google use geographical location and other information about users to target them for advertising. It is the same logic of variability that drives the localization industry, as the chief rationale for localization practices is that of customer or end-user linguistic and cultural customization. Implicit in nonstandard seriality is the rise of a regime of variability and the decline of the paradigm of identicality. So how might these changes in the nature of fundamental processes of production in many developed societies illuminate the process of translation?

Nelson Goodman, in his *Languages of Art*, claimed that all arts are originally autographic, that is, handmade by their authors. Some arts then become allographic, scripted by their authors to be materially executed by others (Goodman 1976: 122, 218–21). The building that I make (autographic) becomes the building that I design to be made by others (allographic). One way of conceiving of the different representations of translation practice is as a tension between the autographic and the allographic. The forms of instant translation to be found in science fiction – from the Babel Fish in *The Hitchhiker's Guide to the Galaxy* (D. Adams 1979) to the Universal Translator in *Star Trek* – speak to a vision of pure, allographic practice where the message is instantly and seamlessly translated into another language (O'Sullivan 2011: 40–69). The digital age would appear at one level to hold this image of what Carol O'Sullivan calls 'the dream of instant translation' (*ibid.*, 40), in which translation leaves the realms of the autographic and the artisanal for the fully developed practice of the allographic, the translation machine materially executing in another language the script of the source language. The problem with this representation is not simply of a practical nature and to do with the nature and limits of existing systems of machine translation, but is situated more fundamentally in the attempt to conscript the digital to an existing regime of identicality. In other words, what characterizes digital reproduction as it is practised is not identicality but variability, not sameness but similarity, and not identicality in repetition but difference in repetition. This means that the typecasting of translation in the digital age as a mechanized, allographic practice fails to capture important dimensions to digital reproduction that are core elements of translation practice: namely, variability, difference, and similarity. In order to establish more clearly how the fortunes of the digital and the translational are intertwined, it is useful to invoke the notion of the 'objectile' as developed by Gilles Deleuze.

In his exploration of the mathematical work of Leibniz, in particular his work on calculus, Deleuze noted that Leibniz's mathematics of continuity introduced and formulated a new conception of the object. Differential calculus does not describe objects as such, but their variations and the variations of variations. In order to describe this new, bipartite definition of the object, Deleuze introduced the term 'objectile'. The objectile is a function that contains a potentially infinite number of objects (Deleuze 1988: 26). Each separate and individual object gives expression to the mathematical algorithim, or objectile, common to all. The objectile is a kind of parametric function which may determine an infinite variety of objects. The objects are all different (one for each set of parameters), yet all similar (the underlying function is the same for all). The objectile, in a sense, is the technical object of the digital age. Infinite variants of the same object can be produced at the same cost as identical copies.

This shift from the object of the age of mechanical reproduction to the objectile of the age of digital reproduction brings us closer to the actual practice of translation. The multiple versions of Montale's 'L'Anguilla', the countless renditions of Dante's *Inferno* or Rilke's *Duino Elegies* or the Bible point to translation as being not so much about (text) objects as objectiles. That is to say, the action of translation on the original textual object transforms the object into an objectile, capable of engendering an infinite number of variants in the target language of translation. What characterizes the translations of, for example, 'L'Anguilla', is that, though there are often quite radical differences in style and interpretation, there is none the less an overall family resemblance or similarity. We know that the translations are, in their diversity, referring back to the same poem. It is, indeed, this sense of similarity that often allows us to intuit or identify an original from a translated text, even if we are unaware beforehand of the identity of the original composition.

Similarity is, of course, much more difficult to define than sameness or identicality, but this is part of the interpretative challenge of a regime of variability. Outside the realm of readily identifiable sameness, similarity means, on the one hand, the possibility for endless variety and, on the other, limits to what can be done (there is, in most cases, a version of the original to work from, so anything does not go). The objectile answers to the particular mixture of constraint and liberty that informs the task of the translator. It is in this respect indeed that the age of digital production and reproduction is the age of translation. In navigating a culture that is increasingly shaped by the paradigms of difference and variability, which require a qualitatively different set of responses than those demanded by the semantic regime of modernity, there can be no richer tradition of recorded human experience and response to the new world of the objectile than millennia of translation practice. A world of standardized objects is a world that targets the average user and introduces a multiplicity of exclusions. The economies of scale of standardization impose their own tax on diversity. The translational paradigm of difference and variability that informs the objectile implies the ability to cater for many different kinds of audience and need, while maintaining a certain integrity with respect to what is being delivered. If Robert Burton lived in an age where translation was an urgent requirement in sourcing the news from elsewhere, we live in an age where translation awareness is even more urgent in sourcing the new from everywhere.

4 Everyware

One of the many paradoxes of late modernity is that, as a suspicion of global or overarching theories became widespread in the humanities and social sciences, globalizing practices proceeded apace (Eagleton 2004). At the beginning of the twenty-first century, there are more nation-states on the planet than ever before, but the emergence of a new state such as Southern Sudan occurs against the backdrop of an unprecedented integration of global economic activities. The totalitarian impulse felt to lurk in any attempt to embrace a totality is increasingly disarmed by the breadth and extent of global economic exchanges and their cultural and political impacts. These impacts need to be understood not only in their partial effects but in their global causes if humans are not to be endlessly bewildered by events that appear random, chaotic, and, in certain instances (global financial meltdown), distinctly menacing. In other words, trying to account for global changes is also an attempt to restore historicity to the picture. What happens happens for a particular reason, and not simply because it is the mysterious working out of an obscure *fatum* or destiny. Taking the broader view is to make sense of, not sacrifice, detail.

Mass provision

It is indeed the preoccupation with local detail that has provided the impetus for the most far-reaching global translation projects of our age. One of the acknowledged world leaders in the management of these projects is SDL. In their literature they describe themselves as:

> The leader in Global Information Management (GIM) solutions that empower organizations to accelerate the delivery of high-quality multilingual content to global markets. Its enterprise software and services integrate with existing business systems to manage the delivery of global information from authoring to publication and throughout the distributed translation supply chain.
>
> (Tridgell 2007)

Among their clients are large, multinational companies such as Best Western, ABN-Amro, Bosch, Canon, Chrysler, CNH, Hewlett-Packard, Microsoft, Philips,

SAP, Sony, Sun Microsystems, and Virgin Atlantic. SDL is a global corporation providing multilingual information management services for other global corporations. In a management briefing paper on 'how today's support manager can deliver a truly global support experience' (*ibid.*), SDL describes the impact of changing technology on the provision of customer support.

In the 1970s and 1980s, companies used the existing communications technology of the time to deal with customer queries, namely, the telephone. The rise of the call centre was a function of the globalization of economic activities paired with an existing technology. Call centres evolved in the 1990s as the increased integration of telephony systems with computers allowed for a variety of different contact methods such as email, web forms, and online chat alongside the traditional telephone conversation. However, using the example of Canon, John Tridgell demonstrates how Canon gradually moved most of its call centre traffic to a multilingual support portal. The move was not simply prompted by the availability of more effective digital technologies, but by a desire to reduce costs. The poor quality and paucity of online support materials were among the factors causing customers to resort to contact or call centre help, and call centres are staffed by what Tridgell elsewhere in his briefing paper calls the 'most expensive resource in the service organization': people. In addition, where materials were available, 'the costs associated with translation were high'. For Canon, 'the breakthrough was to accept that with centralized control and application of translation assets and the adoption of a completely automated workflow, effective multilingual support information now reaches the customer faster than ever in a "win–win" situation; costs are reduced for both online publishing and contact centre throughput' (*ibid.*).

Underlying the solution proposed by SDL to Canon's costly translation dilemma is an interesting tension between the enhancement of linguistic diversity through the provision of content in 'local' languages and the recurrent emphasis on 'centralized control'. Indeed, in the Executive Summary, the concept of Global Information Management (GIM) is presented as centripetal in its form but centrifugal in its consequences:

> This [GIM] encompasses not only the importance of local languages available in all operating territories, but how this can be achieved via a centralized approach to content and content management, yet without sacrificing the ability for the organization to respond to local needs and conditions.
>
> (*Ibid.*)

In the shift or 'migration' from call centre to multilingual support portal, what is stressed, somewhat surprisingly in view of the emphasis on automation, is the centrality of the labour of translation. Tridgell claims that, 'although there is a significant cost associated with hiring, retaining and training a local language contact centre representative, there is no cost involved in the ongoing translation process per se' (*ibid.*). In other words, the call centre staff, by speaking the local language and communicating information predominantly authored in English, are rendering the process of translation invisible. They naturalize translation so that it does not appear as a discrete element of the call centre communicative interaction. On the other hand, the move to dehumanize the customer interaction by generating multilingual content for a portal makes visible and explicit the role of translation in the support systems in various languages. The human incorporation and internalization of translation in the call centre make way for the externalization and explicitation of translation in Global Information Management.

The core rationale for 'centralized control' in the delivery of multilingual content to global markets is reassuringly old-fashioned. The first visual in the management briefing paper (also described somewhat grandiosely as an SDL 'White Paper') is a photograph of a Model T Ford. Although providing multilingual content support for multiple products through the use of digital technologies would seem to qualify SDL's activities as quintessentially post-Fordist, the vision is resolutely Fordist in its enunciation. Standardizing and streamlining the assembly-line production process makes as much sense for translation in the twenty-first century as it is did for automobile production in the twentieth. Output is increased, costs are decreased, the customer gets the car/translation, and the producer pays less for it.

The Fordist paradigm is used to rationalize the mass provision not of undifferentiated content (black Model T) but of differentiated content (multicoloured Model Ts). In order for choice or differentiation to prevail, however, there must be a high degree of homogenization or standardization not only at the level of process or form, but at the level of content. Fordism implies an advanced degree of 'centralized control', and this control is apparent in the solutions proposed for 'local language challenges'. Dealing with large volumes of content demands significant 'translation asset reuse', namely, the use wherever possible of material that has already been translated through recourse to translation memory systems. The need for content to be constantly updated requires the advanced automation of translation workflow. The necessity of using consistent terminology across different languages entails appropriate terminology management. The desire to maintain consistency in documents translated into different languages calls for the use of global authoring tools. Thus, even if the capacity to add 'specialized local products/features' necessitates flexibility in the system of delivery, the overwhelming emphasis is on the paradigm of control.

What is driving this ideology of control, and why is it so central to what would seem like the relatively progressive practice of using translation to promote and enhance linguistic diversity in the digital age? In seeking to answer this question it is useful to examine three factors that underpin contemporary global translation practice: namely, critical mass, time, and cost.

A client of SDL is Case New Holland (CNH), recognized worldwide as a manufacturer of many leading brands of agricultural machinery. It is a global company with a network of 12,000 dealers in 160 countries using 40 languages. As a result of their activities, they generate an extremely large volume of technical support information and problem-solving resources for the dealers who are, in effect, their immediate customers. The sheer volume of material generated across many different languages means that a way must be found to deliver consistently correct technical information over a broad range of subject areas and languages. The information supplied relates to product data (overviews, operating guides, manuals, and training modules) and issues and solutions relating to technical matters (FAQs, knowledge base, technical updates).

In analysing the translation consequences of critical mass, SDL sets up an opposition between industrial and artisanal approaches: 'Translation of written content has been traditionally seen as a "hand crafted" process, which implies a high cost' (Tridgell 2007). The mode of delivery is seen to restrict the domain of application. Translation, as an expensive, artisanal practice, is confined to corporate strategy brochures, sales and marketing leaflets, and higher-level service and support information. As product support operations accumulate information and content at a rate significantly faster than sales and marketing functions, the volume of material to be translated can become quite onerous, hence the emergence of what SDL calls 'the local language factory' with its attendant 'economies of scale'. The very necessity of translation demands a change in the nature of translation agency, the 'hand crafted' and human making way for industrial (semi-)automation. What is particularly striking in this reconfiguration of translation in the digital age of the twenty-first century is that the organizing metaphor is borrowed from the Industrial Revolution of the eighteenth century: the craft work of the hand loom ceding ground to the industrialized production of the cotton mill.

In principle, volume is not a problem if the time available for translation is sufficient. However, constantly changing content is not simply defined by the parameter of mass, but by the parameter of time: 'At any point "24×7" a steady flow of customer interactions are constantly arriving at the service organization via phone, email or web form, each one of which is transforming and generating customer information entered by the service staff' (*ibid.*). These interactions demand the generation of new content or an alteration of existing content. More broadly, two features of the Web, asynchronicity and bi-directionality, have a significant impact on the timescale for translation delivery. Asynchronicity implies that the Web works '24×7'; 'online' means all the time. Before the advent of answering machines, video recorders, and online media archives, making or receiving a telephone call, listening to a radio broadcast, or watching a television programme was a synchronous event that required the transmission and reception of the signal or message to take place at the same time. Conference and community interpreting are still largely synchronous translation practices. What Web-based services allow for is asynchronous exchange where the emitter and recipient of the message do not have to be in contact at the same time. Thus, messages can be delivered or received at any time, which means that digital communication is the quintessential enabler and expression of 24/7 culture.

The potential for bi-directionality, as exemplified by the rise of social media, is maximized by the asynchronous nature of digital exchange. Response is possible at any time of the day or night. One implication is that there is no containment in time of information reception, no 'opening and closing times' that limit and filter in time the quantity of information received that may or may not demand an appropriate response. Another implication is that ease of access alters horizons of expectation. If a message can be sent in seconds at any time, then it seems reasonable to expect that answers can be generated at any time as rapidly as possible. Thus, in the example of CNH, the expected turnaround time (speed of translation) for contact management, dealing with the initial gathering of situation and problem data, was four to eight hours. If the parameter of time is so much to the fore in contemporary translation practice, what are the wider implications for how we might think about translation?

Hannah Arendt once described terror as the accomplishment of the law of movement (Arendt 1973: 67). What is truly terrifying about *Blitzkrieg* is not so much the force as the speed. The tactics of 'Shock and Awe' employed during the invasion of Iraq in 2003 depended for much of their effect on the rapidity with which destruction was visited on Iraqi territory. On a more prosaic level, Arendt's law of movement is manifest in the increased acceleration of communication as the written letter gives way to the fax which is in turn superseded by the email and the text message. At each stage, response times shorten. The result is the terror of the temporal deficit, the feeling that one can never respond quickly enough, that there is always so much more to be done.

The perpetual stress of inadequacy is the inevitable outcome of what another German philosopher, Peter Sloterdijk, has dubbed 'the kinetic inferno' (Sloterdijk 1989: 25). This is the tendency in late modernity for processes of communication and circulation to accelerate at ever increasing speeds as progress is repeatedly defined as going further faster. A concomitant effect of the inferno is the suddenness with which events unfold. A graphic example was the banking collapse of 2008, which, even if predicted by certain commentators, took governments and the media by surprise due to the rapidity of the debacle. The collapse in turn was precipitated by the speed with which events of a global economic nature communicate themselves across international financial markets.

The second half of the twentieth century saw a marked interest in the notion of bio-diversity, the protection of the variety of flora and fauna on the planet in order to ensure ecological sustainability. A similar concern has been manifest in the idea of geo-diversity, the necessity to protect the wide diversity of landscapes on the planet, from the Camargue region of southern France to the Great Barrier Reef in Australia. In the context of the kinetic inferno, it is arguable that an equally crucial form of diversity is what Paul Virilio has termed 'chrono-diversity' (Virilio 2010: 27). By this is meant the need to protect different rhythms, different experiences of time, in order to safeguard and maintain human well-being. In a 24/7 culture dominated by the near instantaneity of text messaging and emails, the sense of being overwhelmed, of being engulfed in the kinetic inferno, is easily reached. The sense of recurrent temporal deficit, of never doing enough fast enough, is a powerful agent of despair, and an important source of stress for translators. Part of the ethical challenge for translators in the digital age is how to incorporate and defend chrono-diversity in their working practices in the context of the time–space compression and near-instantaneous communication.

If mass and time are crucial parameters in the reconfiguration of translation in the digital age, an equally powerful third parameter is cost. This parameter in a sense overdetermines the other two, as it is argued by translation providers that making large volumes of material available in translation as rapidly as possible makes money, rather than loses it. For SDL, the primary rationale for making material available to customers in their own languages is customer satisfaction. Selling products or services is one thing; making sure that the customer returns for the next order or upgrade is another. It is here that the post-sale experience of service and support, it is argued, is crucial. The 'cost/benefit advantages of keeping a current customer versus going out and finding a new one are obvious and well-researched. Generally, re-selling to an established customer is 5 to 10 times more cost-effective than identifying and converting a new prospect to a sale' (Tridgell 2007).

Implicit in the notion of customer satisfaction is trust and, citing the experience of Intel, SDL argues, 'It's difficult for customers to trust someone who doesn't speak their language' (*ibid.*). Corporate translation logic invokes cost at two levels. Firstly, translation is a cost that avoids future costs, for example in the retention of existing customers and reputation enhancement through customer satisfaction. Secondly, the cost of translation need not be so costly if a particular paradigm of localized delivery and centralized organization is pursued. Underlying the latter is a resolutely Fordist conception of increased economies of scale through falling unit costs. The Model T becomes the Model for (T)ranslation. As translation is inevitably perceived as a supplementary cost, the rhetorical alchemy of the translation industry involves changing the nature of the supplementarity, transforming costs into savings.

Dialogue

Crucial to the rationale for translation expenditures is the notion of the dialogical: 'the only way to have a relationship with somebody is by having a dialogue with them' (*ibid.*). Having an ongoing 'conversation' with customers is crucial if they are to remain customers. The dialogical joins the digital in ensuring the possibility of this conversation in another language, and the 'internet provides a very cost-effective communication path for certain aspects of the dialogue, enabling self-help and other user-controlled functions' (*ibid.*). There is, however, an underlying paradox in the construal of translation and the digital as inherently dialogical in conventional localization scenarios.

When CNH redesigned its support infrastructure through a specific blend of automated and human translation to offer 'its global dealers a 24×7 multilingual solution for issue management' the percentage of requests that were handled online via self-service tools rose from 20 to 80 per cent. The dominant ideology of the dialogical implicit in multilingual provision (speaking the language of the customer) is undercut by the cost imperative to minimize human interaction ('the most expensive resource in the service organization'). The notion of dialogue that carries the affective charge of human–human interaction is invoked, but the desired economic outcome is human–machine interaction, where the monological task of serving the self takes primacy over the expensive dialogical overheads of human–human interaction. You can have any language you want ... so long as it is, preferably, not spoken by a human being. In seeking to understand the 'changing role of human communication in an age of rapid technological change' (Littau 2011: 277), it is necessary both to identify the nature of the change and to distinguish between a corporate or institutional discourse of self-justification and the logics that are inherent either in the nature of the tools used or the economic motivation of the translation providers.

An awareness of the limits to versions of the dialogical in the digital age animates the movement towards what has been termed 'out-of-the-ordinary' localization. Anastasiou and Schäler see ordinary or mainstream localization as being driven primarily by short-term sales and return on investment. The economic function of globalization is emphasized at the expense of the social, cultural, and political. Localizers work mainly with proprietary files so that the 'relationship between customers and vendors is one-way tight and protected' (Anastasiou and Schäler 2010: 15). In contrast to this dominant form of localization, they argue for an alternative approach:

> out-of-ordinary localisation is driven by disruptive innovation and has a multi-dimensional global function. Content developers and tool providers promote open standards, such as Creative Commons for content and OASIS-based standards for technology. Content developers and service providers become tool and tool-provider independent, content, linguistic resources and technologies become widely available and the community can easily become involved in projects through crowdsourcing and community-based platforms, thus leading to greater economic activities and wider access to digital information and knowledge.
>
> (*Ibid.*, 15–16)

In this view, middlemen are replaced by open platforms and the sharing of digital content. More broadly, the alternative vision of localization is driven by the existence of a pronounced global digital divide where three-quarters of the world's population do not have access to digital resources (*ibid.*, 24). Not having access to these resources means not having access to useful and potentially life-saving information. A former director of UNICEF, James Grant, has estimated that approximately 2 billion people on the planet lack access to healthcare. As a result, 17 million people die each year and '80% of these preventable deaths occur because of a lack of access to healthcare information' (*ibid.*, 19). Descriptions of medicines, medical equipment user manuals, information about preventing mother-to-child transmission of HIV, and health and nutritional guidelines all require translation into local languages, but this activity is deemed unprofitable or considered a low priority by mainstream localization firms.

To this end, the Rosetta Foundation was launched in 2009 with the aim of making basic information on health, education, and other essential services available to people in their local languages. It wants to make this possible using an open-source intelligent translation and localization platform. Implicit in the rationale of the Rosetta Foundation is that digital and informational poverty are mutually defining, and that the results of exclusion can be a matter of life or death. However, as a founder of the Rosetta Foundation ruefully admits, 'Combating poverty is not an easy task; it is time-consuming and has to be cost-effective' (Anastasiou and Schäler 2010: 24). The question is, of course, cost-effective in whose terms? In other words, is it possible to have an alternative vision of globalization without an alternative theory of power? Spectacular over-concentrations of wealth, marked structural inequalities worldwide, and the inordinate power and influence of transnational pharmaceutical corporations, to take just one example (Lenard, Straehle, and Brooks 2012), suggest that stark digital divides or life-threatening differences in healthcare provision are not unfortunate accidents due to administrative oversight or financial incompetence, but the inevitable outcomes of asymmetrical power relationships between the world's wealthy and impoverished.

In the absence of a theory of power, the danger is that interventions are more akin to the sticking plaster of charity, a random alleviation of particular problems, rather than a fully fledged transformation of the global information order. Without an explicit critique of a neo-liberal market rationale, the suspicion is that corporate largesse is more to do with the expansion of market share than with wholly disinterested benevolence. For example, the company Asia Online has provided its automated translation software technology to the Rosetta Foundation, and it is claimed that 'Asia Online is working towards a goal of eliminating information poverty in many developing markets' (*ibid.*, 23). People live in countries and societies and communities, rather than 'markets' (markets are among the activities in which societies engage, they comprise a subset of human social activities). Is the task of 'eliminating information poverty' about radically altering the distribution of economic and cultural resources in Asian societies, or is it more nakedly about the extension and opening up of markets to corporate penetration? Is there not also the attendant misconception that technology, if attractively priced, can, in and of itself, change the power dynamic informing translation relationships, that it is possible to abstract tools from their social and cultural embedding? Translation rarely eludes the conditions of its production and reception and translation tools are used by humans as social and political beings located in a particular place and a particular time.

Everyware

One of the most notable developments in the last two decades has been the shift from stand-alone PCs, located at fixed work stations, to distributed computing in the form of laptops, wireless PDAs, mobile phones with internet connectivity, and so on. It is not only humans, but their machines, which are on the move. As the British sociologists Dennis and Urry put it, 'This trend in distributed computing is developing towards a shift to ubiquitous computing where associations between people, place/space, and time are embedded within a systemic relationship between a person and their kinetic environment' (Dennis and Urry 2007: 13). Ubiquitous computing, sometimes referred to as the 'third wave of computing', is one 'whose cross-over point with personal computing will be around 2005–20', and it may become 'embedded in walls, chairs, clothing, light switches, cars – in everything' (Brown and Weiser 1996). Greenfield has talked of 'everyware', where information processing is embedded in the objects and surfaces of everyday life (Greenfield 2006: 18). The probable social impact of everyware can be compared to electricity that passes invisibly through the walls of every home, office, and car. The transition from fixed locations of access to increased wireless presence, coupled with the exponential growth of internet capability, means that greatly augmented information flows become part of an information-immersive environment.

A consequence of the emergence of ubiquitous computing is that computing capacity dissolves into the physical surroundings, architectures, and infrastructures. Marcos Novak has developed the term 'transArchitecture' to signify 'a liquid architecture that is transmitted across the global information networks; within physical space it exists as an invisible electronic double superimposed on our material world' (Novak 2010). William Mitchell had already spoken in the 1990s of a 'city of bits', where the combination of physical structures in urban spaces with the electronic spaces and telematics would be known as 'recombinant architectures' (Mitchell 1995: 46–105).

It is difficult to conceive of the trans-architectural in contemporary urban spaces without factoring in the multilingual. That is to say, part of the thinking about next-generation localization and globalization is precisely the role that translation will play in the era of distributed, ubiquitous computing. It is possible to conceive of buildings – government offices, university halls of residence, transport hubs – which would be multilingually enabled. A handheld device such as a mobile phone would allow the user to access relevant information in the language of his or her choice. Thus, rather than the static and serial presentation of information in a limited number of languages, such a development would allow for a customized interaction with the language user with the possibility for continuous expansion in languages and information offered. The existence of applications for smartphones which allow for the translation of signs from one language to another point to the development of network-based interactivity and the move away from serial reception of information.

Advances in peer-to-peer computing and the semantic Web further favour the transition from a notion of translation provision as available in parallel series to translation as part of a networked system, a potentially integrated nexus. In other words, rather than content being rolled out in a static, sequential manner (e.g. separate language information leaflets at tourist attractions), translated material is personalized, user-driven, and integrated into dynamic systems of ubiquitous delivery. The semantic Web points up the potential for forms of collaborative, community translation that are already a conspicuous feature of translation practice in late modernity. In the online social network Second Life, almost three-quarters of the 900,000 monthly users are non-English native speakers. The site has been localized by volunteer translators into German, French, Japanese, simplified Chinese, Turkish, Polish, Danish, Hungarian, Czech, Korean, and Brazilian Portuguese. The volunteer translators are involved not only in translation but in terminology management and in editing and testing localized versions (Ray 2009). Facebook has also used a crowdsourcing model to translate contents into languages other than English, and fan translation is increasingly widespread in everything from the translation of Japanese anime to Korean soap operas (O'Hagan 2009: 94–121).

Wiki-translation

The advent of 'wiki-translation' indicates that the rapid dissemination of online social networking practices not only generates new translation needs, but has far-reaching consequences for the profession of translator in an age of globalization. Interactive, user-generated content, which is a core feature of Web 2.0, is now informing translation practice, and, in this context, translation consumers are increasingly becoming translation producers. The growing prevalence of Web-based machine translation (MT) services in the guise of Google Translate and others calls into question the traditional status of the translator, with norms of professional translator training coming under pressure from collaborative forms of translation practice mediated by new translation technologies such as the Google Translator Toolkit. As regards the visibility of the translator, the move towards Web-based MT services would appear to render invisible the labour of translation, whereas the development of wiki-translation would indicate the making visible of the demands of translation for large groups of global users.

What is especially apparent in the emergence of the interactive Web is that a new medium is not simply an addition to the old one. The traditional media vectors of translation such as the printing press are profoundly reshaped. As Nicholas Carr observes:

> When the Net absorbs a medium, it re-creates that medium in its own image. It not only dissolves the medium's physical form; it injects the medium's form with hyperlinks, breaks up the content into searchable chunks, and surrounds the content with the content of all the other media it has absorbed. All these changes in the form of the content also change the way we use, experience, and even understand the content.
>
> (Carr 2010: 90)

The bi-directionality of Web 2.0, a characteristic of the medium, has begun to determine the nature of translation at the outset of the twenty-first century with the proliferation of crowdsourced translation or open translation projects such as Project Lingua, Worldwide Lexicon, Wiki Project Echo, TED Open Translation Project, and Cucumis. The changes in the form of the content have begun to change the way that content is not only used, experienced, and understood, but also translated. In a sense, bi-directionality is a further development of the emergence of the reader–author in hypermedia in the 1990s. As Karen Littau notes, 'The reader of an electronic text is akin to a writer, because he or she is not the passive consumer of finished product, but – very literally – a collaborator in the process of text production and therefore also an active producer of meanings' (Littau 2011: 275). In pointing to the emergence of crowdsourced translation or wiki-translation, it is possible to define three characteristics of this medium-driven change with implications for thinking about translation.

1. Translation prosumption

Translation debates in recent decades have returned again and again to the question of source- or target-language orientation in translation. Dynamic and formal equivalence, semantic and communicative translation, foreignization versus domestication, *skopos* theory, Descriptive Translation Studies have all been drafted into the polemic over the most appropriate forms of orientation. Implicit in all these models, however, is the notion of an agent who produces a translation for consumption by an audience. It is a production-oriented model of externality. In the case of crowdsourced translation, however, it is the potential audience for the translation that does the translation. The model is a consumer-oriented model of internality. The consumer becomes an active producer, or prosumer. It is no longer a question of the translator, for example, projecting a target-oriented model of translation on to an audience, but of the audience producing its own self-representation as a target audience. Such a shift makes problematic traditional distinctions which generally presuppose active translation agents and passive or unknowable translation recipients.

2. Post-print translation literacy

A study by a team of German researchers on the behaviour of Web users concluded that most Web pages were viewed for ten seconds or less. Even pages with plentiful information and many links were viewed for an extremely brief period (Weinreich, Obendorf, Herder, and Mayer 2008: 1–26). An Israeli company, Clicktale, which supplies software for analysing how people use corporate Web pages, assembled data on the behaviour of a million visitors to sites maintained by its corporate clients. They found that in most countries, people spend between 19 and 27 seconds looking at a Web Page before moving on to the next one, and this includes the time necessary for the page to load into the browser's window (Clicktale 2008). In effect, the internet encourages a shift from steady, cumulative, linear reading to a form of accelerated power browsing.

This sense of acceleration is not new to translation. As Karen Littau reminds us, the advent of the printing press induced a kind of frenzy among readers who demanded access to the new product. In addition to the acclerated output of the presses themselves that was discussed in Chapter 1, the general absence of legal protection of copyright prior to the nineteenth century and the invention of pulp, which allowed for the cheap production of paper from the 1860s onwards, were among the contributory factors in the widespread dissemination of printed books in translation:

> As if in response to the speed of the printing machines themselves, foreign works were picked up swiftly for translation, translators rushed to finish one translation after another, readers hurried from one book to the next and speed-read not one but several books simultaneously.
>
> (Littau 2011: 274)

Indeed, Littau interprets the emergence of fluency as a dominant translation paradigm in late seventeenth- and eighteenth-century Europe as being related to material changes in book form. Word spacing, the systematization and standardization of layout and spelling, and the increasing legibility of typefaces meant that readers could move through texts more quickly than before (*ibid.*, 275).

As translation has a visceral link to prevailing paradigms of literacy, once the paradigms change, we must expect translation to change in nature. In a culture of high print literacy with an emphasis on ordered, linear progression through a text, it is only to be expected that translation pedagogy will place a particular emphasis on the careful, cumulative reading of text and the production of texts answerable to the norms of high print literacy. However, as we move from a technological world defined by the printing press to one defined by the computer, reading practices and literacy norms inevitably change. As Colin Cooper notes in a blog on translation crowdsourcing, crowdsourcing is particularly effective when 'initial quality is not the top priority' (Cooper 2009). The emergence of gist translation, or the acceptance of lower-quality translation output, must be related to shifting reading and literacy norms, as readers of Web-based material have a significantly different approach to their engagement with text, namely, instrumentalized, non-linear, and greatly accelerated. Peer pressure can, of course, be a powerful incentive to improve quality through collaborative correction, but the more important point is that as literacy expectations evolve, so too will translation practices.

3. Translation and pluri-subjectivity

Traditionally, governments have been fearful of crowds. When Baron Haussmann set about the reconstruction of nineteenth-century Paris, he was ever mindful of how the design of his streets might facilitate the control of the revolutionary mob (Schnerb 1993). But like flashmobs, crowds turn up when and where you least expect them. It is useful to locate particular crowdsourcing practices in the context of the subversive potential of the crowd. Whether it is volunteer translators translating alternative media sources from citizen journalists around the world for Project Lingua (http://globalvoicesonline.org/lingua), or translators working to produce translated versions of the documents released on the controversial WikiLeaks site, the politicization of translation through collective volunteer action is present and growing.

At one level, it is possible to locate these translation practices in the type of self-reflexive political agency at work in organizations like Babels (Boéri 2008: 21–50). At another, what is implicitly contested in these practices is a conception of machine–human interaction in translation as fundamentally dehumanizing. If a tendency in localization discourse has been to accentuate the role of automation in translation activity and to minimize the intervention of the human agent, what we are witnessing in these crowdsourcing initiatives is a reinvestment of translation technology by the human, a strategic use of technical resources to further human concerns or agendas. In a sense, what is emerging in the practice is a version of translation technology as a tool of conviviality and an instrument of human political intervention. Implicit in such a representation of translation is a move away from the monadic subject of traditional translation agency – Saint Jerome alone in the desert – to a pluri-subjectivity of interaction.

Information

In 1880, *Scientific American* addressed itself to the topic of 'The Future of the Telephone'. Business houses and the homes of the well-to-do would be interlocked by the new telephone exchanges, not only in cities but in remote areas:

> The result can be nothing less than a new organization of society – a state of things in which every individual, however secluded, will have at call every other individual in the community, to the saving of no end of social and business complications, of needless goings to and fro, of disappointments, delays, and a countless host of those great and little evils and annoyances.
>
> The time is close at hand when the scattered members of the civilized communities will be as closely united, as far as instant telephonic communication is concerned, as the various members of the body are by the nervous system.
>
> (Cited in Casson 1910: 289)

The telephone would indeed revolutionize communication and supersede the previous information technology, the telegraph. When Claude Shannon was looking for a topic for his master's thesis, he looked to the complex relay circuits familiar to telephone engineers as a potential subject for the application of symbolic logic. Shannon's work in symbolic logic would later result in his influential mathematical theory of information (Gleick 2011: 168–232). In his 1949 work, co-authored with Warren Weaver, Shannon argued, 'The fundamental problem of communication is that of reproducing at one point either exactly or approximately a message selected at another point' (Shannon and Weaver 1949: 31).

One could say that, on one level, Shannon was reformulating Samuel Butler's concern with the infinite extension of the written symbol in time and space. Underlying both the utopian promise of the telephone, and Shannon's formulation of the central problem of communication, is the question of translation. In the case of the telephone, the point was illustrated in a famous *New Yorker* cartoon with a slightly nonplussed middle-aged man speaking into the receiver, 'I'm sorry, you've got the wrong language' (cited in Brodzki 2007: 9). The promise of proximity only holds if there is a guarantee of translatabililty. Instant telephonic communication is not the same as instant human understanding. If there is no common language, no means of translation, the 'scattered members' will simply hang up. The problem, as Shannon puts it, although not thinking of translation, is how to reproduce 'at one point either exactly or approximately a message selected at another point'.

This was precisely the concern that brought translation into the heart of the globalizing process from the 1980s onwards. The global expansion of business demanded that translation carry messages from one point to another, leading to the development of the localization industry. This assumption is implicit in the definition of localization offered by Reinhard Schäler:

> [Localization is] the linguistic and cultural adaptation of digital content to the requirements and locale of a foreign market, and the provision of services and technologies for the management of multilingualism across the digital global information flow.
>
> (Schäler 2007: 157)

It is possible, however, to go one step further and argue that when we talk about the information age, information technology, and the information society, we should really be talking about the translation age, translation technology, and the translation society. To see why this might be the case, it is worth considering what happens at crucial moments in the evolution of processes of understanding and transmitting information.

When Charles Babbage, one of the founding fathers of modern computing, began to think about how to get machines to perform mental operations, he was particularly impressed by a loom invented by Joseph-Marie Jacquard. The loom was controlled by instructions encoded and stored as holes printed on cards. Babbage was struck not so much by the beauty of the finished product as by the ingenuity of the process, the translation of patterns from one medium to another (Hyman 1982). When Samuel Morse designed the code that would be used in the telegraph, an invention which would precipitate the great information revolution of the nineteenth century (Standage 1999), he did so by replacing signs (the signs of the alphabet) with other signs (the signs of Morse code). As James Gleick points out:

> This process – the transferring of meaning from one symbolic level to another – already had a place in mathematics. In a way it was the very

essence of mathematics. Now it became a familiar part of the human toolkit. Entirely because of the telegraph, by the late nineteenth century people grew comfortable, or at least familiar, with the idea of codes: signs used for other signs, words used for other words.

(Gleick 2011: 152)

This movement from one symbolic level to another, or encoding, is mirrored by the preoccupation among early pioneers of information science and computing, such as Claude Shannon and Alan Turing, with the mapping of one set of objects onto another, whether logical operators and electric circuits (Shannon), or algebraic functions and machine instructions (Turing).

Replacing signs with other signs, mapping one set of objects onto another, it might be argued, is precisely what translators do. They are continually engaged with forms of encoding, moving from one symbolic level or system to another. It might be objected that to conceive of translation in this way is to return to reductive notions of translation as a form of linguistic transcoding, a kind of brutal substitutionism, where element a in language A is replaced by element b in language B. However, what is clear from the histories of information and translation is that such a conception of what it is to encode is clearly deficient in situating both information and translation in terms of its cultural reception.

When, in unwitting anticipation of the time-compression effects of the internet, a telegraph official in 1860 announces that the telegraph 'enables us to send communications, by means of the mysterious fluid, with the quickness of thought, and to annihilate time as well as space' (cited in Gleick 2011: 148), he is simply affirming the profound socio-cultural consequences of the new medium. Similarly, when the sixteenth-century English translator John Florio speaks of the view that some people held of translations as the 'subversion of the universities', he quotes his '"olde fellow Nolano" who had said and publicly taught that "from translation all Science had its of-spring", since the Greeks had drawn all their science from the Egyptians, who had taken it from the "Hebrews or Chaldees"' (Ginzburg 2000: 40). 'Nolano' was the Italian scholar and translator Giordano Bruno, burned as a heretic in Rome three years before Florio's remarks. Both Florio and Bruno knew, like Adelard of Bath, centuries earlier, that the effects of translation could be radical and far-reaching.

What is striking, therefore, is that reductionist notions of encoding fail to account for the transformative impact of information technology. The history of information and information technologies is, if anything, a history of forms of translation. Information in this sense is a subset of translation rather than translation being a subset of information. When Charles Babbage's collaborator Ada Lovelace wanted to describe what his Difference Engine did, she claimed it performed operations which she defined as 'any process which alters the mutual relation of two or more things' (Morrison and Morrison 1961: 47). This sense of the alteration of mutual relationships which is central to the working out of what constitutes a technology of information is at the core of what translation and translation studies attempt to capture. Seeing our contemporary age as a translation age rather than an information age better defines not only changing understandings of information and technology but also the alteration, the mutability in relations between languages and cultures brought about by new translation media.

Universalization

There is another sense in which the translation age describes the particular form of modernity in the twenty-first century. This sense relates to the impact of digital code on our apprehension of distinctions, as outlined by Emily Apter:

> For it becomes clear that digital code holds out the prospect, at least, of translating everything into everything else. A kind of universal cipher, or default language of information, digital code will potentially function like a catalytic converter, translating beyond the interlingual and among orders of bios and genus, liquid and solid, music and architecture, natural language and artificial intelligence, language and genes, nature and data, information and capital.
>
> (Apter 2006: 227)

As a result of the digital revolution of the late twentieth century, text has become part of digital content, 'digital content, apart from text, contains also audio, video, images and software' and software 'includes websites, programs, or video games and thus implements graphics, animation, and many other widgets' (Anastasiou and Schäler 2010: 11–25). Underlying the informatics revolution is the convertibility, the ultimate translatability, of all content to the binary code of machine language. Computers, which initially only received text, now receive sound and images (both static and animated). At one level, the problem for the translator schooled in written and printed textual traditions is how to deal with these multi-modal textual objects. At another, however, the import of translation studies goes far beyond problem-solving, for example finding the appropriate localization strategy for translating website content. If, to cite Apter, 'translation studies increasingly explores the possibility that everything is translatable' (Apter 2006: 226), rather than being fixated on the fact that nothing is translatable (poetry lost in translation), then the subject acquires a new relevance and urgency.

Just as the notion of translation problematizes simple notions of encoding, so more than two millennia of thought on translation complicates any notion that, because 'everything is translatable', everything is interchangeable. The universalization of translatability through digital code means a renewed sense of purpose for critical translation studies, which can draw on millennia of translation history to show that translation, which has often traded on the rhetoric of commonality ('communicating the same human message'), has more often than not been a powerful factor of differentiation (supporting vernaculars, spreading new ideas, reviving previously discredited traditions). If, as we have seen, translation is shaped by the technical media it employs, from the pen, to the printing press, to the personal digital assistant, it is equally true that these media can be usefully examined through the prism of translation. This is why to speak of translation technology is a tautology, as information technology is unavoidably bound up with translation, and translation as a human activity is inescapably a technology. The presence of technology in Bruegel's *Tower of Babel* is no accident. Its presence does not eliminate but foreshadow differentiation. It is not because the same tools (manual, digital) are used that humans go off and do the same thing. On the contrary, they do something different. And out of this difference comes their humanity.

Transparency

If it is true that 'it becomes clear that digital code holds out the prospect, at least, of translating everything into everything else', then the universalist claim is justified only if it can be verified as true. What the credo of universal translatability implies is a notion of universal verifiability, the ability to determine that something has been translated into something else. In the absence of the possibility of verification, there is no way of determining that what has happened is, in fact, translation and not something else. There is, however, a more readily recognizable way in which transparency has become a central category when reflecting on translation in the digital age.

A notable feature of the impact of new technology and, in particular, new forms of social media is the reconfiguration of the notion of privacy. Facebook is the most prominent of these media in the possibility it offers for users to live a life that is prominently on display to others. Even if stricter controls have been introduced to control access to individual pages, it is none the less apparent that areas of experience and expression that would previously have been seen as belonging to the sphere of the private or, in some cases, the strictly intimate, are now available for public or quasi-public inspection (Turkle 2010). Just as the phone moved from the privacy of the booth to the public broadcast mode of the mobile phone, where conversations are clearly heard, rather than accidentally overheard, the borders between the private and the public are noticeably shifting. Even if overstated on occasion by the agents of moral panic, there is a distinct sense in which whole areas of private life are now on public view. The ultrasound scan of the as yet unborn child posted on the proud parents' Facebook page shows that, even before the child is born, he or she is destined for a private life in the public forums of social media. The bi-directionality of the social media, of course, both encourages (feedback from 'friends') and facilitates (technologically) this new culture of transparency. How does this new culture impact on translation, and what are the consequences of the redefinition of the public and the private for the way in which translation is perceived?

In approaching the topic of transparency, it is worth separating out three potential readings of what it might imply. The first reading is what might be termed the ethical. Ethical transparency is based on the notion that the honest person has nothing to hide, that their life and their work are beyond reproach and that this fundamental probity can be publicly verified at any moment. It is ethical transparency that is the professed justification for the drive towards accountability and transparency in the provision of public services, or the use of Key Performance Indicators to adjudge educational outputs.

A second reading of transparency is ostensible transparency or transparency as spectacle. This is the notion that everything can be shown, everything is available for display, everything is potentially material for spectacle. From the neo-natal snapshot to the sheepish grin to camera at 3 a.m. in a foreign bar, all of life can be rendered transparent for the viewing of others.

The third reading of transparency is the penal. Penal transparency is the idea that transparency is a necessary precondition for surveillance. You cannot survey what you cannot see. The greater the transparency of the observed, the easier the task of the observer, and the easier it is to control what is observed.

Taking the three modes of transparency – the ethical, the ostensible, and the penal – it is possible to see how the cult of transparency in the digital age clearly informs practices and perceptions of translation.

Starting with a common understanding of what translation is believed to be about, one can see clearly a principle of ethical transparency at work. Community interpreting affords the speakers of the non-host language in a society an opportunity to describe their symptoms (medical setting), give an account of their actions (legal setting), or explain their needs (educational settings). Translation makes visible what otherwise would remain hidden, and this ethical transparency allows for communication to take place between human beings who are adjudged to be equal in the transparent commonality of their human experiences and needs. It is the principle of ethical transparency that demands that one can only be charged in a language that one understands, or that one should knowingly consent to a medical procedure. Translation as an activity becomes central to the working out of any notion of ethical transparency in a multilingual world.

Spectacular transparency finds its translation expression in the repeated desire of countries, authors, and publishers to have work translated into other languages. If countries in various parts of the world provide financial support for the translation of their literature into foreign languages (Cronin 2006: 146–57), it is prompted by a desire, implicit or explicit, to show their literary or cultural wares to the world. As Pascale Casanova has argued, a common standard for the evaluation of the literary well-being of a particular culture is the number of polyglots who read the literature of that culture in the original language, or the number of translators who translate the literature of that culture into other languages (Casanova 1999: 37). Translation becomes the shop window for the culture's literary goods. Cultural capital has to be seen to be believed, and translation is what, all other conditions being equal, makes the blind see.

Penal transparency as a core component of translation involves the use of translation for the purposes of control, surveillance, and espionage. From the 'linguists' working with armies in situations of military conflict to the government officials translating reports about what their dissident nationals are getting up to in foreign jurisdictions, making the world transparent and intelligible through translation is central to the function of any power that seeks to assert control over or protect its subjects (Baker 2006). One of the most commonly repeated criticisms of the security services in the United States in the aftermath of 9/11 was that they had catastrophically failed in the area of translation, large volumes of valuable intelligence material being left untranslated and so increasing the vulnerability of the US to attack. Thus, all three modes of transparency can be said to motivate particular forms of translation practice, but how are these modes expressed in a digital age?

In September 2011, WikiLeaks posted the following tweet: 'We wish to bulk translate around 300mil words into 8 languages. That's around $37,000 × 8 using Google. Are there alternatives?' (cited in SymS 2011). The reference to Google was specifically to Google Translate API, the machine translation system for which Google charged a fee of $20 per million characters. South Korean and Arabic translators had already begun to translate the leaked WikiLeaks embassy cables into Korean and Arabic, respectively, and WikiLeaks has a category on its site, 'Pages needing translation' (WikiLeaks.org/wiki/WikiLeaks: Translation). In effect, what the WikiLeaks translation enterprise involves is the alliance of ethical transparency and digital tools. It is not enough to make transparent evidence of fraud, malpractice, illegal activities, or torture by private or public entities, the evidence must also be made transparent linguistically.

As WikiLeaks makes use of digital tools both to obtain and to receive information, it is not surprising that translation should be conceived as another branch of digital activism through, for example, volunteer translation via digital interfaces. Ethical transparency is rarely an uncontested notion, and WikiLeaks has its detractors who argue that indiscriminate leaking of classified information can put people's lives at risk (Leigh and Harding 2011). However, what is clear is that the stated motivation of the organization is a drive towards transparency and the challenging of official or unofficial cultures of secrecy. If the remit of the organization is global, a remit which is facilitated by the global spread of information technology, then, by extension, the remit must include the act of translation, whether this is indirectly through news outlets translating leaked information into different languages for reports, or directly through the activities of volunteer translators translating documents from the site. The failure to translate, in other words, would render opaque any attempt at ethical transparency, no matter how digitally feasible, as information would only be transparent to those who had the language of the original documents. Hence, the various digital supports for translation (including the possible use of Google Translate) are means to make operational and maximize the stated aim of ethical transparency.

In its mission statement, *Words without Borders*, the 'Online Magazine for International Literature' (www.wordswithoutborders.org), explicitly declares its commitment to make particular kinds of literature visible:

> Words without Borders translates, publishes, and promotes the finest contemporary international literature. Our publications and programs open doors for readers of English around the world to the multiplicity of viewpoints,

richness of experience, and literary perspective on world events offered by writers in other languages. We seek to connect international writers to the general public, to students and educators, and to print and other media and to serve as a primary online location for a global literary conversation.

(Words without Borders 2012)

The avowed aim is to start a 'global literary conversation', but that conversation is unlikely to happen if, firstly, the participants cannot access the conversation, and, secondly, if they cannot understand what the participants are saying. This is why, although the technology potentially allows for the conversation (on condition that one has internet access), the conversation cannot take place in the absence of translation. Thus, what ostensible transparency points up is the fiction of digital immediacy or pseudo-transparency, the notion that because a text can be technically accessed, it can be readily understood. Translation as a function of ostensible transparency is in a sense making ostensible or visible the necessity of translation in order to give effect to the global, transmissive possibilities of information technology. Of course, what is being made ostensible is not simply the agency of translation, but particular forms of content that address widely varying motivations.

In the case of *Words without Borders*, the project is predicated on the widely reported Anglophone indifference to literature in other languages and the markedly low percentage of translated titles published in English (Assouline 2011). The ostensible project is one of monolingual internationalism, by which is meant the translation of different literatures in different languages into one language, in this case English. In contrast, the online poetry platform Lyrikline (www.lyrikline.org) engages in what can be termed multilingual internationalism, where poems are translated into German, French, English, Slovene, and Arabic. In both these cases, the inward direction of the translations is not subject to prior selection other than on the grounds of quality. The ostensible project is to make available the literatures of the world in one or more languages. The online magazine and the online poetry platform want to give effect to a form of digital cosmopolitanism where the technology's global promise of access is matched by the cultural contents on offer via the technology. However, as has been remarked on by many commentators, any viable notion of the cosmopolitan must have a credible theory of the local (see Vertovec and Cohen 2002).

The project of ostensible transparency in the context of digital translation practice can be linked to a making manifest of the local to the global, as opposed to presentation of the global to the local. The online website of *Mediterranean Poetry* (www.mediterranean.nu) is specifically devoted to making poetry from writers from Mediterranean countries available in English translation, in addition to contributions from Anglophone poets on Mediterranean themes. *Transcript*, described as 'Europe's online review of international writing' (www.transcript-review.org), is available in German, English, and French and has the specific aim of promoting 'quality literature written in the "smaller" languages [of Europe] and [giving] wider circulation to material from small-language literary publications through the medium of English, French and German'. Thus, special issues of the review have covered writing from Malta, Macedonia, Latvia, Slovenia, Croatia, Brittany, and northern Catalonia. If *Mediterranean Poetry* and *Transcript* practise a form of diffuse localism, giving a platform to a variety of local literatures, the digital presence of other specifically national or quasi-national bodies has a more explicit vision of what constitutes the local.

The Center for Slovenian Literature, the Danish Literature Centre, the Dutch Foundation for Literature, the Finnish Literature Information Centre, Ireland Literature Exchange, the Korean Literature Translation Institute, and the Polish Book Institute, to name but a few such bodies, are dedicated to the promotion through translation of particular national literatures. Joo-Youn Kim, the president of the Korean Literature Translation Institute (KLTI; www.klti.or.kr), makes clear the connection between the promotion of particularism and the enablement of the digital:

> Korean literature has prospered and built up wonderful cultural assets on the soil of its long traditions, and commands a wide pool of works and writers being produced at this very moment. Indeed, literature got in full bloom at an earlier stage in the Korean history, with the first-ever invention of metal movable type-based printing. Now a new chapter is being written with Korea's globally recognised IT power ... In the era of cultural convergence, we simultaneously endeavour to actively accommodate the ever-changing cultural environments within the paradigm of information technology and, thereby, to set forth a new role of literature, which has prospered around the traditional concept of printing.
>
> (Kim 2011)

The institute is seeking to make transparent the ostensible achievements of Korean literature and information technology as the primary medium for the globalization of Korean literature in translation. In Joo-Youn Kim's statement, it is noticeable that the foregrounding of the local is situated in a material history of translation transmission, which goes from the invention of 'metal movable type-based printing' to the emergence of Korea as a 'globally recognised IT power'. The history of tools is seen as inextricably bound up with the fortunes of Korean writing and what is possible through translation. Korean pre-eminence in the field of IT is seen in a national narrative as a logical extension of the country's precocity in the area of printing.

The use of translation for the purpose of ostensible transparency in a digital context brings with it potential tensions that are intrinsic to the interaction between the medium and the message. For example, on the KLTI website, under 'Vision', we find the statement, 'Korea as Cultural leader in Global Community'. The global reach of the medium is explicitly harnessed to the national interests contained in the message of the institute, which sees the promotion of Korean literature in translation as a way of establishing leadership in the global community, an aspiration which is echoed in the presentation of

Korea as a globally recognized IT power. What the KLTI is doing here is no different from what informs the many centres around the world that promote national literatures in translation, namely, the development of a form of digital nationalism which sees the recognition value of national identity as increasingly dependent on a prominent digital presence. In a sense, what is implicit in this digital nationalism is the notion of 'soft power' enunciated by Joseph Nye (1991, 2004). Nye argued that attraction, rather than coercion, was much more effective in the medium to long term for establishing enduring influence in international relations. Although Nye's concept was first developed in the context of thinking about the limits to military and economic coercion ('hard power') as the preferred foreign policy instruments of the United States as a superpower, it was soon apparent that the distinction could be usefully used by a wide range of actors on the world stage.

For smaller nations the options of exercising 'hard power' are generally relatively restricted, either because of a lack of resources or, in certain cases, an unwillingness of populations with colonial or post-colonial histories to exercise such power. In this respect, the notion of 'soft power' – influence through attraction or co-option – appears both more feasible and more desirable or acceptable. Culture is frequently the arsenal that is drawn upon for the weaponry of soft power, even for superpowers, as demonstrated by the long association of Hollywood with the superiority of the American way of life. For countries lacking significant economic or military resources, cultural promotion can be seen as a relatively inexpensive means of exercising soft power. The power, of course, is unlikely to exert any influence if it is not exported beyond the shores of the national culture. To this end, two types of translation are required – spatial (it must be moved from the point of origin to various points around the globe) and semantic (the content must be understood in various points of the globe). Soft power needs a medium (digital connectivity) and a message (translated content). Through the practice of ostensible transparency, as engaged in by multiple government-sponsored translation bodies and institutes across the planet, it is possible to argue that translation has become a key component of the elaboration of soft power in the digital age.

Soft power as a concept is increasingly linked to the notion of 'nation branding' or brand nationalism (Anholt 2007). This was described in the *Boston Globe* as 'shorthand for coordinated government efforts to manage a country's image, whether to improve tourism, investment, or even foreign relations' (Risen 2005). The connection between nation branding and soft power was made explicit by Mikhail Margelov, chairman of the International Affairs Committee of Russia's Federation Council. The Russian government was concerned that the external image of the country was poor, and that public associations with Russia included 'cold weather', 'vodka', and 'authoritarianism'. Margelov argued that the nation's new branding campaign:

> needs to push '*the image of a "good" rather than a "strong" Russia* as part of the "soft power" approach that is now so popular. And to do that it

must have a co-ordinated plan, one that will be *"pro-active rather than defensive"* in order to ensure that Moscow gets in the first word in any dispute'.

(Goble 2009 cited in Volcic and Andrejevic 2011: 599; his emphasis)

The 'nation brand' is one that marries positive associations to the profit imperative. These are associations that help bring foreign investment and tourists into a country, while also acting as stimuli to the sales of nationally produced goods and boosting the international image of the country. The emphasis on image is seen to parallel the transition from modernist industrial production to postmodern consumption, 'a move from the modern world of geopolitics and power to the postmodern world of images and influence' (van Ham 2001). Moreover, as Volcic and Andrejevic argue:

The promoters of nation branding market it as a powerful equalizer – a way that countries without the economic or military clout of superpowers can compete in the global marketplace. They claim that nation branding can help such nations to achieve greater visibility, attract tourists and foreign investors, expand exports, and promote their profile among the member states of various international organizations (such as the EU), all the while cultivating patriotism at home.

(Volcic and Andrejevic 2011: 604)

In the context of a research project, Volcic and Andrejevich interviewed a brand nation marketing specialist in New York who argued:

Branding is *the only* power available to small, unknown, peripheral nations ... it can help them strengthen their economic position, attract investors, skilled labour, and travellers ... Do you honestly believe that Kosovo has any other option than to brand itself? Kosovo *has* to market itself ... this will also strengthen citizens' identity and increase their self-esteem ... there is no other way for Kosovo to persuade the rest of the world that they are a young, peaceful, stable and dynamic country ... even if they are not.

(*Ibid.*, 604–05; his emphasis)

The concert of nations becomes the global trading floor, each nation clamouring for competitive advantage as the notion of political sovereignty becomes subservient to market position or positioning. Although nation branding is generally seen as an instance of the privatization of public functions (promotion of foreign trade, diplomacy), it is possible to see how publicly funded translation institutes and centres can be co-opted into a version of brand nationalism, if only to justify their continued funding in an era increasingly dominated by what Cerny calls the 'competition state', the state that is almost exclusively focused on the economic fortunes of the polity (Cerny 1997: 272).

For the competition state, the perceived added value of distinctiveness means the mobilization of the historical and cultural resources of the nation-state to bring people, goods, and money into the national economy.

A dimension to nation branding in the age of the interactive Web is the role of a form of reciprocity in the construction of the 'brand'. This is, in part, because of the notion that it is only through the active participation of the citizens that the 'brand' will acquire any credibility. As the *Handbook of Brand Slovenia* expresses it, 'The power of the brand lies in the consent and motivation of the Slovene citizens to live the brand' (cited in Volcic and Andrejevich 2011: 610). The use of lateral and participatory, rather than top-down and one-way, message transmission is at one level an expression of the commercial logic of Web 2.0. A version of the lateral and the participatory is the presence of organizations like Ireland Literature Exchange and Books from Lithuania on Facebook. The possibility for interaction that is allowed by social media is not only a way of spreading the message of translation organizations to broader, non-traditional constituencies but also implicitly co-opts Facebook respondents into the pros-elytizing project of the organizations. By expressing an interest in the organization (even through the simple gesture of a 'Like'), Facebook users are mobilized to become a part of the community dedicated to spreading the good news in translation about Irish, Lithuanian, or whatever literature is being promoted by that organization.

Just as brands are primarily about associations, so social media carries its own associative potential in terms of organizations' own expressed 'Likes'. Thus, Ireland Literature Exchange lists among its 'Likes': Sweny's Pharmacy, Lincoln Place, Dublin, Digital Arts Marketing Training, the Festival of World Cultures, the *New York Review of Books*, National Concert Hall, Dublin, Ireland, Irish Arts Center, ABSOLUT Fringe, Dublin Theatre Festival, the National Campaign for the Arts, Theatre Forum Ireland, the *New Yorker*, *Irish Theatre Magazine*, Publishing Ireland, Gallery of Photography, and Abbey Theatre (http://www.facebook.com/IrelandLiteratureExchange). The mixture of national cultural institutions, national representative organizations, national festivals, and a limited number of high-profile journals and magazines, with a more idiosyncratic reference to a pharmacy mentioned in James Joyce's *Ulysses*, positions the informal interactivity of 'Likes' in a strategic economy of national and cultural promotion. If, at present, the engagement with the social media and the mobilization of interactivity are primarily at the level of marketing and publicity, it is possible to imagine how wiki-translation, fansubbing, and other forms of group translation might be incorporated into evolving forms of digital nationalism.

In a trenchant critique of nation branding, Jansen argues that 'Nation branding is a monologic, hierarchical, reductive form of communication' (Jansen 2011: 141). Given that the associative power of brand lies in its simplicity (less is more), the dangers of the conflation of commercial self-interest with national representativity become uncomfortably obvious. Being 'on message' means leaving a lot out, and what must inevitably get left out is what is seen as sending out the 'wrong', that is negative, message. This is where a mission of ostensible transparency in translation enters into explicit conflict with the willed opacity of brand logic. The translated literature of Ireland, Poland, Lithuania, Korea, or whatever literature is supported in translation by a public body from a democratic state cannot be assimilated to 'a monologic, hierarchical, reductive form of communication'. Literature that practised this form of communication would not be literature, but propaganda.

In other words, a project of ostensible transparency in the domain of literary translation must, by virtue of a foundational freedom of expression, contest simple identity narratives that any particular sectional interest might wish to foster for the purposes of narrowly defined economic gain. In this respect, it is important that literary translation, even if predominantly published by private sector or commercial publishers, should be defined as a public good. It is only as a public good in a democratic state that literary translation can be promoted in a way that gives due expression to the multiple and conflicted identities of any body politic. The current capacity for digital interactivity also points to the possibility of a global cybercitizenship for a World Republic of Letters, where nations would be held accountable to citizen-readers for the non-translation of important literary works in different national languages.

Transparency, like most virtues, is rarely unqualified. The most laudable of virtues can become the most tenacious of vices, depending on how you view what is being made transparent. The Ed Wallach Research Group, a US-based firm that specializes in recruitment for US military and intelligence agencies, ran an advertisement in 2011 for 'Senior Language Analysts' in Arabic, Urdu, French, Dari, Pashto, German, Somali, Turkish, Bosnian, and Indonesian Bahasa. The position description stated that, 'as part of a team, the Senior Language Analysts will engage in academic and philosophical discussion while translating foreign language discussions into English'. A more detailed description required that the 'Senior Language Analysts will provide an understanding of the specific geographic region through maintenance of social, academic or business contacts; through the reading and understanding of native-language publications; and/or through open-source research'. The analysts were also expected to have '[s]trong skills in computer-based applications' and the ability to 'conduct independent research and familiarity with open-source research and analysis' (Ed Wallach Research Group 2012).

The explicit task of the analsysts is one of the oldest assigned to translators from the time of Alexander the Great: intelligence gathering. Meaningful action in everything from the distribution of foreign aid to military invasion implies prior deliberation, and effective deliberation requires relevant information. In a multilingual world, there is no information without translation or mediated translation (verbal summaries, précis writing). If this were not the case, there would be no need for the senior language analysts.

In the case of penal transparency, the use of translation for surveillance and information-gathering purposes, it is important in a digital context to focus not so much on product, as on process. That is to say, when it comes to translation and surveillance, the tendency can be to dwell on new configurations of hardware or ingenious pieces of software that can effectively monitor all that is being written or communicated via a particular device. However, such an approach is fundamentally linked to a way of viewing tool use that is highly reductive and not especially illuminating. The social anthropologist Tim Ingold has pointed to the necessary synergy of practitioner and tool in an essay on using a saw entitled 'Walking the Plank':

> What does it mean to say that in carrying out some task, a tool is used? We might suppose that use is what happens when an object, endowed with a certain function, is placed at the disposal of an agent, intent on a certain purpose. I want to cut a plank, and I have a saw. So I use the saw to cut the plank. However, from the account I have already presented [of cutting a piece of wood] it is clear that I need more than the saw to cut wood. I need the trestle to provide support, I need my hands and knees respectively to grip the saw and to hold the plank in place, I need every muscle of my body to deliver the force that drives the saw and to maintain my balance as I work, I need my eyes and ears to monitor progress. Even the plank itself becomes part of the equipment for cutting, in that the evolving groove helps to guide the work. Cutting wood, then, is an effect not of the saw alone but of the entire system of forces and relations set up by the intimate engagement of the saw, the trestle, the workpiece and my own body.
>
> (Ingold 2011: 56)

It is not the object itself, therefore, or its intrinsic attributes that define it as a tool. When a thing becomes a tool, it is because it has been placed in a relationship with other things in a field of activity where it can have a particular effect. This expanded understanding of what constitutes tool usage is implicit in the job description of the language analysts. They are expected to 'engage in academic and philosophical discussion while translating foreign language discussions into English' and maintain 'social, academic or business contacts' as well as 'reading and understanding ... native-language publications' and engaging in 'open-source research'. The use of digital tools, here, is embedded in a field of relationships with other things, peoples, and practices, without which the use of the digital tools in open-source research would have neither effect nor meaning. Reports of widespread cyber-espionage and the inexorable rise of cyber-crime (Clarke and Knake 2010; Glenny 2011) means, of course, that translation as a core activity of surveillance, licit and illicit, will continue apace. The digital tools that are used in this translation activity acquire their effect and relevance from the field of relationships in which they are embedded. In other words, whether current and future forms of penal transparency are to expand or severely limit (for political and/or criminal reasons) the exercise of human rights is determined by the entire system of forces and relations in which translation finds itself embedded. The system, like the analysis needed to understand it, is now, more than ever, inescapably global.

5 Details

Tranzlashun turns up in all kindz ov place in r brave new wurld. The opening sentence in this chapter, despite appearances, is not misspelled. It is a translation, an automatic translation of a recognizably English sentence into 'lolcat', produced by the Lolcat Translator (http://speaklolcat.com). Lolcat is described on the Speaklolcat site as a 'made up language that is said to be spoken by fluffy animals such as pets'. The site enjoins the user to learn to speak lolcat, 'the language of all animals. not just cats, dogs, kittens and puppies. communicate with your pet dog or cat. docta dolittle eat ur hart out!' Lolcat, of course, is a quintessentially virtual creation, the texting acronym lol (laugh out loud) matched to the viral spread of pictures of domestic animals with slick captions on internet forums and Facebook pages. The advent of an automated translator for this invented language confers a recognizable, if ironic, legitimacy on lolcat. In the digital age, it is the very translatability of a language that would appear to constitute part of its definition. In the Universal Translator Assistant Project (http://uta. mrklingon.org), an open-source translation tool for a variety of science-fiction languages, the tagline reads, 'Using the technology of today to bring the theories of yesterday to the languages of tomorrow.' The implicit claim is that it is translation that provides a link between the technology of today, the theories of yesterday, and the languages of tomorrow.

Details

In examining what the technology of today will do to the languages of tomorrow, it is useful to consider what particular 'theories of yesterday' might tell us about the nature and practice of translation. In an article that first appeared as a Xerox PARC Working Paper in 1980, Martin Kay claimed that 'history provides no better example of the improper use of computers than machine translation' and he went to imagine a scene of sorry hubris:

> There was a long period – for all I know, it is not yet over – in which the following comedy was acted out nightly in the bowels of an American government office with the aim of rendering foreign texts into English. Passages of innocent prose on which it was desired to effect this delicate

and complex operation were subjected to a process of vivisection at the hands of an uncomprehending electronic monster that transformed them into stammering streams of verbal wreckage. These were then placed into only slightly more gentle hands for repair.

(Kay 1997: 7)

Kay believed in the possibilities of machine translation, but he did not believe in its impossible ambitions. He described translation as a 'fine and exacting art', but he also thought that 'there is much about it that is mechanical and routine' and that, if these mechanical and routine parts could be given over to machines, translators would not only be more productive, but the work would become 'more rewarding, more exciting, more human' (*ibid.*, 3). The problem, of course, was deciding what was mechanical and routine. Kay's main critique of approaches to machine translation (MT) was that they favoured solutions that were approximate and tended in the absence of human intervention to multiply errors in catastrophic chain reactions. So it was assumed that if a machine translated a pronominal reference correctly 90 per cent of the time, this was an acceptable outcome. The problem is: how does the machine know that it is translating the pronominal reference correctly or not? If there is no reliable way of knowing which 10 per cent have been incorrectly translated, then 100 per cent of the pronouns must be examined by the human editor or translator. As Kay observed, 'it does not matter very much if the program is right 90, 99, 80, or 50 per cent of the time. The amount of work that it leaves for the repairman is essentially the same' (*ibid.*, 10). Kay's proposal, the 'Translation Amanuensis', a translation editor that worked in conjunction with, rather than tried to replace, the human translator, became the template for the forms of computer-assisted technology that have come to dominate the translation profession in the years since Kay's working paper was first published.

What is significant in Kay's critique is the nature of his criticism. He sees the fallacy of particular approaches to machine translation lying not in the entirely reasonable ambition to automate certain sub-routines in the translation process but in its indifference to details. The question of details, the translation of a pronoun, for example, is related to reliability: 'If it [the translation system] falls short of the acceptable standard, *to any degree whatsoever*, it might as well fail grossly because the burden it places on the proofreader will be very large' (*ibid.*, 11; his emphasis). He sees the role of the human translator interacting with the Translation Amanuensis as being primarily to do with a close attention to linguistic and translation detail, so as to prevent the 'cascading errors' that are all too common in 'language processing' (*ibid.*, 22).

This notion of 'detail' takes on a wider significance if we situate it within a particular discussion around the universal. Jean-Claude Milner, in a discussion of Walter Benjamin, sets up a distinction between 'thinking in a massive way' (*penser de manière massive*) and 'thinking in details' (*penser en détails*) (Milner 2011: 31). For Milner, one of the pitfalls, for example, of progressive thinking is the 'rhetoric of massiveness': the tendency to employ specific terms, such as 'freedom', 'democracy', and 'empowerment', with a supposedly mass or broad effect in ways that silence the hearers. If details such as mass fingerprinting at ports of entry and the decreased importance of parliamentary accountability through the rise of executive power seem to contradict the effective purchase of these terms, they are readily dismissed as mere details with respect to the defence of what is seen as the more fundamental achievement of parliamentary democracy itself.

On a darker but analogous note, a frequent claim of French negationists has been to dismiss the Holocaust as a 'detail'. As Milner claims, 'When a subject notices a detail, no matter how small, and when he or she is told to ignore it, he or she can be sure that something very important is going on there'[1] (*ibid.*, 32). What thinking in a massive way results from is what Milner describes as '*l'universel facile*', whereas 'if thinking through details leads to the universal, it is of necessity a difficult universal'[2] (*ibid.*, 32). For Milner, Freud's psycho-analytic explorations in the *Traumdeutung* or the *Psychopathology of Everyday Life* are examples of detailed thinking that take massive notions like hysteria, neurosis, and psychosis and tracks them through a series of illuminating details. At the end, the notions may still bear the same name but their internal structure and the nature of the universal claims they make have radically changed. The difficult universal is arrived at not by systematically identifying what each case has in common, as each case is very different, but by moving towards a notion of emergent commonality based on difference, rather than similarity.

Alan Melby in his 'Notes' on Martin Kay's classic paper sets up a distinction between two kinds of text-type that produce very different results in machine translation. The first text-type is 'controlled domain-specific language' and the second is 'dynamic general language' (Melby 1997: 29). We have already encountered controlled domain-specific languages in our discussion of SDL and Sun Microsystems (Chapters 2 and 4). In the case of these languages, MT systems are capable of producing high-quality raw output that requires relatively little post-editing. This is not the case, Melby argues, with dynamic general-language texts. The results are frequently uneven and disappointing and require an advanced degree of human post-editing to bring them up to the standard of high-quality output. This leads him to a second set of distinctions, in which he sets up an opposition between high-quality and what he terms 'indicative' translation:

> It has often been assumed that for a translation to be useful it must be of sufficiently high quality to be comparable to the work of a professional human translator. Not so. Low-quality MT that is produced quickly and used only to get an indication of the content of the original text and which is then often discarded is sometimes called 'indicative translation'. Surprisingly, indicative translation is perhaps the fastest growing use for MT.
>
> (*Ibid.*, 29)

In the case of indicative translation, one is primarily concerned with the overall or 'massive' effect of the text. As Melby notes, 'who cares about grammar or word choice when a motivated human can, with a little practice, form an approximate idea of what the document is about?' (*ibid.*, 30). The details are unimportant; it is the overall effect that counts. By inputting Melby's passage into one of the most popular online MT services, Google Translate, and translating it into French, we get an idea of what particular kinds of indicative translation might look like:

> Il a souvent été supposé que pour une traduction soit utile, il doit être de qualité suffisante pour être comparable à l'œuvre d'un traducteur professionnel. Pas du tout. Faible qualité MT qui est produite rapidement et utilisé uniquement pour obtenir une indication de la teneur du texte original et qui est alors souvent mis au rebut est parfois appelée 'traduction indicative.' Étonnamment, traduction indicative est peut-être l'utilisation la plus forte croissance pour les MT.

Opinions will vary as to the usability of this translation and how much 'practice' or prior knowledge one would need to understand the text, but it would not be unreasonable to claim that it does provide the reader with some notion of what was in Melby's original paragraph. The proliferation of translation applications for smartphones, in addition to the now almost axiomatic invitation to translate when Google searches throw up content in foreign languages, are powerful multipliers for the practice of indicative translation. What is implicit in the widespread availability of automatic translation is a notion of translation as potentially instantaneous and universal. This availability is of course facilitated by changing approaches to MT and the relentless increase in the processing capacity of computers themselves.

Until the late 1980s, MT was largely dominated by rule-based systems where grammar and syntax rules were combined with cross-language dictionaries. In the 1990s, the shift was to experimenting with sets of parallel texts. In statistical-based MT, algorithms analyse large collections of previous translations or parallel corpora to estimate the statistical probabilities of words or phrases in one language ending up in another. A model is then constructed on the basis of these probabilities and used to evaluate new text. By implication, these systems perform best on the types of texts on which they have been trained. The greater the coverage, the greater the need for more and more extensive corpora (Ratliff 2006: 2–3). The paradigm implicit in the statistical approach is one of the analysis of massive amounts of data available on the Web or elsewhere. One could argue, in effect, that it is an example of the particular kind of effectiveness of 'thinking in a massive way'. The result is that, in both of Melby's oppositions, we can see the emergence of the easy universal that Milner describes. In the case of controlled domain-specific language we have what might be described as pre-emptive universality. As we saw in Chapter 2, one of the goals of controlled language is to remove 'accidental content', the many different ways in which the same thing can be said and which generates new content to be translated. This 'accidental content' comprises the details that must be removed if the MT system is to run effectively. Once the language is sufficiently controlled, the universal rolling out of translations in the language pairs catered for is eminently feasible.

In the case of indicative translation, the details are not removed, but they are no longer deemed to matter. It is the cumulative effect of meaning based on human ingenuity in dealing with less than intelligible texts that legitimates the roll-out of online translation services on smartphones or laptops. The implicit goal is the vision of the universal translator described by Evan Ratliff in his discussion of a new MT approach developed by Jaime Carbonnell, science officer with the IT company Meaningful Machines:

> Right now, the Global Autonomous Language Exploitation program run by Darpa [Defense Advanced Research Projects Agency] is aiming to complete an automated text and translation system in the next five years. Meaningful Machines is part of a team participating in that challenge, including the 'surprise language' segment (in which teams are given a more obscure language and asked to build a translation system). The challenge sounds like another attempt to create the sort of universal translator that has eluded MT for 60 years. But success seems much more plausible than ever before.
>
> (*Ibid.*, 4)

It is important to understand that the notion of the easy universal has nothing to do with the very considerable technical complexity involved in the construction of controlled natural languages or the development of MT systems underlying the provision of online indicative translation. Rather, the difference lies in the role of detail and the relationship between translation and detail in positing another notion of universality.

Detail explains why there is such a thing as a translation profession, and why students will spend years acquiring the requisite language and other skills to become translators. It is the attention to detail that is seen time and time again to characterize the competent translator. When translators give voice to a characteristic, if not always enabling, modesty about what they do, it is often in the awareness of the sheer enormity of detail that crowds into the rendition of a text.

In her introduction to the 1886 and 1892 editions of her translation of *Madame Bovary*, Eleanor Marx claims, 'Certainly no critic can be more painfully aware than I am of the weaknesses, shortcomings, the failures of my work' (Flaubert 1886: xxi). As a translator who becomes her own critic, she knows that the painful awareness lies in the multiplicity of detailed decisions or choices she has had to make to bring Flaubert's text to the English reader. She also anticipates in a way the nature of translation criticism which focuses on the aesthetic, cultural, and political implications of the choices that are made at micro-levels by the translator. When Vladimir Nabokov subjects Marx's translation to the withering ire of his analysis, he will single out one tense, the imperfect, crucial to conveying a sense of unity and continuity in time, as a significant detail that weakens the force of the translation (Nabokov 1980: 173). Emily Apter, in her discussion of Marx's translation, sees a political philosophy underpinning certain lexical choices made by the daughter of Karl Marx and a significant activist in her own right. Whereas Alan Russell, in his later 1952 Penguin translation, consistently translates Flaubert's 'la richesse' as 'riches', Eleanor Marx always renders the word as 'wealth'. Apter argues, 'Eleanor Marx's consistent rendering of "riches" as "wealth" would seem to enhance the latent critique of wealth in Flaubert' (Apter 2008: 75).

The Italian translation of the *Rough Guide to New York City* is taken up by Lawrence Venuti as an example of how, through detailed modifications or interpolations, translators can both amplify and critique conventional representations of place:

> Whereas the English text illustrates Manhattan's 'massive romance' by referring to the '4am half-life Downtown, or just wasting the morning on Staten Island Ferry' the Italian version resorts to a lexicon that is both melodramatic and lyrical: 'il Greenwich Village, dove la vita *ferve ancora* alle 4 del mattino, il traghetto di Staten Island in un mattino *luminoso*.'
>
> (Venuti 2008: 26; original emphasis)

If *ferve ancora* (still rages) and *luminoso* (luminous) add markedly to the romance of Manhattan, the translators are considerably more sceptical about the fulsome, public-order rhetoric of the New York public authorities. The English text claims that the crime rate in the city dropped significantly, 'especially during the Mayor Giuliani years', while the Italian translation drops the specific reference to the mayor and notes that, as a result of lower crime figures, 'le autorità di Manhattan recentemente si sono lasciate andare a avventate manifestazioni di autocongratulazioni e pacche sulle spalle' (the Manhattan authorities have recently allowed themselves to sink to the level of rash expressions of self-congratulation and pats on the back) (cited in *ibid.*, 26). What emerges from readings of the translation of a literary classic and the translation of a popular travel guide is the centrality of details not only to the production of a translation, but to the possible receptions of the translated text. To paraphrase Milner, if the subject notes a translation detail, no matter how small, and is told to ignore it, he or she can be sure that is where something is going on. It is indeed the necessary care for, and attention to, detail that makes research in translation studies arduous and time-consuming (see, for example, in the case of the multiple English translations of a single Jules Verne text, O'Driscoll 2011).

At another level, implicit in the examples of translation production and analysis discussed above is the presence of the difficult universal, the universal that is arrived at through the enumeration of difference, rather than the restatement of commonality, and which problematizes the 'massive' notions of fidelity, equivalence, and meaning. There is a sense, then, in which the easy universalism of particular representations of translation in the digital age runs directly counter to another form and reception strategy of translation based on the idea of a difficult, asymptotic universal. This difficult universal recognizes that there is a communicative life beyond particulars or details, otherwise the translation enterprise would be doomed to a plaintive solipsism, but that any move towards the universal must take account of the endless interrogation of the details of language and culture. Lawrence Venuti argues that the 'political intervention performed by translation in postmodern culture may be more usefully imagined as a local, small-scale activity of resistance against dominant discourses and institutions' (Venuti 2008: 22).

The resistance that is situated at the level of detail has an interesting corollary in terms of the nature of the institutional or political investment in the universalism of MT. As we saw above in the reference to the Global Autonomous Language Exploitation program, the Defense Advanced Research Projects Agency, a research wing of the US military, is particularly interested in the possibilities of machine translation. Language Weaver, a Californian firm that specializes in statistical MT systems, 'got an investment from the CIA's venture firm In-Q-Tel in 2003', and 'now has customers in intelligence agencies here and abroad' (Ratliff 2006: 4). In the words of the CEO of Language Weaver, Bryce Benjamin, the software 'is being used day in and day out to catch bad guys' (*ibid.*, 4). The ultimate political problem, of course, is defining who the 'bad guys' are, and for whom. More significant, perhaps, than the cavalier moral dualism of the comments is that from the Cold War to the 'War on Terror', a certain kind of universalist vision of translation has accompanied military bids for strategic and territorial advantage. It is as if the massive thinking behind the tactics of 'Shock and Awe' were seeking a congenial home in the field of translation, and that a theory of global power and influence cannot forgo a theory of what translation should be and do.

Gaps

In developing an approach to translation predicated on the difficult universal, the question that might be asked is: what for? In a digital world of accelerated, quasi-instantaneous exchange, is there not a compelling case to be made in terms of time and efficiency for the easy universalism of controlled language and indicative translation? Is there not a sense in which some communication, however imperfect, is better than none? To try to answer this question, it is helpful to ask what we put into communication when we translate. In the case of interlingual translation, we might respond that two languages and cultures are typically placed in dialogue, and there may be sub-languages of these languages (legal, scientific, commercial) or subcultures (based on, for example, ethnicity or class) that are party to this dialogue. Looking more closely at the word 'dialogue', there are two components, 'dia', from the ancient Greek, meaning 'across', and 'logue', related to 'legein', 'speak'. Implicit in the term is the acknowledgement of a distance that needs to be crossed (dia) and the possibility that the distance can be crossed through the intelligibility of speech (legein). Therefore, translation as a dialogue between languages and cultures must be as much about the necessary recognition of distance as it is about the communicative possibilities of intelligible speech, oral or written.

The notion of difference is the stock-in-trade of any debate on intercultural communication and is a powerful vector for one of the world's major economic activities, tourism. However, a difficulty arises when the so-called typical differences (Japanese formality, American informality, Caribbean *joie de vivre*) become barriers rather than aids to understanding as they harden into the exportable cliché of mass tourism, or the semiotic shorthand of commercial soap operas. As the sinologist and philosopher François Jullien argues:

> Between cultures, I would not trust these supposedly characteristic *differences*, labelled as such and presented as standard (the most obvious traits are often the least interesting): as they become ossified, they become an obstacle to thought. But, I said it before, I make the *gaps* work – the notion is exploratory not classificatory. Opening up a gap is to break with conformism, to bring tension back into thinking, in short, to set our reason back to work.[3]
>
> (Jullien 2010: 15; his emphasis)

The notion of 'gaps' here is as much within, as between, cultures. In other words, cultures are not uniform blocs reified under the sign of difference which are assimilated by translators and then bridged by their irreproachable sense of tact. They are dynamic entities, constantly in a state of flux. For this reason, the notion of 'identity' becomes highly problematic, as the question is what kind of identity are we talking about, given that any given culture or language is a product of endless mixing and cross-fertilization, and that new ways of working, generational change, and new forms of technology subject the language and culture to continuous transformation. In this context, Jullien argues not for the promotion of 'identity', which, in many cases, is, to a greater or lesser extent, fictive, but for the idea of 'fecundity' (*fécondité*) (*ibid.*, 12). Fecundity carries within it a dynamic sense of plurality that foregrounds the resources (*ressources*) of a culture. The notion of 'resources' here is not to be confused with that of 'values': 'values are the vectors of an affirmation of self. They are bound up, whatever one might claim to the contrary, in a relationship of power whereas resources are indefinitely exportable (exploitable) and available to everyone'[4] (*ibid.*, 15). Confucianism, for example, offers the thinker the resources of subtlety of expression, sense of balance, the importance of a notion of 'regulation', the avoidance of overly dogmatic thinking but, as a value system, Jullien argues, it can be less attractive in promoting social conformism, a servile attitude towards those in power, and so on (*ibid.*, 16).

The form of difficult universalism that works through the details of language and culture in translation both reveals the 'gaps', those distances that need to be crossed in translation, and the resources which are made available to world languages and cultures through the translational circuits of intelligibility. In order to see how this form of universalism might be related to translation practice, I will examine two very different accounts of what it is to translate.

The narrative poem *Meghadūta* or 'Cloud Messenger' was written in Sanskrit by the famed poet Kalidasa in the fourth or fifth century CE. It was translated into English in 1813 by Horace Hayman Wilson. Although sympathetic to the aims of Empire, Wilson was at pains to point out how different was the world represented in the Sanskrit poem. As David Damrosch notes, 'he follows the sixty pages of the poem with over a hundred pages of detailed and informative notes, explaining religious and geographical references, the symbolic significance of birds and plants, and the social and literary assumptions of the poet and his audience' (Damrosch 2008: 44). In his copious notes Wilson is paying attention to the 'details' of Sanskrit language and culture that inform the poetic production of Kalidasa, the necessary 'gaps' in Western attempts to grasp the poem. He pursues the project of difficult universalism using a dual strategy of repudiation and analogy. The repudiation is the direct challenge to Western stereotypes about Indian culture, stereotypes that he feels are undone by the import of the poem. When Kalidasa refers to the virtue of gratitude, Wilson notes:

> The *Hindus* have been the object of much idle panegyric, and equally idle detraction; some writers have invested them with every amiable attribute, and they have been deprived by others of the common virtues of humanity. Amongst the excellencies denied to them, gratitude has always been particularized; and there are many of the *European* residents in *India*, who scarcely imagine that the natives of the country ever heard of such a sentiment. To them, and to all detractors on this head, the above verse is a satisfactory reply.
>
> (Wilson 1814: 91)

In his comment, Wilson is undercutting a notion of typical difference and opening up a gap in received thinking about Indian culture.

The other component of Wilson's strategy is analogy, in which he refers to classical writers of antiquity, such as Ovid, Catullus, and Horace, to make Kalidasa comprehensible to his Western readers. After the 'dia' of distinctive difference, he moves towards the 'logos' of intelligibility, the attempt to make the meanings of the poem circulate in his culture of origin:

> the analogies between the poetry of the East and the West are given especially for the benefit of those liberal critics, who admire, upon the strength of prescription, the beauties of classical and modern writings, and deny all merit to the same or similar ideas, when they occur in the works of oriental writers. It is also entertaining to observe how much men resemble each other, in spite of the accidental varieties of complexion or education, place or time.
>
> (*Ibid.*, xix–xx)

Wilson's move here towards a notion of the universal is not based on the repudiation of difference or an attempt to fill in the gaps, but on a repeated desire to open up a breach in conformism, bring tension back into Western perceptions, and challenge the foundations of Empire's way of 'reasoning' about its colonial subjects.

This is not to argue that Wilson was not in many other ways wholly complicit in the project of Empire, but rather to show how his translation enterprise is founded on a notion of 'thinking through details' that by and large eschews the 'massive' effects of colonial stereotyping. Unfortunately, for Wilson, his 'logos' was not quite up to the task of translating the *Meghadūta* into English. Captivated by the translation poetics of neo-classical writers like Dryden and Pope, Wilson renders the poem into English in less than heroic couplets. As Damrosch notes, 'Translations notoriously age as their language becomes dated, but Wilson's style was dated even in his own time' (Damrosch 2008: 45). What Wilson reveals in his detailed presentation of the poem is not so much a static notion of Sanskrit identity as an image of the abundance of 'resources' in Sanskrit culture and language. Indeed, it is precisely in terms of a resource-oriented approach to intercultural contact that Wilson presents his translation project in his preface:

> The efforts of *Sanscrit* scholars have hitherto, however, been directed rather to the useful than the pleasing, rather to works of science than imagination. The complicated grammar of the *Hindus* has been most successfully investigated, their mythology amply illustrated, and much of their philosophy satisfactorily explained; their astronomical works have been exhibited to the philosophers, whose modern attainments have rendered ancient science an object of curiosity rather than information, and their laws are no longer concealed behind the veil of an unknown tongue, from the knowledge of those who are charged with the administration of justice in *Hindoostan*. It only remains to explore the field of their lighter literature, and transfer some of its most elegant flowers to a European soil.
>
> (Wilson 1814: x–xi)

Wilson's comments, of course, are replete with a particular kind of imperial hubris ('successfully investigated', 'amply illustrated'), and he is not averse to spelling out the coercive possibilities of knowledge ('administration of justice in *Hindoostan*'). On the other hand, as revealed by his prefatory comments and his detailed annotations to the translation, he is interested in the multiplicity rather than the unity of the culture he investigates. What is made apparent, above all, is the fecundity of the culture and language which informs the *Meghadūta*. The question that might be asked, however, is: what relevance does this particular form of 'thick translation' by a nineteenth-century British Orientalist have for translation in the twenty-first century?

What is paramount in Wilson's approach to his translation of the Sanskrit text is an attention to, and a concern with, detail. This, indeed, is often seen as an integral part of how translators go about their business. Daniel Gouadec claims that 'Translators must first and foremost strive to avoid making serious errors' and he gives as examples 'mistranslating drug dosages, switching around the connections in a wiring diagram, confusing a rise with a fall or clockwise with anti-clockwise' (Gouadec 2007: 10). Of course, what might seem like a detail, a missing zero or a misplaced term, could in all of these cases have dramatic consequences. However, the concern with detail in the digital age should not simply be reduced to the 'War on Error'. This is because the nature of what might be considered 'detail' is changing, and this is related to the reconfiguration of two basic parameters: time and space.

Dominique Estival, in a discussion of the development of a language translation interface for the Australian Defence Organization (ADO), describes how a greater spatial or geo-political sensitivity, and an increasing concern with timescale, meant that translation became a major preoccupation for the ADO. Crucially, it is the nature of contemporary conflict that motivates the move towards translation, 'the shift of focus from "defence of Australia" to "national security" implies an increased awareness of the international environment around Australia' (Estival 2005: 178). The three activities that result from the shift in the defence paradigm are intelligence gathering, coalition operations, and foreign operations (peace-keeping, humanitarian, and relief operations). For example, in relation to intelligence gathering, the implication of translation in a New Intelligence Order is made particularly clear:

> There have been many discussions for better and more timely intelligence since the intelligence failures shown to precede the tragedy of 9/11 in the USA and requests for more translators and tools to help translators have been widely publicised. Australia is in the same situation as all other countries in this respect, although the Bali bombings in September 2002 and September 2005 and the bombing of the Australian embassy in Jakarta in October 2004 mean that there are also specific threats and concerns for Australia with particular linguistic implications.
>
> (*Ibid.*, 178)

The notion of intelligence vulnerability that is universalized ('Australia is in the same situation as all other countries in this respect') means that the notion of intelligence itself, rather like information, cannot be thought of outside the operation of translation. '[I]ncreased awareness of the international environment around Australia' leads to a greater engagement with the linguistic detail of the Asia-Pacific region. In other words, whereas previously traditional ties to the UK and US had led to English being the sole language of use of the ADO, different political circumstances and new allies (Japan, Republic of Korea, Thailand, France), as well as new areas of non-combat operations (Solomon Islands, East Timor, Aceh (Indonesia)), meant that there was not only a greater contextual sensitivity to language use but an acknowledgement of growing complexity. The default universalism of English as a global *lingua franca* no longer functioned. Translation was as inevitable as it was necessary. If translation was necessary because of changing geo-political or spatial orientations, what were the implications for time?

According to Estival, it takes one to two years to train someone to function in a spoken foreign language, and another two to three years to produce an effective translator/interpreter, depending on the language pair. He adds, 'it is very difficult to predict which languages are going to be of interest in a three-year time frame and even more difficult to predict the extent of the potential demand for translation for those languages' (*ibid.*, 180). Given the size of the Australian population, the ADO cannot be increased beyond a particular size, so there 'will never be enough personnel available to be trained and the range of languages of interest cannot be predicted in time to perform the training required to produce skilled translators in those languages' (*ibid.*, 180). Estival is drawing our attention back to the question of chrono-diversity (see Chapter 4), the tension between the short timeframe of translation demand and the long timeframe of translator training or education. What is apparent in the Australian example, as elsewhere, is that a shift in scale at a spatial level has immediate consequences at a temporal level. As the linguistic demands, in a sense, become more detailed and more complex, the ability to deliver on them in real time becomes more and more problematic.

The response of the research wing of the Australian military, the Australian Defence Science and Technology Organization (DSTO), to this scalar shift was to develop a Language Translation Interface (LTI) that brought together the resources of existing MT systems, including free, online MT translation services. Time and money are invoked as the principal reasons for the development of the LTI: 'The development of a new translation engine requires enormous efforts and resources and is beyond the scope of a research project at DSTO. In any case, it is not possible to predict which languages might become of interest and the results of such efforts would most likely not meet actual needs' (*ibid.*, 189). At one level, the results and the basic philosophy of the LTI would appear to fall under the rubric of the easy universalism that informs the MT translation projects of the US military. The need to think in detail about new geo-political situations leads to a form of 'massive' translation through the widespread use of available MT tools. The overall conclusion in the Australian case was that the users were broadly happy with the kind of indicative translation output provided by the LTI. The translation devil does, however, intervene at the level of detail. In the one example provided of output from an LTI session, where a number of alternative English translations are provided for a Japanese sentence, the MT output that has been post-edited clearly provides the most satisfactory translation. The repeated references to 'quality', and the desirability of developing and building translation memories to enhance the quality of the LTI output, show that the concern with detail is not so much removed as displaced. That is to say, in an age of the widespread deployment of IT, there may increasingly be a sense in which translation, or what we tend to think of as translation, may not be where we expect to find it; indeed it may be going under another name for much of the time. The concern with detail that is part of that move towards difficult universalism may not be an inevitable casualty in the digital age and may re-emerge in a different guise.

Quality

In the 1980s and 1990s, the use of post-editing on machine-generated text was largely for the purpose of making the translated text minimally comprehensible. The text was intended for dissemination rather than assimilation, akin to the indicative translation mentioned above by Alan Melby. As Garcia notes, 'Full post-editing was considered to involve more effort than translating directly from the source text' (Garcia 2011: 218). However, as MT systems improved and became more widespread in their use, 'full post-editing is now encroaching into areas that had been dealt with up to now by translation assisted by TM [translation memory]' (*ibid.*, 218). Two factors are behind this development, both relating again to space and time. The global connectivity of economic activities means not only that economic power is shifting with the emergence, for example, of the Chinese, Brazilian, Indian, and South African economies, but that the demand for certain language pairs, such as Chinese–English, has risen dramatically. Given the paucity of English native speakers with an adequate command of Chinese, the tendency is for Chinese-language speakers to translate from their mother tongue into English.

Garcia argues in a study of the effectiveness of post-editing that translators working into their weaker tongue particularly tended to benefit from post-editing MT output, as opposed to translating directly from the source language: 'should the quality be high enough, the MT version may save translators time in the process of understanding the source and provide them with a draft on which to work' (*ibid.*, 221). Spatial reconfiguration of economic relations means increasing traffic between non-cognate languages with consequent translation challenges. At the same moment, as economies in the information age are connected in real time, the response times to demands of various kinds are endlessly foreshortened. In this context, TAUS, a think-tank for the translation industry, claims that post-editing for publication should be able to process about 5,000 words per day, twice as many as conventional translation, even if they admit the quality is likely to be lower. The other caveats are that the figure supposes experienced, professional post-editors working on the output of engines trained in domain-specific areas and with the possibility that some of the text has been pre-edited (TAUS 2010: 6–9).

What is striking in the discussions around post-editing and translation automation generally is the recurrent concern with 'quality'. In a report on a TAUS Execuive Forum held in Japan in April 2012, Jaap van der Meer notes, 'The adoption of MT technology makes translation more efficient but what about the quality? This question creeps [*sic*] up in every presentation of machine translation solutions of course. We dedicated a special session to the problematic area of translation quality evaluation' (van der Meer 2012: 2). Quality is, in a sense, the return of the repressed translation detail. The careful, detailed attention to text, language, and meaning that is implicit in the act of translation re-emerges in the context of automation in the debates about the extent and role of post-editing, and about how to achieve acceptable quality in translation output.

The 'massiveness' of the move towards automation is repeatedly wrong-footed by the detailed susceptibilities of 'quality'. Haunting discussions around translation automation in the digital age is the spectral presence of the thickness of detail that goes to make up languages and cultures. This is not to say that translation automation is impossible. It can be highly effective in certain circumstances, and its use and practice will continue to grow for the spatio-temporal reasons described above. However, it is important to note that translation is a scalar concept which covers a wide variety of practices, and that our expectations of what it should or can do may ultimately be traced back to competing versions or understandings of the universal.

Jean-Claude Milner, in a discussion of Jean-Jacques Rousseau's famous declaration at the beginning of his *Social Contract*, 'L'homme est né libre et partout il est dans les fers' (Man is born free and everywhere he is in chains), claims that the opposition appears initially to be chronological: man is born free at birth, and then he becomes enslaved. Milner argues that a deeper opposition resides at a logical level:

> I hear the sound of the clash between the universal proposition in the singular, *Every man is free* and the proposition in the plural, *All men are free*. The first one is true, the second false. But, at the same time, we understand that the proposition in the singular is only true in an intensive sense. It is universal in the strict sense that it brings out the maximum intensity in the name *man*. It would still be universal even if men were nowhere to be found free.[5]
>
> (Milner 2011: 36)

The kind of 'intensive' universality evoked by Milner, where there is an exploration of the maximal meaning or meanings of what a word might signify, contrasts with an extensive universality primarily concerned with extension and plurality, as in mass consumer products, where what is most characteristic is their interchange-ability and omnipresence (the Starbucks phenomenon). Translation in the digital age is faced with the tension between forms of extensive universality that drive the translation industry worldwide and the claims of intensive universality which underline the maximally difficult and maximally complex nature of words and their use. This tension is referred to by Brian McConnell from the software company Worldwide Lexicon Inc. when he recommends a watchword for translation in the future, 'Don't let perfect be the enemy of the good':

> His example of a model platform for a world of ubiquitous translation functionality where simplicity is the watchword is Twitter. The focus should be exclusively on defining conventions for the most common tasks and interactions between the various [*sic*] involved, and then regularly improving them.
>
> (Joscelyne 2011: 1)

If the 'perfect' is the drive towards intensive universality, the 'good', as defined here, is the move towards extensive universality, where the prior definition of conventions will allow for the cheap, fast, and efficient circulation of messages in a 'world of ubiquitous translation'.

Digital humanism

The very notion of 'a world of ubiquitous translation' brings us close to the fundamental dilemma for any student or scholar of translation trying to understand what is happening in the digital age. This is the experience of living whithin a profoundly hybrid culture, where, on the one hand, we have established notions of what constitutes text, knowledge, and identity, while, on the other, all of these notions are being challenged by new digital realities and practices (hypertext, wikipedias, avatars). Translation is one of these notions that is, in a sense, caught in the hybrid gallery of the familiar image of the lone translator seated at her desk working her way methodically through the text, and the profusion of images suggested by the following: 'Translation is now delivered to the end user via a variety of workflows: MT-only, MT built from TMs plus LSP-enabled post-editing; MT and crowd-enabled post-editing, or simply hand-crafted via the community, all of which might draw on various data resources, increasingly from the cloud' (Joscelyne 2011: 1). The word we are using is the same, but in our contemporary hybrid culture, are we talking about the same thing? Are we not caught inevitably between the cultural formation of translation in one form of civilization, and emergent forms of translation in another?

To help us answer these questions it is useful to consider a historical categorization introduced by the anthropologist Claude Lévi-Strauss in response to a request by UNESCO to draw up a document on the contribution of the social sciences to humanism in a technical age (Lévi-Strauss 2008: 25–28). Lévi-Strauss distinguished three forms of humanism: the aristocratic humanism of the Renaissance, based on the rediscovery of the texts of classical antiquity; the bourgeois humanism of exoticism, based on the discovery of the cultures of the East and Far East; and the democratic humanism of the twentieth century, linked to the activity of anthropology and including the totality of human cultures. What is significant about Lévi-Strauss's tripartite division is that all three forms of humanism have forms of translation at their heart. The Renaissance, Orientalism in its various guises, and anthropology as a viable practice were all deeply connected to translation. Without translation, in effect, they would not have happened. There would have been no Lucretius to turn the Renaissance world upside down, no comparative grammars to challenge ethnocentric accounts of linguistic origins, no field reports to discredit colonial stereotypes about 'primitive' peoples. Each of these forms of humanism both shaped and responded to changes in the culture and technology of the time (astrolabe, railways, cinema).

In the wake of Lévi-Strauss's periodization, Milad Doueihi has proposed a fourth form of humanism that corresponds to our contemporary period: digital humanism. The totality of the effects of the digital on every aspect of human life – from the access to knowledge (Google), to the nature of romantic attachment (internet dating), and forms of popular insurrection (social media and the Arab

Spring) – point to civilizational shifts which call for a new type of humanism. In Doueihi's words:

> Digital humanism, because it deals with a global technology that is bound up with the human and produces wholly new objects, while at the same time changing the way we view existing objects, is the sign of a significant change and, above all, of an emerging discipline.[6]
>
> (Doueihi 2011: 36)

As we saw in the last chapter, the notions of translation prosumption, post-print translation literacy, and translation pluri-subjectivity demonstrate how we are forced to change our views of classical objects of translation study as a result of changes in the digital environment. Smartphone translation apps like Word Lens, the Phraselator developed by the US military, and the Language Translation Interface elaborated by the Australian armed forces are some of the multitude of 'new objects' which are appearing in the field of translation. What is particularly striking is that the form of digital humanism outlined by Doueihi has translation once again at its core. This is primarily because the need for a way of thinking about culture, society, and technology is driven by a concept that is inseparable from translation itself: namely, convertibility. The possibility that text, image, and sound can be converted/translated into digital code means that representations, identities, and objects become inherently unstable as they can potentially be converted/ translated into anything else, emerging as new objects or circulating in new contexts. The rare book that could only be consulted in the fixed, institutional setting of the Rare Books and Manuscripts section of the library can now be consulted from a deck-chair on a beach over an internet connection. What digital humanism has to engage with, above all else, is how are we to conceive of the personal, the social, the political, and the ideal in an era of potentially limitless convertibility or, to put it another way, in an age of potentially endless translation or translatability?

One of the major figures to emerge in the aristocratic humanism attributed by Lévi-Strauss to the period of the Renaissance was the philologist. Poggio Braccioloni, Leonardo Bruni, Pier Paolo Vergerio, Cencio Rustici, Bartolomeo Aragazzi da Montepulciano, and Benedetto da Piglio were among the humanist scholars in the fifteenth century who would distinguish themselves by their knowledge of classical languages, but also, of course, by their translation abilities (Greenblatt 2011: 155–81). This relationship between nascent humanism and the emergence of the philological method leads Doueihi to argue for a similar development in the context of a developing digital humanism. What Doueihi calls the 'philological imperative' (*impératif philologique*) is basically the attempt to pin down changing fields of meaning and changing understandings of the sense and use of keywords associated with a proper historical under-standing, 'which enrich the context and allow for a more measured assessment of some of the promises of technology'[7] (Doueihi 2011: 27). Given the centrality of the practice of translation to the work of philologists, and the philological sensibility at work in the practice of translators from Jerome to Luther to Eleanor

Marx, it is only to be expected that the notion of a 'philological imperative' should find a place in translation studies as a key area of enquiry within this new digital humanism. Situating translation in a material history, and exploring the changing understandings, implicit and explicit, of what translation means in the twenty-first century, is a way of responding to this philological imperative.

Part of the impetus for philological exploration in the period of Renaissance humanism was to mount a challenge to received wisdom about the nature of biblical truth or the construction of the universe. Detailed exploration of texts in their original languages and the making available of the fruits of these researches in translation would strengthen the case for the autonomy of the human intellect and the right to enquire without fear of coercion or the tyranny of precedent (in the case of science, see Lindberg 2007 and Montgomery 2000). Thus, the history of translation is, among other things, the history of the quest for human autonomy. However, there is something of a paradox at the heart of this quest, which has implications for how we are to respond to the burgeoning growth of online automated translation. Susan Bassnett, in an examination of the issue of status anxiety for translators, makes an observation which has long been voiced by professional organizations representing translators:

> Those people who assume that translators have the power to interpret for them are reluctant to see this skill as worth paying for, and when the same people talk about books they have read that were originally written in other languages, one can be sure that they will mention the author's name, not the name of the translator without whom they would not have been able to read the book at all.
>
> (Bassnett 2011: 28–29)

In effect, Bassnett is speaking both of the reluctance to accord autonomous existence to the translator, and of the unwillingness to pay the price of the autonomy granted through the work of the translator. In describing the work of the translator, Bassnett speaks of craftsmanship: 'many translators are happy with the idea of craftsmanship in translation, which carries connotations of a long apprenticeship served and a deep understanding of primary materials which the expert translator can then shape as he or she thinks fit' (*ibid.*, 30). The emergence of the translator as an autonomous, functioning agent is the result of a long, arduous preparation, and in a society dominated by the notion of exchange-value, it is only to be expected that the translator is duly rewarded. What happens, however, to the craft paradigm of translation in a digital age? Or to put the question rather differently: what becomes of the relationship between translation and autonomy in the wake of translation automation?

Conviviality

The social theorist Ivan Illich was greatly preoccupied by the relationship between humans and their tools. He felt that rather than humans working with tools, they had ended up working for them. By 'tools', Illich understood 'all rationally designed devices' in a society, such that the term covered simple hardware (drills, pots, syringes, building elements, and motors), but also productive institutions, such as factories that produce tangible commodities like breakfast cereals, and productive systems that produce intangible commodities such as 'education', 'health', and 'knowledge' (Illich 1990: 17–18). What was necessary was to 'invert the present deep structure of tools' and to 'give people tools that guarantee their right to work with high, independent efficiency, thus simultaneously eliminating the need for either slaves or masters and enhancing each person's range of freedom' (*ibid.*, 12). Tools, in Illich's view, had become wholly subordinate to an ideology of industrial productivity that limited, rather than enhanced, human flourishing:

> I choose the term 'conviviality' to designate the opposite of industrial productivity. I intend it to mean autonomous and creative intercourse among persons, and the intercourse of persons with their environment; and in this contrast with the conditioned response of persons to the demands made upon them by others, and by a man-made environment. I consider conviviality to be individual freedom realized in personal interdependence, and, as such, an intrinsic ethical value. I believe that, in any society, as conviviality is reduced below a certain level, no amount of industrial productivity can effectively satisfy the needs it creates among the society's members.
>
> (*Ibid.*, 12)

The stress in Illich's presentation of conviviality is on the development of autonomy, but an autonomy that is situated within the wider context of human interdependence. Tools which further this object are those which enhance conviviality. On the other hand, 'manipulatory' or 'destructive' tools are tools which 'increase regimentation, dependence, exploitation, or impotence, and rob not only the rich but also the poor of conviviality' (*ibid.*, 20). Thus, the bicycle or, under certain conditions, the phone can become a tool for conviviality, whereas, Illich argues, the private motor car and the television are more often than not manipulatory or destructive tools.

For Michael Slattery, writing on personal computing and conviviality, the PC is incontrovertibly a tool for conviviality: 'When the only computers were huge mainframes owned by large companies or organizations, these large owners inevitably exercised a certain form of control over access to and use of computing power. The PC put this computing power directly into the hands of the individual, thus liberating personal access and use from external control' (Slattery 2012). The internet represents a further stage in the emancipation of the individual, in particular from the institutionalization of knowledge. Slattery sees the internet as inherently subversive of the monopolization of knowledge by elites:

> Just as the personal computer delivered computing power into the hands of the individual, so internet delivers to each user unprecedented access to

information and knowledge. The internet revolution has introduced a radical democratisation of access to information. Perhaps even more significant is the new power it gives to individuals to distribute and to share the information that they have.

(Slattery 2012)

It is arguable that it was the 'radical democratisation of access to information' that had the most immediate effect on the lives of translators, as they began to have access to a quantity and range of reference material which had been unimaginable before the advent of personal computing and the internet. As Minako O'Hagan observes, 'every day remunerated translators rely on the vast amount of free user-generated content and information available on the Internet, be it glossaries of terms or technical information of all kinds in a given language' (O'Hagan 2011: 15). If we take the example of fan translation, notably the fansubs of Japanese anime (O'Hagan 2009: 94–121), it is clear that, for the fans producing the translated subtitles, translation is an indispensable part of what Illich describes as 'autonomous and creative intercourse among persons, and the intercourse of persons with their environment'. More generally, as Bassnett points out with respect to world literature, without translation on a multilingual planet, creative intercourse would be a dead letter. So it would appear reasonable to argue that translation is a tool for conviviality, a type of productive system that produces an intangible commodity such as 'intercultural understanding'.

The tools of the translators, translation technology, in this view would become part of translation's contribution to the construction of forms of global conviviality. In the re-humanization of translation that was discussed in the case of wiki-translation (Chapter 4), and the potential contribution of translation technology to the promotion and enhancement of language diversity (Chapter 2), it is feasible to make a case for the translators' tools as parts of a new, emancipatory culture of the convivial. For the casual user of Google Translate or any of the many smartphone translation apps, it is possible to claim that these forms of automatic translation are enhancing the autonomy of the user. In other words, they are permitting him or her to interact in effective or meaningful ways with his or her environment, whether real or virtual. The advent of collaborative translation or community translation – 'translation performed voluntarily by Internet users and ... usually produced in some form of collaboration often on specific platforms by a group of people forming an online community' (O'Hagan 2011: 14) – means that the users are able to assess collectively the quality of translations that are proposed, as in the example of Facebook translations (Jiménez-Crespo 2011: 131–52). In this way, autonomous and creative intercourse among persons can enhance quality, just as the collaborative and peer-review potential of social networking can be an invaluable part of the 'learning webs' that Illich envisaged for genuinely emancipatory forms of education (Illich 1995: 35–37). In 'learning webs', groups of like-minded people come together in communities of learning that are not beholden to the constraints and power dynamics of institutionalized settings.

The philological imperative demands, however, that we ask another question: can there be a sense in which particular kinds of translation tool become destructive or manipulatory? This question demands different responses depending on what aspect of the current digital scene we examine. It is possible, none the less, to group the concerns under the broad heading of what might be described as a 'translation ecology'. In an earlier volume, I advanced the concept of translation ecology to describe the types of translation practice that would allow speakers of minority languages to exercise control over what, when, and how texts would be translated into and out of their languages (Cronin 2003: 165–72). Central to this notion of translation ecology are notions of autonomy, power, and how translation can contribute to cultural and linguistic diversity. In what ways can translation become a destructive or manipulatory tool, damaging to the linguistic and cultural ecology of societies?

In the case of online, automated translation, one difficulty is that while it promotes autonomy at one level (the user can understand the text), it, of course, encourages dependency at another. The user becomes dependent on the translation provided by the MT system, and thus enters into a heteronomous relationship with the system. The tension between autonomous and heteronomous forms of translation has long haunted the practice of translation, and dependence on translations provided by others has long troubled the conscience of Empire (Cronin 2002: 45–62). The automatic, real-time production of the translation tends not only to abstract or dematerialize the labour of translation and conceal the nature of dependence, but can also lead to a representation of translation as an effortless form of substitutive transfer.

As a number of high-profile online translation services are free, there can be even greater reluctance to pay for translation services supplied by professional translators. The demonetization of translation in this context makes its status even more uncertain in economies dominated by the logic of exchange value, where what is valuable is what you pay for. As has been noted earlier, many commentators on translation automation have described its main impact as in the area of indicative translation or gisting. One of the most notable casualties in indicative translation or gisting for non-controlled language is, not surprisingly, language itself. The instrumental, purposive drive of gisting implies a particular notion of what it is that language does. Language becomes primarily about getting information from point A to point B. In this transitive vision of the translation task the particular stylistic integrity of a language, the long apprenticeship in the nuances of a tongue, are of little consequence. If the direction of translation is predominantly from more powerful languages, then the unchecked consequences on the target languages can be all the more marked as both the volume and rapidity of translation automation increase. In other words, it is not enough simply to have a language present on the internet to ensure its linguistic viability and thereby guarantee future linguistic diversity. The speakers and users of the language must be aware of the hidden, heteronomous bias of forms of translation automation, overdetermined by the linguistic structures and cultural assumptions of the source language and culture. The risk is all the greater, in that the increased use of translation memories brings with it the potential for initial translation choices to become embedded in texts, which are then replicated endlessly in different contexts, as well as a tendency to favour the sentence as the unit of translation over overall textual cohesion (Bowker 2007: 175–87; Alves and Liparini Campos 2009: 191–218).

As translation moves from a more traditional notion of translation, edit, and publish organized by a project team to the different translation model based on a more bottom-up, organically formed 'project community', then crowdsourcing or wiki-translation assumes a greater importance (Kelly, Ray, and De Palma 2011: 75–96). This development brings with it an inevitable status anxiety around the profession of the translator. As noted above, demonetization in a market economy implies de-professionalization. When Facebook asked its users for help in translating its website, a 7,000-member-strong protest group emerged called 'Leave Translation to Translators', which was highly critical of a for-profit organization exploiting the goodwill of its users to enhance its profitability. The members of the group also made much of what they saw as the delusional thinking that made inept but well-meaning amateurs believe they could do the work of professionals. When LinkedIn made a similar move to use crowdsourcing to meet its translation needs, its translator members set up a group known as 'Translators against Crowdsourcing for Commercial Business' (Kelly 2009).

Underlying the concerns of professional translators about the economic viability of their profession and the simplistic notions of what it is that translators do, there is a more profound crisis which the internet critic Andrew Keen attributes to what he calls the 'cult of the amateur' (Keen 2008). Keen argues that the plethora of user-generated content on the internet has made finding high-quality, professionally produced and researched material increasingly difficult. In effect, what is purportedly free comes at a high cultural cost, as the migration of advertising revenue and modes of access to the internet has had catastrophic effects on the newspaper industry and countless record labels. In the absence of gatekeepers or expert-based filtering processes, what results is the universalization of ignorance or a kind of pseudo-democracy of response, where anyone's opinion is as valid as anyone else's, irrespective of their degree of knowledge of the subject. The difficulty with Keen's argument is that he often falls victim to the particular failing he describes, offering a highly partial view of internet developments that is not always based on what is actually happening. On the other hand, the democratization of access to knowledge that Illich called for brings with it particular dilemmas for the status of expertise and informed opinion, in terms of both economic sustainability and its role within the public sphere.

In this context, Milad Doueihi calls for the necessity to revisit what he describes as the 'ambivalent legacy of the Enlightenment':

> This heritage appears to legitimate at least two contradictory trends, one rooted in the development of the culture of the book and its institutions

(the academy, publishing, the press) and the other based on the idealism of the free sharing and circulation of knowledge.[8]

(Doueihi 2011: 15)

The idealism of the free circulation of knowledge, which finds its expression in late modernity in Illich's demand for educational tools for conviviality, creates something of a crisis for those professions and institutions which have traditionally been engaged with the elaboration and dissemination of knowledge, such as the university, publishing, and last, but by no means least, translators. Indeed, the Enlightenment idealism of knowledge dissemination can be exploited in the translation context by less scrupulous agents who use the rhetoric of collective emancipation to mask the private accumulation of profit (McDonough Dolmaya 2011: 97–110). In terms of a translation ecology, the illusion of freedom may conceal more insidious forms of control. Identifying whether translation tools are at the service of conviviality or 'increase regimentation, dependence, exploitation, or impotence' demands the forms of philological attentiveness which Doueihi sees as integral to an emerging digital humanism. However, the notion of humanism must be qualified if we are to move beyond the destructive hubris that often accompanied the use of the term to justify imperial crimes and ecological ravaging.

Consensualism

One of the repeated features of hegemonic humanism is consensualism, the notion that the human community is united by a set of self-evidently superior values (see Benasayag and del Rey 2007). An agonistic conception of human community, on the other hand, runs directly counter to the beatific visions of universal understanding underlying many public pronouncements on the topic of globalization, which were critiqued earlier in the borderless utopianism of particular representations of translation (Chapter 3). The agonistic conception takes as a starting premise the incomprehensibility of the Other. That is to say, human interaction is not simply the revelation of what is already there. In the movement to engage with the complex being of others, in the creation of some form of shared sense, some degree of commonality, the operation is not one of uncovering a universal substrate, waiting to be revealed in its pre-formed state, but the contingent construction of bottom-up commonality. This kind of bottom-up commonality is akin to the difficult universalism invoked earlier in this chapter.

It is useful in this context to employ the distinction made by François Jullien between the universal, the uniform, and the common. For Jullien, the universal is the universal of scientific reason, the claim, for example, that the atomic composition of water does not change wherever it is studied in the universe. Universal reason cannot suffer exceptions; there cannot be two hydrogen atoms in water in the United States and three in Australia, otherwise the claim is not universally valid. The uniform is a kind of perverse double of the universal, a phenomenon which has universal impact not because of the necessary implications of reason, but because of a skilfully engineered ease of access. An example would be global fast-food chains or the proliferation of similarly branded retail units in pedestrianized zones the world over. When it comes to defining the common, Jullien characterizes it as *fons* not *fundus*. What he means by this is that the common is not what is left at the bottom (*fundus*) once everything has been taken away and all the differences have been removed, but rather the source (*fons*) of what is potentially shareable through mutual intelligibility (Jullien 2008: 213). A group can work out what it has in common, what are common interests and concerns, but this work is processual. In other words, the working out is not the mechanical application of a pre-defined prescriptive agenda, but the constructed emergence of shared ideals, preoccupations, values. The common, then, is best understood not from a building perspective, as the ready implementation of a blueprint, but as a form of what Tim Ingold would call 'weaving', the negotiated, imminent emergence of sense through interactivity (Ingold 2000: 346).

This sense of the constructed nature of the common is caught in Georges Braque's comment on the two nineteenth-century landscape painters Émile Corot and Paul Trouillebert: 'The common is true. The similar is false. Trouillebert looks like Corot but they have nothing in common' (cited in Jullien 2008: 215). As becomes all too apparent when you travel abroad, being similar to someone (e.g. sharing the same nationality) does not mean that you necessarily have anything in common with them. This constructed nature of the common, which is conflicted and processual, must be at the core of any digital humanism if the latter is not to be indiscriminate, 'massive', and manipulatory in its effects. Given that much of what translation involves is attempting to construct a kind of commonality between different languages and cultures through a process of endless negotiation of meaning (no translation is ever definitive), the type of humanism it might espouse in the digital age must, of necessity, be *fons*, not *fundus*.

Progeneration

The convergence of the human and the material, the interaction between humans and technology in successive ages of translation, situates translation at one level in the emerging intellectual and cultural movement of transhumanism (Hansell and Grassie 2012; Blake, Molloy, and Shakespeare 2012). A core tenet of transhumanism is that evolving technologies will greatly enhance human intellectual, physical, and psychological capacities, and it was indeed in the context of 'augmented humanity' that the CEO of Google presented Conversation Mode, the translation app mentioned in Chapter 2). Posthumanist thinkers, for their part, share the transhumanists' belief in the significance of technology in our lives, but they are deeply critical of the unreflective scientism they see at work in transhumanist philosophy and are more anxious to situate humans and human reason within an overarching ecological framework (Wolfe 2009). It is obvious that the form of digital humanism advocated here for translation studies will become part of the dialogue around transhumanism and posthumanism, if only because of the fundamental interplay between human language and technology in past and present developments in translation practice.

One of the recurrent topics of debate in the area of the transhuman and the posthuman is of course the human body, not only how the body itself mutates through interactions with the digital tools it manipulates, but also how human bodies do or do not come into contact with each other in digital worlds. The notion of connectivity in a digital age bears directly on the position of translation within both culture and the academy. To see why this might be the case, I shall begin by looking briefly at an episode from James Joyce's *Ulysses*. In the Nestor section of the novel, Stephen Dedalus, in the guise of teacher, observes the slow progress of one of his less able students, Cyril Sargent. The pupil's first name is an ironic allusion to the saint who invented an alphabet and was also a translator. Sargent has been punished by the headmaster, Garret Deasy, for his failure to solve mathematical problems and has been set to writing out algebraic solutions from the blackboard into his copybook, entitled 'Sums':

> In long shaky strokes Sargent copied the data. Waiting always for a word of help his hand moved faithfully to the unsteady symbols, a faint hue of shame flickering behind his dull skin. *Amor matris*: subjective and objective genitive.
>
> (Joyce 1922: 163–64)

Stephen repeatedly reflects in this section of the novel on his own 'amor matris', his own relationship with his mother and his biological family. As Barry McCrea notes, Stephen finds parallels between his own situation and that of the hapless Sargent:

> Stephen, who is generally given to seeing parallels and symbols, immediately identifies the slow, unrealized Sargent with his own situation. He associates Sargent's abjection with what he imagines to be his own imprisonment in his biological family and the paradigms associated with it. Sargent's 'Sums', his book of selves, is a *copy*book, and a copied, genealogical self is what Stephen feels gloomily condemned to.
>
> (McCrea 2011: 112; his emphasis)

Of course, one of the most common reasons for a failure to appreciate the complexity of translation is that it is viewed as the activity of the hack, a kind of slavish copying of the original that deserves all the scorn the romantic critic can muster for the curse of the derivative. Cyril Sargent may be an unworthy successor to the gifted Cyril, who was one of the inventors of the first Slavic alphabet and a translator of the Bible into Old Church Slavonic. His association, however, with the rote activity of copying suggests the reductive, almost dismissive approach to translation that may be further strengthened by the seemingly mechanical reproducibility of the online translation service. There is, though, another dimension to the episode which is of equal importance when examining potential futures for translation.

To see how this might be the case, it is worth examining briefly the distinction the social anthropologist Tim Ingold makes between 'genealogy' and 'relation'. In the genealogical model, individuals are seen as entering the life-world with a set of ready-made attributes which they have received from their predecessors. The essential parts which go to make up a person, his or her 'culture', are handed on, more or less fully formed. The popular image for this conception of personhood and community is that someone has something in their 'blood' or, more recently, 'in their genes'. The relational model, on the other hand, relates to the concept of 'progeneration' which Ingold defines as the 'continual unfolding of an entire field of relationships within which different beings emerge with their particular forms, capacities and dispositions' (Ingold 2000: 142). That is to say, whereas the genealogical model is concerned with past histories of relationship, with the unfolding development of a bundle of preset attributes in a given space, the progenerative model is primarily concerned with current sets and fields of relationships for persons in a given lifeworld.

The genealogical model has obvious affinities with the notion of 'family' or, indeed, 'diaspora', in both a narrow nuclear and wider kinship definition of the notion. It is the model which clearly informed the 2004 Citizenship referendum in Ireland that introduced the notion of bloodline into definitions of Irish citizenship. In the genealogical model the descent line is separate from the life line, and life and growth become the realization of potentials that are already in place. So being Irish is being a member of a family which through immediate (domestic) or extended (diasporic) bloodline is endowed with a culture that is determined by essence rather than context.

One consequence of this model is that cultural difference is almost invariably construed as 'diversity'. That is to say, the notion of diversity, which is becoming something of a mantra of beatific official pronouncements on our multi-cultural world, supposes that different groups are possessed of different sets of ready-made attributes. These are juxtaposed in the shop windows of different contemporary states, and each group acting out their pre-defined cultural script contributes to the effervescent display of cultural diversity. So the invocation of diversity which is often seen as a way of countering nativist genealogical exclusiveness simply multiplies the examples of genealogical inheritances, rather than challenges the basic logic.

McCrea argues that what marks the emergence of the modernist narrative is the move away from the genealogical model towards alternative forms of kinship, whether it be Stephen Dedalus's relationship with Leopold Bloom, or Marcel leaving his much-loved family to enter into the transformative worlds of Swann and Charlus. It is arguable that the function of translation of many societies and cultures is to introduce speakers of a language into the 'company of strangers'. It is to move outside or beyond the genealogical model towards a mode of development that is progenerative. It is precisely the progenerative dimension to translation that must make it a recurrent object of suspicion for genealogical narratives of community and nation. In 1905, when Douglas Hyde, the future President of Ireland, went on a fundraising trip for the Irish language to the

United States, he paid a visit to then President of the United States Theodore 'Teddy' Roosevelt. Entertainment was not lavish, and after a simple main course they proceeded to a dessert of apples and green grapes washed down by a cup of tea and a glass of sherry. Roosevelt was in garrulous form and was no stranger to strongly held opinion. He revealed to his Irish guest his own vision of the multicultural:

> He was of the opinion that there was still too much 'colonialism' in America, that it was a nation made up of a lot of other nations and because there were so many Irish in the country, Americans should take anything that was good or worthwhile or interesting in the Irish and make it into their own.[9]
>
> (Hyde 1937: 15)

Roosevelt's primary concern was to construct a national community, but a community that would make a virtue of appropriative diversity. In order for this post-'colonialism' society to emerge he was, like Hyde, greatly preoccupied with the question of language, but his concern was not to see minority languages triumph, but to see English, the dominant host language of the United States, prevail. It was English that would allow for 'anything that was good or worthwhile' to be assimilated into the body politic. In a statement to the *Kansas City Star* in 1918, Roosevelt offered a précis of his thinking on the issue: 'Every immigrant who comes here should be required within five years to learn English or leave the country.' A year later, in a letter he wrote to the president of the American Defense Society, he declared, 'We have room for but one language here, and that is the English language ... and we have room for but one sole loyalty and that is a loyalty to the American people' (Pearson 1920: 19). The objective, in a sense, was to subordinate the progenerative energies of the translation contact with the foreign to a controlled project of genealogical continuity of one people speaking one language. A more contemporary manifestation of this form of recuperation is the extraordinary lack of interest that continues to be shown by many English literature departments throughout the English-speaking world in the phenomenon of translation, despite the fact that translation has been central to the evolution of literature and language in English (Ellis 2008; Braden, Cummings, and Gillespie 2010). It is as if to teach English literature in a predominantly chronological fashion is to imply a sense of genealogical relation or continuity, a role which was, in a sense, allotted to English 'polite letters' in the nineteenth century in British universities as part of the project of fashioning national and imperial subjects (Readings 1997).

The scale, extent, and spread of users of the internet mean, of course, that the company of strangers is now global. One of the challenges for translators and for translation studies is how to unleash the progenerative potential of the global, digital community to allow for the emergence of new forms of expression and engagement. If we are moving to 'the unsteady symbols' of the future, chief among those symbols will be the ever-changing, self-renewing figure of translation. More broadly, we will have to negotiate the perpetual challenge of what it means to be human in the translation age, knowing that the only certainty in our digital world is that there is none.

Notes

1 The house of translation

1 Entre les membres d'une même société des interactions sont constamment nécessaires, justement pour reproduire en permanence le lien social. L'éloignement freine ces possibilités d'interactions. Si un élément d'une société se trouve trop loin des autres, il risque fort de s'autonomiser. Le social est tissé en permanence par tout un ensemble de liens, tout un systèmes de ligatures, structures de parenté, langues, relations de production et de pouvoir ... Ces interactions ne supportent pas l'étirement, l'éloignement.

2 Plain speaking

1 Quoi qu'il en soit, que sa langue dominante soit ou non celle dans laquelle il rêve, cette aptitude des langues à fonctionner comme supports de pensée, de l'imagination et du rêve surplombe absolument, sans évidemment l'annuler, leur fonction d'instruments de communication

2 Sur le plan psychologique, faire le choix du français [c'est là] le signe d'une attitude combative, le contraire de l'esprit d'abandon et de renoncement ... Bien sûr, un esprit combatif ne garantit pas le succès, mais il est nécessaire. Comme dit le proverbe chinois, les seuls combats perdus d'avance sont ceux qu'on ne livre pas.

Sur le plan moral, c'est-à-dire sur le plan des valeurs qui est plus important encore, le choix du français, ou plutôt l'attitude détachée vis-à-vis de langue actuellement dominante dans le monde, signifie qu'on accorde plus d'importance à la recherche en elle-même qu'à sa communication. En d'autres termes ... l'amour de la vérité passe avant la vanité. Il ne s'agit pas de renoncer à communiquer avec les autres: la science est une aventure collective qui se poursuit de siècle en siècle, et même le plus solitaire des chercheurs dépend complètement de tout ce qu'il a appris et continue à recevoir chaque jour. Mais refuser d'accorder trop d'importance à la communication immédiate, c'est se souvenir du sens de la recherche scientifique.

3 Quatres grands aspects présents dans cette critique du conformisme au nom d'une véritable démocratie fondée sur l'individualisme sont relayés par la contre-culture puis par l'idéologie de l'internet: le refus de la conformité aux normes dominantes, l'exaltation du mouvement, le caractère fondamental de la voix et de la conversation et la remise en cause des catégories sociales du public et du privé.

3 Translating limits

1 mettre de l'ordre, à partir d'un point, dans le monde environnant.

2 Cette servitude volontaire est le commencement de la liberté. Il n'y a pas de meilleure manière d'arriver à prendre conscience de ce qu'on sent soi-même que d'essayer de

recréer en soi ce qu'a senti un maître. Dans cet effort profond, c'est notre pensée elle-même que nous mettons, avec la sienne, au jour.

3 Inn diesen reden allen / obs gleich die Lateinische oder Griechische sprache nicht thut / so thuts doch die Deudsche / und ist ihr art / das sie das wort (Allein) hinzu setzt / auff das / das wort (nicht odder kein) deste völliger und deutlicher sey / Den wiewol ich auch sage / Der Bawer bringt korn und kein gelt / So laut doch das wort (kein gelt) nicht so völlig und deutlich / als wenn ich sage / Der Bawer bringt allein korn und kein gelt / und hilfft hie das wort (Allein) dem wort (kein) so viel / das es eine völlige Deudsche klare rede wird / denn man mus nicht die buchstaben inn der Lateinischen sprachen fragen / wie man sol Deudsch reden / wie diese Esel thun / Sondern man mus die mutter ihm hause / die kinder auff der gassen / den gemeinen man auff dem marckt drümb fragen / und den selbigen auff das maul sehen / wie sie reden / und darnach dolmetschen / so verstehen sie es denn / und mercken / das man Deudsch mit ihn redet. (Translation by Michael Marlowe.)

4 Lieber / nu es verdeudscht und bereit ist / kans ein jeder lesen und meistern / Leufft einer itzt mit den Augen durch drey odder vier bletter / und stösst nicht ein mal an / wird aber nicht gewar / welche wacken und klötze da gelegen sind / da er itzt uber hin gehet / wie uber ein gehoffelt bret / da wir haben müst schwitzen und uns engsten / ehe denn wir solche wacken und klötze aus dem wege reumeten / auf das man kündte so fein daher gehen. Es ist gut pflügen / wenn der acker gereinigt ist. Aber den wald und die stöcke ausrotten / und den acker zurichten / da wil niemand an. Es ist bey der welt kein danck zu verdienen. (Translation by Michael Marlowe.)

5 Gentibus est aliis tellus data limite certo: Romanae spatium est Urbis et orbis idem.

5 Details

1 Quand un sujet note un détail, éventuellement minime, et quand on lui demande de ne pas y faire attention, alors il peut être sûr que c'est là que ça se passe.

2 si penser par détails mène à l'universel c'est nécesairement à l'universel difficile.

3 Entre cultures, je ne me fierai pas à ces *différences* prétendument caractéristiques, étiquetées comme telles et formant standard (les traits les plus voyants sont souvent les moins intéressants): en se figeant, elles font barrière à l'intelligence. Mais, je l'ai dit, je fais travailler des *écarts* – la notion n'est pas de rangement mais exploratoire: ouvrir un écart, c'est pratiquer une brèche dans le conformisme, réintroduire de la tension dans la pensée, bref, remettre raison en chantier.

4 les valeurs sont les vecteurs d'une affirmation de soi, elles s'inscrivent, quoi qu'on prétende, dans un rapport de forces; tandis que les ressources sont indéfiniment exportables (exploitables) et sont disponibles à tous.

5 J'entends résonner un entrechoc entre la proposition universelle au singulier *Tout homme est libre* et la proposition au pluriel *Tous les hommes sont libres*. La première est vraie, la seconde est fausse. Mais du même coup, on comprend que la proposition au singulier n'est vraie qu'en intensité. Elle est universelle dans la mesure exacte où elle porte le nom *homme* à son intensité maximale. Elle demeurerait universelle, quand bien même les hommes seraient libres nulle part.

6 L'humanisme numérique, parce qu'il a affaire à une technique globale indissociable de l'humain, et qu'il produit des objets inédits, tout en modifiant notre regard sur les objets classiques, représente une nouvelle evolution et, surtout, une discipline naissante.

7 qui enrichit le contexte et permet une évaluation plus équilibrée de certaines des promesses de la technique.

8 Cet héritage semble autoriser au moins deux tendances contradictoires, ancrées, l'une, dans l'accomplissement de la culture du livre et de ses institutions (l'université,

l'édition, la presse), l'autre, dans l'idéalisme du libre partage et de la circulation du savoir.

9 Badh é a bharamhail féin go raibh an iomarcaidh 'coilíneachta' i nAmerice fós, go mbadh náisiún é a raibh móran náisiún fighte le chéile ann, agus ó bhí oiread sin Éireannach 'na measg gur cheart d'Americe gach rud maith nó fiúntach nó spéisamhail ar bith do bhí i mbeatha na nGaedhael do ghlacadh uatha, agus a gcuid féin a dhéanamh de.

Bibliography

Adams, D. (1979) *The Hitchhiker's Guide to the Galaxy*. London: Pan Macmillan.

Adams, J.N. (2008) *Bilingualism and the Latin Language*, Cambridge: Cambridge University Press.

Adams, R.M. (1966) *The Evolution of Urban Society: Early Mesopotamia and Prehispanic Mexico*, Chicago: Aldine.

Adkins, L. and Adkins, R.A. (2000) *The Keys of Egypt: The Obsession to Decipher Egyptian Hieroglyphs*, New York: HarperCollins.

Agamben, G. (2009) *'What is an Apparatus' and Other Essays*, tr. D. Kishik, Palo Alto, CA: Stanford University Press.

Agassi, A. (2010) *Open: An Autobiography*, New York: HarperCollins.

Alves, F. and Liparini Campos, T. (2009) 'Translation Technology in Time: Investigating the Impact of Translation Memory Systems and Time Pressure on Types of Internal and External Support', in Göpferich, S., Jakobsen, A.L. and Mees, I.M. (eds) *Behind the Mind: Methods, Models and Results in Translation Process Research*, Copenhagen: Samfundslitteratur Press, 191–218.

Anastasiou, D. and Schäler, R. (2010) 'Translating Vital Information: Localisation, Internationalisation and Globalisation', *Syn-Thèses*, 3, 11–25.

Anderson, B. (2006) *Imagined Communities: Reflections on the Origins and Spread of Nationalism*, revised edition, London: Verso.

Andrews, C. (1985) *The British Museum Book of the Rosetta Stone*, London: British Museum Press.

Anholt, S. (2007) *Brand New Justice: The Upside of Global Branding*, Oxford: Butterworth Heinemann.

Apter, E. (2006) *The Translation Zone: A New Comparative Literature*, Princeton, NJ: Princeton University Press.

——(2008) 'Biography of a Translation: *Madame Bovary* between Eleanor Marx and Paul de Man', *Translation Studies*, 1, 1, 73–89.

Apuleius (1989) *Metamorphoses*, tr. J.A. Hanson, 2 vols, Harvard, MA: Loeb Classical Library.

Arendt, H. (1973) *The Origins of Totalitarianism*, London: Harcourt.

Assouline, P. (2011) *La Condition du traducteur*, Paris: Centre National du Livre.

Atkinson, W.K. (1952) *The Lusiads* [Camões], Harmondsworth: Penguin.

Bacon, F. (1863), *Novum Organum*, tr. James Spedding, Robert Leslie Ellis, and Douglas. Denon Heath in Francis Bacon, *The Works*, Vol. VIII, Boston, MA: Taggard and Thompson.

Baker, M. (2006) *Translation and Conflict: A Narrative Account*, London: Routledge.

Bassnett, S. (2011) *Reflections on Translation*, Bristol: Multilingual Matters.

Bates, E.S. (1943) *Intertraffic: Studies in Translation*, London: Cape.

Beckett, S. (1983) *Disjecta: Miscellaneous Writings and a Dramatic Fragment*, London: Calder.

Bellos, D. (2011) *Is That a Fish in Your Ear: Translation and the Meaning of Everything*, London: Penguin.

Belot, L. (2012) 'Souriez, vous êtes achetés', *Le Monde*, Cahier du monde, 20935, 12 May, 1, 4–5.

Benasayag, M. and del Rey, A. (2007) *L'Éloge du conflit*, Paris: La Découverte.

Benjamin, W. (1973) *Illuminations*, tr. H. Zohn, London: Fontana.

Bernal, M. (1987) *Black Athena: the Afro-Asiatic Roots of Ancient Civilisation*. Vol. I: *The Fabrication of Ancient Greece 1785–1985*, London: Free Association Books.

——(1991) *Black Athena: the Archaeological and Documentary Evidence*, London: Free Association Books.

Bessonne, M. (2011) 'Culte de l'internet et transparence: l'héritage de la philosophie américaine', *Esprit*, 376, July, 145–59.

Blake, C., Molloy, C., and Shakespeare, S. (eds) (2012) *Beyond Human: From Animality to Transhumanism*, London: Continuum.

Blondeau, O. and Allard, L. (2007) *Devenir Média*, Paris: Éd. Amsterdam.

Boéri, J. (2008) 'A Narrative Account of the Babels vs. Naumann Controversy: Competing Perspectives on Activism in Conference Interpreting', *The Translator*, 14, 1, 21–50.

Bowker, L. (2007) 'Translation Memory and "Text"', in Bowker, L. (ed.) *Lexicography, Terminology and Translation: Text-Based Studies in Honour of Ingrid Meyer*, Ottawa: Ottawa University Press, 175–87.

Braden, G., Cummings, R., and Gillespie, S. (2010) *The Oxford History of Literary Translation in English*, Vol. II, Oxford: Oxford University Press.

Bradley, A.C. (1901) *Poetry for Poetry's Sake*, Oxford: Clarendon Press.

Braunstein, P. and Doyle, W.D. (2001) (eds) *Imagine Nation: The American Counterculture of the 1960's and the 70's*, London and New York: Routledge.

Breton, P. (2000) *Le Culte de l'internet: une menace pour le lien social?*, Paris: La Découverte.

Bridges, R.S. (1916) *Ibant Obscuri*, Oxford: Clarendon Press.

Brodzki, B. (2007) *Can These Bones Live? Translation, Survival and Cultural Memory*, Stanford, CA: Stanford University Press, 2007.

Brook, T. (2008) *Vermeer's Hat: The Seventeenth Century and the Dawn of the Global World*, London: Profile.

Brower, R. (ed.) (1959) *On Translation*, Cambridge, MA: Harvard University Press.

Brown J.S. and Weiser M. (1996) 'The Coming Age of Calm Technology'. Available at: http://www.ubiq.com/hypertext/weiser/acmfuture2endnote.htm (accessed 18 July 2010).

Büchler, A., Guthrie, A., Donahaye, J., and Tekgül, D. (2011) *Literary Translation from Arabic, Hebrew and Turkish into English in the United Kingdom and Ireland, 1990–2010*, Aberystwyth: Literature Across Frontiers.

Burke, P. (1998) *The European Renaissance: Centres and Peripheries*, Oxford: Blackwell.

——(2004) *Languages and Communities in Early Modern Europe*, Cambridge: Cambridge University Press.

——and Po-chia Hsia, R. (eds) (2007) *Cultural Translation in Early Modern Europe*, Cambridge: Cambridge University Press.

Burton, R. (1927) *The Anatomy of Melancholy*, ed. Dell, F. and Jordan-Smith, P., New York: Tudor.

Butler, S. (1970) *Essays on Art, Life, and Science*, Port Washington, NY: Kennikat Press.

Calderini, R. (1953) 'De interpretibus quaedam in papyris', *Rivista di filologia e di instruzione classica* 33, 341–46.

Cano, E. (2011) '2011, 2.0: Le village planétaire', *Libération*, 30 December, 22–23.

Carpo, M. (2011) *The Alphabet and the Algorithim*, Cambridge, MA: MIT Press.

Carr, N. (2010) *The Shallows*, London: Atlantic.

Casanova, P. (1999) *La République mondiale des lettres*, Paris: Seuil.

Casson, H.N. (1910) *The History of the Telephone*, Chicago: A.C. McClurg & Co.

Cerny, P. (1997) 'Paradoxes of the Competition State: The Dynamics of Political Globalization', *Government and Opposition*, 32, 2, 251–74.

Cerquigini, B. (1989) *Éloge de la variante: histoire critique de la philologie*, Paris: Seuil.

Childe, G. (1964) *What Happened in History*, Harmondsworth: Penguin.

Clapham, M. (1957) 'Printing', in *A History of Technology: From the Renaissance to the Industrial Revolution c.1500–c.1750*, Vol. III, Oxford: Oxford University Press, pp. 377–416.

Clarke, R.A. and Knake, R. (2010) *Cyber War: The Next Threat to National Security and What to Do about It*, New York: HarperCollins.

Clicktale (2008) 'Puzzling Web Habits across the Globe', Clicktale Blog, 31 July. Available at: http://www.clicktale.com/2008/07/31/puzzling-web-habits-across-the-globe-part-1 (accessed 8 September 2010).

Cohen, J.M. (1950) *Don Quixote* [Cervantes], Harmondsworth: Penguin.

Cooper, Colin (2009) 'Is Translating Crowdsourcing Unethical?' Available at: http://colincooper.net/?p=31 (accessed 23 September 2010).

Coppens, Y. and Picq, P. (2001) *Aux Origines de l'humanité*, Paris: Fayard.

Cronin, M. (2002) 'The Empire Talks Back: Orality, Heteronomy and the Cultural Turn in Interpreting Studies', in Gentzler, E. and Tymoczko, M. (eds) *Translation and Power*, Boston and Amherst: University of Massachusetts Press, 45–62.

——(2003) *Translation and Globalization*, London and New York: Routledge.

——(2000) *Across the Lines: Travel, Language, Translation*, Cork: Cork University Press.

——(2005) 'Double Take: Figuring the Other and the Politics of Translation', *Palimpsestes*, 17, 13–24.

——(2006) 'Currencies of Exchange: Literature and the Future of European Language Diversity', *Futures*, 38, 2, 146–57.

Crowley, J. (2003) *The Translator*, New York: HarperCollins.

Crowley, R. (2011) *City of Fortune: How Venice Won and Lost a Naval Empire*, London: Faber and Faber.

Crystal, D. (2003) *English as a Global Language*, Cambridge: Cambridge University Press.

——(2006) *Language and the Internet*, 2nd edition, Cambridge: Cambridge University Press.

Damrosch, D. (2003) *What is World Literature?*, Princeton, NJ: Princeton University Press.

——(2008) 'What Could a Message Mean to a Cloud? Kalidasa Travels West', *Translation Studies*, 1, 1, 41–54.

Davie, M. (2005) 'The Venetian Version', in Barron, W.J.S. and Burgess, G.S. (eds) *The Voyage of St. Brendan. Representative Versions of the Legend in English Translation*, 2nd edition, Exeter: University of Exeter Press, 155–230.

Debray, R. (2010) *L'Éloge des frontières*, Paris: Gallimard.

Deleuze, G. (1988) *Le Pli: Leibniz et le baroque*, Paris: Éditions de Minuit.

Delisle, J. and Woodsworth, J. (1995) *Translators in History*, Amsterdam: John Benjamins.

Dennis, K. and Urry, J. (2007) 'The Digital Axis of Post-Autombility', Department of Sociology, Lancaster University, 1–74. Available at: http://www.kingsleydennis.com/The%20Digital%20Nexus%20of%20Post-Automobility.pdf (accessed 5 September 2010).

de Vere White, T. (1967) *The Parents of Oscar Wilde: Sir William and Lady Wilde*, London: Hodder and Stoughton.

Dixon, K.R. and Southern, P. (1997) *The Roman Cavalry*, London: Routledge.

Dodds, E.R. (1936) *Journal and Letters of Stephen MacKenna*, London: Constable.

Doueihi, M. (2011) *Pour Un Humanisme numérique*, Paris: Seuil.

Eagleton, T. (2004) *After Theory*, London: Penguin.

Eco, U. (2010) *The Search for the Perfect Language*, London: Fontana.

Eddy, M. (2012) 'Unlikely Surge of Upstart Pirate Party Complicates German Political Landscape', *New York Times*, 9 May, A6.

Edgerton, D. (2006) *The Shock of the Old: Technology and Global History since 1900*, London: Profile.

Ed Wallach Research Group (2012) 'Senior Language Analysts'. Available at: http://www.dc-jobs.jobfox.com/government/intel/senior (accessed 22 December 2011).

Eisenstein, E.L. (1980) *The Printing Press as an Agent of Change*, Cambridge: Cambridge University Press.

Eliot, T.S. (1928) *For Lancelot Andrewes: Essays on Style and Order*, London: Faber and Gwyer.

Ellis, R. (2008) *The Oxford History of Literary Translation in English*, Vol. I, Oxford: Oxford University Press.

Ellis-Fermor, U. (1950) *Hedda Gabler/The Pillars of the Community/The Wild Duck* [Ibsen], Harmondsworth: Penguin.

Ellmann, R. (1987) *Oscar Wilde*, London: Penguin.

Engels, F. (1934) *Dialectics of Nature*, tr. C. Dutt, Moscow: Progress.

Engle, P. and Engle, H.N. (1976) *Writing from the World*, Iowa: Iowa University Press.

Estival, D. (2005) 'The Language Translation Interface: A Perspective from Users', *Machine Translation*, 19, 2, 175–92.

Feuerbach (1839) *Towards a Crtiique of Hegel's Philosophy*, tr. Z. Hanfi. Available at: http://www.marxists.org/reference/archive/feuerbach/works/critique (accessed 25 May 2012).

Flaubert, G. (1886) *Madame Bovary: Provincial Manners*, tr. E. Marx Aveling, London: W.W. Gibbings.

Förster, M., Jesuit, D., and Smeeding, T. (2003) *Regional Poverty and Income Inequality in Central and Eastern Europe: Evidence from the Luxembourg Income Study*, World Institute for Development Economics Research, Dsicussion Paper No. 65. Available at: http://www.wider.unu.edu/publications/dps/dps2003/dp2003–65.pdf (accessed 11 December 2011).

Foster, T. (2010) 'Using Translation Technology at Sun Microsystems'. Available at: http://developers.sun.com/dev/gadc/technicalpublications/whitepapers/translationtechnologyun.html (accessed 15 May 2012).

Frazier, J.G. (1921) *The Library* [Appollodorus], Cambridge, MA: Harvard University Press.

Friedman, T. (2006) *The World is Flat: The Globalized World in the Twenty-first Century*, London: Penguin.

Friel, B. (1981) *Translations*, London: Faber and Faber.

Garcia, I. (2011) 'Translating by Post-editing: Is it the Way Forward?', *Machine Translation*, 25, 217–37.

Gavan Duffy, C. (1883) *Four Years of Irish History, 1845–1849*, London: Cassell.

Gazagnadou, D. (1994) *La Poste à relais: la diffusion d'une technique de pouvoir à travers l'Eurasie*, Paris: Kimé.

Ginzburg, C. (2000) *No Island is an Island: Four Glances at English Literature in a World Perspective*, New York: Columbia University Press.

Gleick, J. (2011) *The Information: A History, a Theory, a Flood*, London: Fourth Estate.

Glenny, M. (2011) *Dark Market: Cyberthieves, Cybercops and You*, London: Vintage.

Globalization and Localization Association (GALA) (2012) 'About the Localization Industry'. Available at: http//www.gala-global-org/about-localization-industry (accessed 16 April 2012).

Goble, P. (2009) 'Kremlin Assumes Control for Promoting Russia's Image Abroad'. Available at: http://politicom.moldova.org/news/kremlin-assumes-control-for-promoting-russiasimage-abroad-201549-eng.html (accessed 20 September 2012).

Godelier, M. (2004) *Métamorphoses de la parenté*, Paris: Fayard.

Goodman, N. (1976) *The Languages of Art: An Approach to a Theory of Symbols*, 2nd edition, Indianapolis, IN: Bobbs-Merill.

Goody, J. (2006) *The Theft of History*, Cambridge: Cambridge University Press.

Gouadec, D. (2007) *Translation as a Profession*, Amsterdam: John Benjamins.

Graddol, D. (2001) 'English in the Future', in Burns, A. and Coffin, C. (eds) *Analyzing English in a Global Context: A Reader*, London: Routledge, 26–37.

Grataloup, C. (2011) *Faut-il penser autrement l'histoire du monde*, Paris: Armand Colin.

Greenblatt, S. (2011) *The Swerve: How the Renaissance Began*, London: The Bodley Head.

Greenfield, A. (2006) *Everyware: The Dawning Age of Ubiquitous Computing*, Berkeley, CA: New Riders.

Grin, F. (2004) 'On the Costs of Cultural Diversity', in van Parijs, P. (ed.) *Cultural Diversity versus Economic Solidarity*, Brussels: De Boeck Université, 189–202.

Gura, P.F. (2008) *American Transcendentalism: A History*, New York: Hill and Wang.

Hagège, C. (1985) *L'Homme de paroles*, Paris: Gallimard.

——(2012) *Contre La Pensée unique*, Paris: Odile Jacob.

Hansell, G.R. and Grassie, W. (eds) (2012) *H+/–: Transhummanism and its Critics*, Xlibris, New York.

Héran, F. (2009) *Figures de la parenté*, Paris: Presses Universitaires de France.

Hermann, A. (1956) 'Dolmetschen in Altertum. Ein Beitrag zur antiken Kulturgeschichte', in Theime, K., Hermann, A., and Glässer, E., *Beiträge zur Geschichte des Dolmetschens*, Munich: Iser Verlag, 25–29.

Hughes, T. (1983) *Modern Poetry in Translation*, Modern Poetry in Translation: New York.

Hyde, D. (1937) *Mo Thurus go Meiriceá nó i measg na nGaedheal ins an Oileán Úr*, Dublin: Oifig Díolta Foilseacháin Rialtais.

Hyman, A. (1982) *Charles Babbage: Pioneer of the Computer*, Princteon, NJ: Princeton University Press.

Illich, I. (1990) *Tools for Conviviality*, London: Marion Boyars.

——(1995) *Deschooling Society*, new edition, London: Marion Boyars.

Ingold, T. (1986) *Evolution and Social Life*, Cambridge: Cambridge University Press.

——(2000) *The Perception of the Environment: Essays in Livelihood, Dwelling and Skill*, London and New York: Routledge.

——(2011) *Being Alive: Essays on Movement Knowledge and Perception*, London: Routledge.

Internet World Stats by Language (2012). Available at: http://www.internetworldstats.com (accessed 2 February 2012).

Italiano, F. (2012) 'Translating Geographies: The *Navigatio Sancti Brendani* and its Venetian Translation', *Translation Studies*, 5, 1, 1–16.

Jansen, S. (2011) 'Redesigning a Nation: *Welcome to E-stonia, 2001–2018*', in Kaneva, N. (ed.) *Branding Post-Communist Nations: Marketizing National Identities in the 'New' Europe*, London: Routledge, 120–44.

Jidejian, N. (1991) *Tyre through the Ages*, Beirut: Librairie Orientale.

Jiménez-Crespo, M.A. (2011) 'From Many One: Novel Approaches to Translation Quality in a Social Network Era', *Linguistica Antverpiensia*, 10, 131–52.

Joscelyne, A. (2011) 'Interoperability and Open Tools'. Available at: http://www.trans lationautomation.com/technology/interoperability-and-open-tools.html (accessed 28 May 2012).

Joyce, J. (1922; 1971 edition) *Ulysses*, Harmondsworth: Penguin.

——(1939) *Finnegans Wake*, Lonodon: Faber and Faber.

Judet de la Combe, P. and Wismann, H. (2004) *L'Avenir des langues: repenser les humanités*, Paris: Éditions du Cerf.

Judt, T. (2010) *Ill Fares the Land*, London: Penguin.

Jullien, F. (2008) *De L'Universel, de l'uniforme, du commun et du dialogue entre les cultures*, Paris: Fayard.

——(2010) *Le Pont des singes: de la diversité à venire*, Paris: Galilée.

Kaufmann, J.-C. (2011) *Le Coeur à l'ouvrage: théorie de l'action ménagère*, 2nd edition, Paris: Nathan.

Kay, M. (1997) 'The Proper Place of Men and Machines in Language Translation', *Machine Translation*, 12, 1/2, 3–23.

Keen, A. (2008) *The Cult of the Amateur: How Blogs, MySpace, YouTube and the Rest of Today's User-Generated Media Are Killing Our Culture and Economy*, 2nd edition, London: Nicholas Brealey.

Kelly, N. (2009) 'Freelance Translators Clash with LinkedIn over Crowdsourced Translation'. Available at: http://www.commonsesneadvisory.com/Default.aspx?Contenttype=Article DetAD&tabID=63&Aid=591&moduleId=391 (accessed 22 September 2012).

——, Ray R., and De Palma D.A. (2011) 'From crawling to sprinting: Community translation goes mainstream', in O'Hagan, M. (ed.) *Translation as a Social Activity, Community Translation 2.0*, New Series: Themes in Translation Studies, *Linguistica Antverpiensia*, 10, 75–96.

Kim, J.-Y. (2011) 'President's Message'. Available at: http://www.litkorea.net/ ke_01_02_011.do (accessed 20 December 2011).

Koehn, P. (2009) *Statistical Machine Translation*, Cambridge: Cambridge University Press.

Kurz, I. (1986) 'Dolmetschen in Alten Rom', *Babel*, 32, 4, 215–20.

Lafforgue, L. (2005) 'Le Français, au service des sciences', *Pour la Science*, March, 32.

Lanchester, J. (2012) 'Marx at 193', *London Review of Books*, 34, 7, 5 April, 7–10.

Lash, S. (2010) *Intensive Culture: Social Theory, Religion and Contemporary Capitalism*, London: Sage.

Lee, D. (1955) *The Republic* [Plato], Harmondsworth: Penguin.

Leigh, D. and Harding, L. (2011) *WikiLeaks: Inside Julian Assange's War on Secrecy*, London: Guardian Books.

Lenard, P.T., Straehle, C., and Brooks, T. (eds) (2012) *Health Inequalities and Global Justice*, Edinburgh: Edinburgh University Press.

Leroi-Gourhan, A. (1965) *Le Geste et la parole: la mémoire et ses rythmes*, Paris: Albin Michel.

Lévi-Strauss, C. (2008) 'How the Social Sciences Have Humanised Technical Civilisation', *Unesco Courier*, 5, 25–28.

Lindberg, D.C. (2007) *The Beginnings of Western Science: The European Scientific Tradition in Philosophical, Religious and Institutional Context, Prehistory to AD 1450*, 2nd edition, Chicago: University of Chicago Press.

Littau, K. (2011) 'First Steps towards a Media History of Translation', *Translation Studies*, 4, 3, 261–81.

Luther, M. (1909) 'Ein sendbrief D.M. Luthers. Von Dolmetzschen und Fürbit der heiligenn', in *Dr Martin Luthers Werke*, Weimar: Hermann Boehlaus Nachfolge, Book 30, Vol. II, 632–46.

Lyons, J. (2010) *The House of Wisdom: How the Arabs Transformed Western Civilization*, London: Bloomsbury.

McCrea, B. (2011) *The Company of Strangers: Family and Narrative in Dickens, Conan Doyle, Joyce and Proust*, New York: Columbia University Press.

McDonough Dolmaya, J. (2011) 'The Ethics of Crowdsourcing', in O'Hagan, M. (ed.) *Translation as a Social Activity, Community Translation 2.0*, New Series: Themes in Translation Studies, *Linguistica Antverpiensia*, 10, 97–110.

McElduff, S. (2009) 'Living at the Level of the Word: Cicero's Rejection of the Interpreter as Translator', *Translation Studies*, 2, 2, 133–46

McGilchrist, I. (2009) *The Master and His Emissary: The Divided Brain and the Making of the Western World*, New Haven, CT: Yale University Press.

McGrath, A. (2001) *In the Beginning: The Story of the King James Bible*, London: Hodder and Stoughton.

McLuhan, M. (2001) *Understanding Media: The Extensions of Man*, 2nd edition (first edition 1964), London: Routledge.

Meadows, D.H., Meadows, D.L., Randers, J., and Behrens, W.W. (1972) *The Limits to Growth*, New York: Universe Books.

Mehrez, S. (ed.) (2012) *Translating Egypt's Revoluton: The Language of Tahrir Square*, Cairo: The American University in Cairo Press.

Melby, A. (1997) 'Some Notes on *The Proper Place of Men and Machines in Language Translation*', *Machine Translation*, 12, 29–34.

Melville, J. (1999) *Mother of Oscar: The Life of Jane Francesca Wilde*, London: Allison and Busby.

Mercier, P. (2011) *Perlmann's Silence*, London: Atlantic.

Mihalache, I. (2008) 'Community Experience and Expertise: Translators, Technologies and Electronic Networks of Practice', *Translation Studies*, 1, 1, 55–72.

Milner, J.-C. (2011) *Clartés de tout: de Lacan à Marx, d'Aristote à Mao*, Lagrasse: Verdier.

Mitchell, W. (1995) *The City of Bits*, London: MIT Press.

Montgomery, S.L. (2000) *Science in Translation: Movements of Knowledge through Cultures and Time*, Chicago: University of Chicago Press.

Morrison, P. and Morrison, E. (1961) *Charles Babbage and His Calculating Engines*, London: Dover.

Mulcaster, R. (1582) *The First Part of the Elementarie Which Entreateth Chefelie of the Right Writing of Our English Tung*, London: Thomas Vautroullier.

Murray, A.T. (1924) *The Iliad* [Homer], London: Heinemann.

Nabokov, V. (1955) 'Problems of Translation: *Onegin* in English', *Partisan Review*, 22, 496–512.

——(1980) *Lectures on Literature*, New York: Harcourt.

Newmark, P. (1981) *Approaches to Translation*, Oxford: Pergamon Press.

——(1993) *Paragraphs on Translation*, Clevedon: Multilingual Matters.

——(1996) *More Paragraphs on Translation*, Clevedon; Multilingual Matters.

Novak, M. (2010) 'The Meaning of Transarchitecture'. Available at: http://www.fen-om.com/network/2010/03/05/the-meaning-of-trans-architecture-marcos-novak/ (accessed 1 October 2010).

Nye, J. (1991) *Bound to Lead: The Changing Nature of American Power*, New York: Basic Books.

——(2004) *Soft Power: The Means to Success in World Politics*, New York: Public Affairs.

O'Connor, U. (ed.) (2004). *The Joyce We Knew*, Dingle: Brandon.

O'Driscoll, K. (2011) *Retranslation through the Centuries: Jules Verne in English*, Bern: Peter Lang.

O'Hagan, M. (2009) 'Evolution of User-Generated Translation: Fansubs, Translation Hacking and Crowdsourcing', *Journal of Internationalization and Localization*, 1, 1, 94–121.

——(2011) 'Introduction', in O'Hagan, M. (ed.) *Translation as a Social Activity, Community Translation 2.0*, New Series: Themes in Translation Studies, *Linguistica Antverpiensia*, 10, 11–23.

Oldfather, W.A. (1926) *The Discourses as Reported by Arrian, the Manual and Fragments* [Epictetus], New York: G.P. Putnam.

Olohan, M. (2011) 'Translators and Translation Technology: The Dance of Agency', *Translation Studies*, 4, 3, 342–57.

O'Neill, P. (1985) *Ireland and Germany: A Study in Literary Relations*, Bern: Peter Lang.

Ostler, N. (2011) *The Last Lingua Franca: The Rise and Fall of World Languages*, London: Penguin.

O'Sullivan, C. (2011) *Translating Popular Film*, Basingstoke: Palgrave Macmillan.

Pearson, E.L. (1920) *Theodore Roosevelt*, New York: Macmillan.

Phillimore, J.S. (1919) *Some Remarks on Translation and Translators*, Oxford: Oxford University Press.

Phillipson, R. (2003) *English-Only Europe? Challenging Language Policy*, London: Routledge.

Pym, A. (2001) 'Against Praise of Hybridity', *Across Languages and Cultures*, 2, 2, 195–207.

Quest Visual (2012) *Word Lens*, iPhone app. (accessed 28 January 2012).

Rahman, Z.H. (2006) 'Hope of Escape Lost in Translation', *Sunday Times*, 17 December, p. 22.

Ramadan, S. (2002) *Leaves of Narcissus*, Cairo: The American University in Cairo Press.

Rastier, F. (2007) 'Les Langues sont-elles des instruments de communication', in Fernandez-Vest, J. (ed.) *Combat pour les langues du monde/Fighting for the World's Languages*, Paris: L'Harmattan, 415–30.

Ratliff, E. (2006) 'Me Translate Pretty One Day', *Wired*, 14, 12, December, 1–3.

Rawnsley, A. (2011) 'Military's Newest Recruit: C-3PO', *Wired*, 19, 4, April, 14. Available at: http://www.wired.com/dangerroom/2011/04/milit (accessed 10 April 2012).

Ray, J.D. (2007) *The Rosetta Stone and the Rebirth of Ancient Egypt*, Cambridge, MA: Harvard University Press.

Ray, R. (2009) *Crowdsourcing: Crowd Wants to Help You Reach New Markets*, Romainmôtier: Localization Industry Standards Association.

Readings, B. (1997) *The University in Ruins*, Cambridge, MA: Harvard University Press.

Reeves, N. (2002) 'Translation, International English and the Planet of Babel', *English Today*, 18, 4, 21–28.

Remnick, D. (2005) 'The Translation Wars', *New Yorker*, 7 November, 35–49.

Richards, I.A. (1953) 'Towards a Theory of Translating', in Wright, A.F. (ed.) *Studies in Chinese Thought*, Chicago: University of Chicago Press.

Rieu, E.V. (1946) *The Odyssey* [Homer], Harmondsworth: Penguin.

Risen, C. (2005) 'Re-branding America: Marketing Gurus Think They Can Help "Re-position" the United States – and Save American Foreign Policy', *Boston Globe*. Available at: http://www.boston.com/news/globe/ideas/articles/2005/03/13/re_branding_america (accessed 3 November 2011)

Robinson, D. (1997) *Western Translation Theory from Herodotus to Nietzsche*, Manchester: St Jerome Press.

Rotondo, J.P. (2011) 'Literature Knows No Frontiers: John Galsworthy and the Shaping of PEN', *Daily Pen American*, 11 August. Available at: http://www.pen.org/blog/?p=2086 (accessed 22 January 2012).

Rusten, J., Cunningham, I.C., and Knox, A.D. (1993) *Characters Herodas Mimes Cercidas and the Choliambic Poets* [Theophrastus], Cambridge, MA: Harvard University Press.

Samuelsson-Brown, G. (2006) *Managing Translation Services*, Clevedon: Multilingual Matters.

Sanders, R. (2010) *German: Biography of a Language*, New York: Oxford University Press.

Savory, T.H. (1957) *The Art of Translation*, London: Cape

Schäler, R. (2007) 'Localization', in Baker, M. and Saldanha, G. (eds) *Encylopedia of Translation Studies*, 2nd edition, London and New York: Routledge.

Schell, M. (2008) 'What is Global English?' Available at: http//www.globalenglish.info/global.html (accessed 23 March 2010).

Schmidt, E. (2010) 'IFA International Keynote'. Available at: http//www.m.youtube.com/?reload=3&rdm=4q07vhs (accessed 3 April 2012).

Schnerb, R. (1993) *Le XIXè Siècle*, Paris: PUF.

Schonfeld, E. (2009) 'Facebook Spreads its Crowdsourced Translations across the Web, and the World'. Available at: http://techcrunch.com/2009/09/29/facebook-spreads-its-crowdsourced-translations-across-the-web-and-the-world (accessed 3 July 2011).

Schröder, H. (1989) *Additions and Corrections to Richard Ellmann's Oscar Wilde*, privately published.

Scientific American, (1880) 'The Future of the Telephone', 10 January.

Sennett, R. (1993) *The Uses of Disorder: Personal Identity and City Life*, New York: W. W. Norton.

Shannon, C. and Weaver, W. (1949) *The Mathematical Theory of Communication*, Urbana: University of Illinois Press.

Shields, K. (2000) *Gained in Translation: Language, Poetry and Identity in Twentieth-Century Ireland*, Bern and Oxford: Peter Lang.

Simpson, J. (ed.) (2007) *The First English Dictionary, 1604: Robert Cawdrey's A Table Alphabeticall*, Oxford: Bodleian Library.

Slattery, M. (2012) 'Illich Foresees the Internet'. Available at: http://conviviality.ouvaton.org/article.php3?id_article=31 (accessed 1 June 2012).

Sloterdijk, P. (1989) *Eurotaoismus: Zur Kritik der Politischen Kinetik*, Frankfurt: Suhrkamp.

Sonzogni, M. (ed.) (2009) *Corno inglese: An Anthology of Eugenio Montale's Poetry in English Translation*, Jokeredizioni Novi Ligure.

Standage, T. (1999) *The Victorian Internet: The Remarkable Story of the Telegraph and the Nineteenth Century's Online Pioneers*, London: Phoenix.

Steiner, G. (1975) *After Babel: Aspects of Language and Translation*, Oxford: Oxford University Press.

Stevenson, A. (ed.) (2010) *The Oxford Dictionary of English*, 3rd edition, Oxford: Oxford University Press.

Susam-Sarajeva, S. (2006) *Theories on the Move: Translation's Role in the Travels of Literary Theories*, Amsterdam and New York: Rodopi.

SymS (2011) 'Wikileaks – Google Translation', 12 September. Available at: http://www.proz.com/forum/machine_translation_mt/207403-wikileaks_google_translation.html (accessed 20 December 2012).

Tadié, J.-Y. (1996) *Marcel Proust*, Paris: Gallimard.

Tahir Gürçaglar, S. (2008) *The Politics and Poetics of Translation in Turkey*, Amsterdam and New York: Rodopi.

Tapscott, D. (2009) *Growing up Digital: How the Net Generation is Changing Your World*, New York: McGraw-Hill.

TAUS (2010) *Postediting in Practice*. Available at: http://www.translationautomation. com/best-practices/postediting-in-practice.html (accessed 28 May 2012).

Taviano, S. (2010) *Translating English as a Lingua Franca*, Milan: Mondadori Education.

Taylor, T. (2010) *The Artificial Ape: How Technology Changed the Course of Human Evolution*, New York: Palgrave Macmillan.

Teilhard de Chardin, P. (1966) *The Vision of the Past*, New York: Harper and Row.

Thom, C. (2006) *Early Irish Monasticism: An Understanding of its Cultural Roots*, London and New York: T. & T. Clark.

Tosi, A. (2007) *Un italiano per l'Europa: la trduzione come prova di vitalità*, Rome: Carocci.

Tridgell, J. (2007) '"Any Language You Want – so Long as it's English" – how Today's Support Manager Can Deliver a Truly Global Support Experience'. Available at: http// www.sdl.com (accessed 20 September 2011).

Turkle, S. (2011) *Alone Together: Why We Expect More from Technology and Less from Each Other*, New York: Basic Books.

Tymoczko, M. (1999) *Translation in a Postcolonial Context*, Manchester: St Jerome.

——(2007) *Enlarging Translation, Empowering Translators*, Manchester: St Jerome.

Urry, J. (1999) *Sociology beyond Societies: Mobilities for the Twenty-first Century*, London and New York: Routledge.

Vanbremeersch, N. (2009) *De La Démocratie numérique*, Paris: Seuil.

van der Meer, J. (2012) 'Translation Automation in Japan'. Available at: http://translation automation.com/best-practices/translation-automation-in-Japan.html (accessed 28 May 2012).

van Ham, P. (2001) 'The Rise of the Brand State', *Foreign Policy*. Available at: http://www.globalpolicy.org/component/content/article/162/27557.html (accessed 24 December 2011).

van Parijs, P. (2004) 'L'Anglais lingua franca de l'union européenne: imperative de solidarité, source d'injustice, facteur de decline?', *Économie Politique*, 15, 13–32.

Vellacott, Philip (1953) *Alcestis and Other Plays* [Euripides], Harmondsworth: Penguin.

Venuti, Lawrence (2004) *The Translation Studies Reader*, London: Routledge.

Venuti, L. (2008) 'Translation, Simulacra, Resistance', *Translation Studies*, 1, 1, 18–33.

Vertovec, S. and Cohen, R. (eds) (2002) *Conceiving Cosmopolitanism: Theory, Context, Practice*, Oxford: Oxford University Press.

Virilio, P. (2010) *L'Administration de la peur*, Paris: Textuel.

Volcic, Z. and Andrejevic, M. (2011) 'Nation Branding in the Era of Commercial Nationalism', *International Journal of Communications*, 5, 598–618.

Wallerstein, I. (1997) 'The National and the Universal: Can There be such a Thing as World Culture?', in King, A. (ed.) *Culture, Globalization and the World-System: Contemporary Conditions for the Representation of Identity*, Minneapolis: University of Minnesota Press, 97–105.

Waquet, F. (1998) *Le Latin ou l'empire d'un signe*, Paris: Albin Michel.

Watson, P. (2011) *The German Genius: Europe's Third Renaissance, the Second Scientific Revolution and the Twentieth Century*, New York: Simon and Schuster.

Webb, B. (1997) 'Eva of the Nation and the Young Ireland Poets', unpublished M.Phil. in Irish Studies dissertation, National University of Ireland, Galway.

Weinreich, H., Obendorf, H., Herder, E., and Mayer, M. (2008) 'Not Quite the Average: An Empirical Study of Web Use', *ACM Transactions on the Web*, 2, 1, 1–26.

Wignall, G. (2009) 'Authoring for Consistency and Reuse'. Available at: http//www.sdl. com (accessed 12 September 2011).

Wilde, J. (1864) *Poems*, Dublin: James Duffy.

——(1884) *Driftwood from Scandinavia*, London: Richard Bentley and Son.

——(1893) *Social Studies*, London: Ward & Downey.

Wilde, O. (1973) *De Profundis and Other Writings*, Harmondsworth: Penguin.

Wilks, Yorick (2008) *Machine Translation: Its Scope and Limits*, Berlin: Springer.

Will, F. (1973) *The Knife in the Stone*, The Hague: Mouton.

Wilson, H.H. (1814) *The Mégha Dúta; or Cloud Messenger; a Poem, in the Sanscrit Language: by Cálidása*, Calcutta: Black, Parry & Co.

Wolfe, C. (2009) *What is Posthumanism*, Minneapolis: University of Minnesota Press.

WordReference.com (2005) 'Cream Cheese', 1–2. Available at: http://www.forum.wordreference.com/showthread.php?t=17827 (accessed 29 January 2012).

Words without Borders (2012) 'About *Words without Borders*'. Available at: http://www.wordswithoutborders.org/about (accessed 4 January 2012)

Wrangham, R. (2007) 'The Cooking Enigma', in Pasternak, C. (ed.) *What Makes Us Human?*, Oxford: Oneworld, 182–203.

Wyndham, H. (1951) *Speranza: A Biography of Lady Wilde*, London and New York: T.V. Boardman.

Yates, F. (2002) *Giordano Bruno and the Hermetic Tradition*, Routledge Classics Series, London: Routledge.

Zhong, W. (2003) 'An Overview of Translation in China: Practice and Theory', *Translation Journal*, 7, 2, 33–46.

Index